The fruit of over two decade
research, this book explores t
human rather than horticultu
on the practice of church pl
planting, which sits at the inte ....gy,
is not just a growth strategy bu... .... opportunity to reflect on the nature
and priorities of the church. And he advances the bold and striking
suggestion, deeply rooted in biblical exegesis and theological reflection,
that reproduction is an essential and defining feature of an authentic
ecclesiology. This is a book I have been waiting for, and it has not
disappointed.

Stuart Murray Williams, Tutor in Mission, Bristol Baptist College

George Lings has used his forensic thinking to help us understand
that the Church was created to be reproducing by its very nature. It is
a masterly account of this issue, based on George's insights from the
Bible, Christian tradition and church history. This is a deeply argued
thesis which demands that we engage with it, both in our thinking and
above all in our missionary practice.

Revd Canon Dave Male, National Advisor for Pioneer Development

George's appetising combination of breadth of vision, insight and
humour combine in this book with passion and conviction. It reads
like the enthusiastic but precisely written result of many years of
observation, prayer, research and insight. There's also a sense of
benign frustration that the idea of reproduction—something so obvious
in nature, theology and biblical studies, and proven to be effective in
the ministry of so many fresh expressions of Church—seems to be
overlooked by so many.

Lucy Moore, Messy Church founder and team leader

This is a delightful piece of theological reflection from George. It distils
George's wisdom from reflecting on the nature of the Church, God and
mission through what he has observed and researched over the last few
decades. I found it both stimulating and helpful.

Jonny Baker, Director of Mission Education, Church Mission Society

In this insightful book, George Lings offers a helpful and engaging lens to reunite what should have never been separated—the Church and mission. Indeed, growing in a truly loving, authentic and Jesus-centred community, though demanding, will always be attractive and have a missional effect. A great encouragement for existing churches to explore giving birth to new churches!

Catherine Askew, Chaplain-in-Residence, Northumbria Community

George Lings is internationally renowned for his research into church planting, which has been vital in bringing the Fresh Expressions movement to birth. This book provides an ecclesiological foundation for fresh expressions of Church in the calling and capacity of the Church to reproduce. George's writing is characteristically humble and simultaneously excitingly audacious. If it is true that it is the Church's vocation to reproduce, this has profound and wide-reaching implications for every church. A must-read for all who wish to think seriously about the nature of God's mission in relation to Church and kingdom.

Sally Gaze, Fresh Expressions Facilitator for the Diocese of Norwich, and author of *Mission-Shaped and Rural*

REPRODUCING CHURCHES

GEORGE LINGS

The Bible Reading Fellowship
15 The Chambers, Vineyard
Abingdon OX14 3FE
brf.org.uk

The Bible Reading Fellowship (BRF) is a Registered Charity (233280)

ISBN 978 0 85746 464 4
First published 2017
10 9 8 7 6 5 4 3 2 1 0
All rights reserved

Cover images © Thinkstock

Acknowledgements
Unless otherwise stated, scripture quotations are taken from The Holy Bible, New International Version (Anglicised edition) copyright © 1979, 1984, 2011 by Biblica. Used by permission of Hodder & Stoughton Publishers, an Hachette UK company. All rights reserved. 'NIV' is a registered trademark of Biblica. UK trademark number 1448790.

Scripture quotations from The New Revised Standard Version of the Bible, Anglicised edition, copyright © 1989, 1995 by the Division of Christian Education of the National Council of the Churches of Christ in the United States of America. Used by permission. All rights reserved.

Scripture quotations from The Revised Standard Version of the Bible, copyright © 1946, 1952, 1971 by the Division of Christian Education of the National Council of the Churches of Christ in the United States of America. Used by permission. All rights reserved.

Every effort has been made to trace and contact copyright owners for material used in this resource. We apologise for any inadvertent omissions or errors, and would ask those concerned to contact us so that full acknowledgement can be made in the future.

A catalogue record for this book is available from the British Library

Printed and bound by CPI Group (UK) Ltd, Croydon CR0 4YY

Contents

Foreword

This book is a rarity. It has been written by a genuinely reflective church leader who has also been a genuine practitioner. The phrase 'reflective practitioner' can all too often mean someone who has thought a little bit about a little bit of life. In George's case we have a man who has reflected for decades on a long and rich experience of pastoral work, church planting and church growth. You hold the fruit of that reflection in your hand.

Handbooks on church growth are not rare. Nor, sadly, are books persuading us that the growth of the church is mistaken or irrelevant. What George has written is better than both, because it begins in the depths. It takes us deep into the scriptures and into the traditions and fundamental marks of the Church. And it shows us that the Church can indeed be one, holy, catholic, apostolic—and reproducing.

I do promise you that George knows what he is talking about. He has travelled the church for many, many years, listening, questioning, analysing, blessing, consulting and loving the churches he has seen.

As a church planter myself, I remember George's visit as if it were yesterday. We were working away, doing our best but not entirely sure what we were doing, planting a small-group-based church in an overspill town in Hampshire. When George came, it was as if a man drew alongside us in our thirsty work, opened a case of cold and refreshing water, and helped us to see, as we drank, that what we were doing was theologically rooted and embedded in the traditions of the wider Church, and was fruitful. We returned to our work deeply refreshed. George can do that for you, as you read this book.

You will be given a language to think in, models to consider, scriptures to reflect on and historical examples to learn from. But most of all you will receive a glimpse into the heart of God—that there should be more people knowing Jesus and more kingdom-justice in the world. George has received this heartbeat through his own discipleship, and he will impart it to you.

Be careful! If you catch this vision, you will be empowered and encouraged and provoked to step outside whatever box you may be in, and to walk with God into a delightful, fruitful, reproductive future. You will be on an adventure. You will be on mission. May God bless you on that journey!

Paul Bayes, Bishop of Liverpool

Introduction:
why this book?

I hope the title of this book has intrigued you. What was your reaction to its claim that churches should reproduce? Were you delighted, puzzled, surprised, or shocked? You may wonder where such a way of talking came from. Here's my story.

Where do our thoughts come from?

Some say our selfish genes produce our thoughts. Others argue that they arise from the way we grew up. I've heard it all blamed on eating too much cheese the night before. Yet there is another possibility: I'd call it prompts from God. We don't have to believe that these prompts occur independently of the other reasons. God shows remarkable humility in communicating with us. He knows we have mixed motives and limited understanding of his ways. Moments of inspiration can occur while we are seeking him or, equally, while we are quite unaware of him.

I've started the book this way because it goes back to one moment when a surprising thought came to me. I have mainly kept it to myself for over 20 years, but at last I'm daring to make it known. So I am putting the thought, its meaning and its consequences before readers in the wider Church. I'll have to await your verdict on whether the book contains something of truth and value.

Called to observe

The background to my surprising thought is my own history, with its twists and turns. When it came to me, I was serving as vicar of St George, Deal, in Canterbury diocese. My family and I lived there from 1985 to 1997. In the first few months of 1992, I was given a sabbatical. But let me tell you the story that led up to it.

Before then, back in 1984, late in my second curacy, I had become interested in the topic of planting churches. It started when I read the earliest British book on the topic, *How to Plant Churches*, edited by Monica Hill.[1] With a small group of other Anglicans, I began to collect details of examples and invented a simple database to record them. I mentioned the 40 cases that we were aware of in 1987 at the first national Anglican Church Planting Conference, held at Holy Trinity Brompton (HTB). That led to a surprise. The chairman, Revd John Collins, immediately proclaimed me the data collection officer of this barely existing movement. In shock I duly complied. Over the next five years, as the spare-time hobby of a jobbing vicar, I received piecemeal bits of information from around the country.[2] I presented the patterns I saw in the data to the succeeding conferences for several years.

Back in 1984, I misunderstood what I now see was the start of a more specific vocation. I wondered then whether I was being prompted to begin a church plant somewhere, and was willing to try. Fortunately, all explorations of that route became dead ends. I now doubt if I ever possessed the get up and go, the vision and courage, and the skills to start a church from nothing. I now also look back with horror, mixed with relief, at how ignorant I was about how it is done wisely. We now call these initiatives 'fresh expressions of Church'.

Having become a vicar in 1985, it seemed as though my role was not to start something but to observe others doing it. I tried to track the patterns, variables and dynamics in a new development that, even in 1984, Monica Hill called complex and controversial.

Until recent years those within the Christian tradition have resisted, and some still do resist, any kind of Church planting which introduces new models. Every new expression, from Methodism to Pentecostalism, has received opposition in the past.[3]

That controversy was particular and tense for the Church of England in 1991–92. Four unauthorised church plants had crossed a parish boundary in a twelve-month period. 'Invaded' incumbents publicly protested. An attack on the very parish system was feared. The press loved the controversy.

So we come to my 1992 sabbatical. I visited the four controversial plants. I deliberately widened my experience by visiting cases of good practice both in the UK and in New Zealand. I also studied the limited amount of emerging literature. In the spring, I retreated to the peace of our remote granite-walled Welsh cottage, high in the hills above Blaenau Ffestiniog, to try to write it all up.

What a day!

Curiously, perhaps ominously, it was April Fool's Day, 1992. I was sitting in a tiny upstairs bedroom, converted into a temporary study by turning the window shutters into a sort of desk. I remember sitting in front of the computer screen trying to make sense of all I had seen and read. I can only say that then a loud thought occurred to me: *God's Church should and can reproduce.*

Why was that a weird thought, back then? Today's reader needs to realise that most literature up till then only tackled the practicalities of planting churches. They focused on starting churches, more than sustaining them. The practice was unrelated to any doctrine about the Church, much less how church planting might amend that doctrine. It was novel to think that the very nature of the Church included both the calling and the capacity to reproduce—and to call something 'novel' is pretty close to theological suicide or, at least, highly suspicious. At that time no one made this doctrinal claim. Church planting was only a bold tactical option in local ministry, perhaps done as a response to mission needs. It was not seen as part of Church identity, yet this growing phenomenon[4] was starting to pose questions about what should be allowed. As I looked in 1992 at some biblical texts, I detected the possibility that scripture broadly supported that bombshell thought which had arrived unbidden.

More surprises

I wrote up the visits I had made and added some biblical and theological comments. The report was sent to my supervisor, Bishop Colin Buchanan, and my diocesan bishop, Archbishop George Carey. So matters rested as I returned to a full parochial life. Over a year later I received a letter. On opening it I must have sounded like Victor Meldrew, exclaiming, 'I don't believe it.' The Archbishop wished to confer upon me a Lambeth MLitt, saying it was for my 'theological contribution to church planting'. There can't be many people who get given an Oxford Masters degree for merely indulging their hobby.

Yet that gift proved more significant than I knew. Because of it, I could apply for my current role in research for Church Army. It gave me the qualification to teach at higher education level. Later, it became the passport to seven years of diffidently tackling a part-time PhD, based at Cliff College under Dr Martyn Atkins.

Since that groundbreaking moment in 1992, I have only rarely aired my thought, which still seemed audacious and unproven. However, I did serve from 1992 to 1994 on the Church of England group that produced the report *Breaking New Ground*. The group drew upon some parts of my sabbatical research, but their report left aside my claim about the Church. Ten years later, I found myself on the working party that produced *Mission-shaped Church*, which came out in 2004. By a twist of history I was asked to write its first draft. In the most directly theological chapter of the report, I included some biblical material on the calling and capacity for Church to reproduce. The editorial process, rightly conducted by others, kept the heart of that case, showing that the idea was gaining some approval. The chair of the group, Bishop Graham Cray, confirmed that, when the draft was before the House of Bishops, no one took exception to this section.[5]

How do you test your own ideas?

By then I was into the early years of PhD study, completed in 2008. I knew that the possibly crazy idea that had flashed across my mind in 1992 needed testing, but how could I test whether it was true? To suggest an almost novel amendment to Church doctrine, with its 2000-year tradition, is tricky. At the Reformation, such suggestions turned out to be life-threatening, whereas today they are likely only to be dismissed as frivolous. There was another danger: in designing my tests, would I only choose criteria that backed up what I already wanted to be so? I know that when you buy a certain kind of car, you immediately begin to notice who else has been wise and discerning enough to choose the same type. How would I get beyond wish-fulfilment and my prejudices?

I knew I had noticed something that, on the surface, looked intriguing and promising, but did it really have foundations? I needed to dig deeper into scripture, the overall Christian tradition and wider theological thinking. I then got a gift. During my 1992 sabbatical I had learnt to value Avery Dulles' book *Models of the Church*, reading it closely from cover to cover. I returned to it and, beyond the most well-known sections about his six models of the Church, I found what I needed. To my delight, pages 191–92 gave a series of questions deliberately designed to test any proposed new contribution to a better understanding of the Church.

To find this in Dulles' book was so helpful. He wrote his tests years before my idea had occurred. Moreover, he is respected as a Church thinker but from a different tradition to my own, and he had designed the tests to appeal across a variety of theological traditions. I could be confident that they were objective enough. I salute their breadth and summarise them for you in the slightly strange order Dulles gives:[6]

1 a clear and explicit basis in scripture
2 the testimony of tradition—the broader the better
3 fostering corporate identity and mission
4 fostering virtues and values admired by Christians
5 correspondence with contemporary human experience
6 theological fruitfulness, thus solving some past problems and lack of linkages
7 fruitfulness in relating to those outside the Church

Tests 1, 2 and 6 deal more with the questions of whether the new idea is true and how universal it is. That's why I would have grouped them together. Tests 3, 4, 5 and 7 relate more to practical theology, testing how useful a concept is. 'Is it true?', 'Is it universal?' and 'Is it useful?' are all right and important questions to grapple with when faced with a new idea.

Notice, too, that Dulles' seven tests overlap with the four ways Christians have often decided what is true: scripture, tradition, reason and experience. Anglicanism has long tried to hold the first three together, although we haven't always agreed which was the most important. The role of the fourth factor, experience, is now being taken more seriously. We more freely admit today that our experience is involved in encountering scripture, tradition and reason, but also that experience makes a contribution of its own.

I came, I saw, I wondered

Experience has been important in my story. I feel like a Church equivalent of those explorers who found the first duck-billed platypus. There could be no doubt in their mind that it existed, but what animal family it fitted into was a conundrum, for it defied prior classifications.

Similarly, I was seeing what I could not deny were examples of young churches, but they did not look like the churches that had gone before. There were a load of differences: they not only varied in size, but they could occupy different habitats—different networks and cultures. They held their gatherings in different ways from congregations. They sustained their communities in a diversity of styles. Many were led by unauthorised people. They were at the same time like and unlike what we had known before. Since 1997, my working life has been to visit them, write up their stories and ponder what their existence means.[7] Since 2012, the Church Army Research Unit, which I lead, has interviewed the leaders of over 1000 of these young Anglican churches, across the breadth of England.

Those experiences obviously showed that further churches can be started, but was it only like Tesco opening a new store or Barclays Bank starting a new branch? Should we understand the start of another church as just the organisational spread of an institution, or could it be different from that? Could we see this widespread phenomenon of 'fresh expressions of Church' in a better way? I think it is more accurate and more helpful to see the Church as profoundly interpersonal. One reason is that biblical terms for the Church include phrases like 'the people of God' and 'the body of Christ'. Also, we humans are made in the image of God, and God, as three persons of the Trinity, in some ways resembles a community. So we should think of his Church in communal, interpersonal terms.

Key words act like lenses: they affect everything you see. When we look at the Church through the interpersonal lens, not the institutional one, it changes the way we should talk. New things don't just start; you might say they are born. The Church does not just expand like a store or bank, where each one is pretty much like the others, only varying in size, like the Tesco Express or the superstore.

Perhaps the best way of talking about this is to say that the Church reproduces. Something organic comes out of it, which inherits the family likeness and yet is also itself. This is how it is with families:

parents remain parents, but their children are both related to and different from them. For me, that picture fitted with what I was seeing, both in my academic study and in my field research. By its nature, or its being, the Church is meant to reproduce, but it does so in a non-identical fashion. If we truly started to think in that way, then seeing fresh expressions of Church come to birth would be entirely normal, with nothing to fear in their difference from their parent body, and much to be applauded. Such a doctrine of the Church makes sense of the creativity we currently see. It explains why these young churches display the variety that we observe. Of course, the question still remains, is this idea true?

Another question I had to face was whether it was legitimate even to pose a fresh way to understand the Church. At that point, Dulles was helpful to me once more. His work, starting in the 1970s, has become a classic text in understanding the Church. He showed that there were a number of different views, which he called 'models'. The number of them, their diversity and their interaction revealed that each one was only part of the overall picture. His work proved that no one model does everything. Each is incomplete. What we need to notice, as well, is that five out of his six ways of understanding the Church have arisen since the middle of the 20th century. Dulles argues that the inherited institutional view was dominant, beginning with the fourth-century Emperor Constantine, but only up till around 1940. The other views represent a rapid and recent rise. Such recent disturbance and diversity indicates ferment. It brings humility and openness to further ways of thinking. Dulles' tale leaves space to add what might still be missing.

So the principle of adding a previously unrecognised idea—that the Church is by nature reproductive—is possible and legitimate. It fits with the creative period in which we find ourselves. But, as only one among a number of incomplete additions to our knowledge about the nature of the Church, it should be judged by similar criteria.

Not overclaiming

I am not claiming that there is a reproductive *model* of the Church to be added to Dulles' list. The claim that the Church is reproductive seeks only to add something to all his models, not to explain the whole of what the Church is. A similar distortion would be to claim that the capacity for having babies, though essential to the future of the species, explains what it is to be human. This book therefore does not offer a full theology of the Church. It is only adding a missing strand of its identity.

Even then, I know that attempting to add, with good intentions, can be fatal. It has always been the case, in cross-cultural work, that the danger of syncretism lurks. Syncretism means to add, but in such a way that the nature of the original substance is compromised. Adding milk or sugar to coffee might not be to everybody's taste but the original drink is still coffee. Adding tea to it might well be syncretism, and adding petrol certainly would be. I am conscious that I am adding to prior views, and I need to show that, in doing so, the essential nature of Church is enhanced, not compromised.

The power of models, images and paradigms

Another reason for using Dulles' tests is that he knows about the power of models and the related words 'images' and 'paradigms'. These are all varying terms that have something in common: they are like a mental lens. Everything you see can be affected by a lens—for example, by using sunglasses, or 'seeing the world through rose-tinted spectacles'. Pick up a particular theological lens and you will see all aspects of Church through this filter. Yet quite often we need more than one way of seeing things.

There is a parallel in scientific understanding. Light is partially understood through complementary models, using analogies of light as a particle and light as a wave. I am glad that Dulles and another scholar of the Church, Paul Minear,[8] both know how evocative images are. As Minear puts it, 'To some extent they are self-fulfilling; they make the Church become what they suggest the Church is'.[9] The advertising industry has known the power of images for years. I recognise that to talk about 'a reproducing Church' is such an image. Precisely because imagery is powerful, and this image of the reproductive Church touches upon its essence, it needs something like Dulles' tests to investigate if it is true. The image exists alongside the thought that the nature of the Church is interpersonal, not primarily institutional. That, too, is a change of image and may even be a change of paradigm, or whole way of thinking, which I will open up in the next chapter.

Obsession with the Church?

I am aware that there is suspicion and distrust of the Church. There are many reasons why such negativity is deserved. I know that some people are much more energised by the call to mission or the values of the kingdom. I will explore in Chapter 11 what could be a good way to relate these three ideas together. I don't rate the Church above the other two, but I do refuse to separate it from them.

You will also find that I make a number of references to the Church of England. I don't think it is the only way to be Church but it's the one I have grown up in. I've researched its practice for a particular reason, though not a very honourable one. The Church of England is reluctant to learn from denominations younger than itself or from outside Europe. It is more open to learning from what it is already doing. That was the view we took when we wrote the report *Mission-shaped Church* and it seemed to help.

Now ponder this reality. It is not an accident that the new things we are seeing are normally called fresh expressions of *Church*. We live at a time when we are reimagining what a local church can look like. I think it is time to have some positive and creative thinking about the Church. This book tries to establish some deeper theological foundations for an understanding of the Church and why it is normal to have fresh expressions of Church. It goes beyond seeing new churches starting as just a consequence of mission, or as one agent for the kingdom. Unless we can rediscover a positive view of God's purposes for the Church, we will perpetuate an unhelpful, untrue and unwarranted divorce between three intended partners: mission, kingdom and Church.

So read on and decide for yourself:

- Does this idea, that the Church is intended by God to reproduce, make sense?
- Can the idea pass Dulles' tests?
- If true, what does it tell us?

Notes

1 M. Hill (ed.), *How to Plant Churches* (MARC Europe, 1984).
2 Many came from Revd Bob and Mrs Mary Hopkins, who had a travelling ministry.
3 Hill, *How to Plant Churches*, p. 9.
4 The number of Church of England church plants begun per year had increased from two in 1982 to 37 in 1992.
5 Interview at Canterbury Cathedral International Study Centre, 18 October 2006.
6 A. Dulles, *Models of the Church* (Gill & Macmillan, 1988), pp. 191–92.
7 Between 1999 and 2012, Church Army published 55 of these extended stories through the *Encounters on the Edge* series. They are still available as PDFs: see www.encountersontheedge.org.uk.
8 P.S. Minear, *Images of the Church in the New Testament*, 2nd edition (Westminster Press, 2004).
9 Minear, *Images of the Church*, pp. 22–26.

1

Different lenses, different views of the Church

When I was 30 I had to go to the optician for the first time. It was annoying, but I could no longer read a book easily, though driving and playing sport were fine. So I got my first bifocals, and I sharply noticed that what you look through affects what you see. Something similar happens when you put on sunglasses. Some kinds highlight the colours in the world around. They make you think that what you are seeing is warmer and more vibrant.

Our assumptions are similar to spectacles. Both affect the way we are looking at things and, therefore, what we think we are seeing. The Introduction introduced this idea through some related terms— models, images and paradigms—and noted how powerful they are.

As I reflect on my varied church leadership experience since 1974, and how I was supposed to understand the Church, I have come to realise that my theological spectacles have been altered several times. At each stage I saw something different or differently. My underlying paradigm, or worldview, was quite profoundly changed. I have found also that, with each change, it becomes harder to go back. I can remember when colour television came in. You could still opt for black and white, but why would you? Surely watching in colour was more like the real world.

Four successive lenses

Let me trace for you four successive paradigms, or ways of under-standing, that I think have operated in my lifetime. Most of them are not drawn from Dulles and his famous book, or from Minear's book about 96 images of the Church found in the New Testament. What I am talking about lies behind and beneath those sorts of categories. In each one, I will headline what the key term suggests and how growth is understood within that way of seeing.

Tracking this movement may be important because, in many denominations, including the Church of England, a high value is put on stability and being settled. Perhaps that is partly why fresh expressions of Church unsettle a number of people. We all know what it is to value cherished traditions, and we prefer known ways of operating. A mythology can grow up around both, such that people say, 'It has always been like that and so shouldn't change.' A trivial classic example is the belief that churches have always had pews. In reality, they only became popular a couple of hundred years ago. Here I want to show that there have been significant changes in much bigger assumptions about the Church.

The institutional paradigm

This view is venerable, longstanding and still around. Its advocates might well argue that it keeps the show on the road. Unexciting things like committees, stewardship schemes, rules and regulations are like a flywheel that keeps the Church engine turning over. I don't think that institutions are necessarily bad. Economic and legal considerations have a part to play, and we can't live totally without them. But, since the writings of Max Weber, we are aware that there is a well-known tendency for all adventures to drift slowly towards bureaucracy. Institutions can be deadening.

The nature of institutional thinking is monopolistic and unitary: it thinks it is the only show on the road and the only way things can be done. Therefore, I have noticed that, in this way of seeing, any new people wanting to join the Church as institution do so by being incorporated into exactly its style, under its rule. *Star Trek* fans might think of the malign force, the Borg, who assimilate anyone they come into contact with. The message is 'You join us on our terms.' The notion that new people coming in might change us is considered ridiculous. You may even have heard that said explicitly, by longstanding church members. The institutional Roman Church, in particular, understood itself as the perfect society, the only one true Church. Any departure from it was thought to be, at best, divisive and probably heretical. But other denominations have taken such an approach, too. The Anglican description of those outside the Church of England as 'Dissenters' is evidence of this attitude, and these sorts of views have not disappeared.

It will be immediately obvious that the following set of ideas just don't fit with this way of thinking. By the institutional paradigm, churches don't 'reproduce' or get 'born'; all that might happen is that a further local branch of the institution might be opened. Any new branch—say, for an area of new housing—should not be different in any significant way from its parish church. If 'reproduction' is fanciful, then non-identical reproduction is impossible and undesirable.

As I mentioned in the Introduction, Dulles teaches that this model lost its dominance around 1940. He holds that Vatican II, 20 years later, completed its relegation to a secondary place and was the death knell for that image as primary or adequate by itself.[1] But Catholic critics from within, like the consultant Gerald Arbuckle, counter that the institutional is fighting back. He argues that 'renewal' will be an inadequate term for what is needed. Twenty years ago, he even said, 'A fresh expression is necessary.'[2] Dulles' more optimistic book charted the rise of five other models in the 30 years after World War II. This is a serious admission that we live in times when the reimagination of the Church is going on. Notice that the words 'image' and 'imagination' are related.

The managerial or mechanical paradigm (Church Growth)

I recall the arrival in Britain in 1975, in the same decade as when Dulles was writing, of 'Church Growth' thinking. It was brought in by the Bible Society, in the humorous and persuasive style of Revd Eddie Gibbs. Although he is English, Gibbs brought the idea from the USA. The controlling image was an American one, in a period when plans dictated outcomes. Looking back now, perhaps unsurprisingly, it was managerial and rather mechanical.

I remember well that the Church Growth view was shocking to traditional church leaders in several ways. It suggested that the Church could be improved and, indeed, that it should be, because it was far from perfect. That was naked criticism and leaders were offended. Just as bizarrely at the time, it held that growth should occur. It taught that growth was normal for churches—a controversial thought. I remember other Anglicans disapproving. Growth was thought of as rather crass. It was a dirty word, rather like talking about how much you earned. Others simply dismissed the idea as not worthy of consideration because it came from America.

This was very different from the institutional view, which didn't do change and simply sucked others into what already existed. Church Growth was done in two related ways. One was by making internal improvements to the existing local church community and its building, in order to make both more attractive to others. The other way was to seek numerical growth by the addition of new members. This raised the spectre of the three 'E' words that the Church of England doesn't like: evangelism, enthusiasm and earnestness.

However, this paradigm was the same as the institutional in its assumption that others would come to us. In the institutional view, that was because the institution was all that existed, but in the Church Growth view, it was because the improved Church was worth joining. Both practised inward attraction. A mathematical symbol to write alongside the Church Growth view would be the plus sign, standing for the desire to add, together with an inward facing arrow. Mission and evangelism were a matter of going out from the Church in order to bring others back to it, having introduced them to Jesus along the way.

Church Growth thought of change in modernist terms: growth was analysed, planned, timed and costed. It was as though a church was a machine to be tinkered with and tuned up. There were critiques then that its thinking was too close to the consumerist language of customers. It was criticised, perhaps unfairly, for its lack of holistic mission. Rage even came from others about the view that it encouraged Homogeneous Unit Practice or its principle—an idea spotted by another American, Donald McGavran. He taught that people like to become Christians without changing their cultural background.

Church Growth's overall way of operating is now castigated by writers such as Frost and Hirsch, as being merely attractional.[3] Moreover, Eddie Gibbs himself and his English colleague, Ian Coffey, later listed many features relating to available space, resources, serving niches and the pursuit of excellence, which mean that models from the USA do not translate easily to the UK context.[4]

Despite some criticisms, Church Growth thinking is still alive and well. It informs a number of churches, larger and smaller, as well as particular strategies like Back to Church Sunday and the much wider programme that many find helpful, 'Leading your Church into Growth'. The books of Bob Jackson spell out researched findings about what helps to reduce decline and what is likely to assist numerical growth as well as growth in depth.[5] It would have been astonishing, if not shocking, to the Church of England in 1975 to know that, 40 years later, the same national Church would make numerical growth one of its goals for the next five years. Whether that derives more from Church Growth thinking or from alarm at a 40-year decline is a good question.

Because the focus was on improving the attractiveness of what already existed, this second paradigm did not so much reject creating further churches as fail to consider that it could be important. Because it came after the institutional paradigm, the emphasis fell on the churches we already had, and on making them fit for purpose. The energy was inwards, in order to improve current churches, as well as outwards, to bring people back to what had been improved. During that period, my own limited research across the country found but a handful of further new Church of England churches,[6] other than the so-called house churches. The latter began mainly through people leaving existing denominations. Yet, even during the 1980s, the sufficiency of this paradigm began to be challenged and, in my view, it was eventually subverted to some extent by its successor.

The horticultural paradigm (Church Planting)

Monica Hill was the editor of the first English church planting book, in 1984.[7] A few years later, Bob Hopkins wrote a pair of Grove booklets: the first in 1988, followed closely by a second in 1989, written from his own planting experience and wider thinking.[8] Drawing on presentations I had made, he coined, in the first booklet, a set of horticultural terms for different kinds of plants: Runners, Grafts, Seeds and Transplants. This classification got taken, in modified form, into the 1994 Church of England report *Breaking New Ground*. In some senses, Church Planting was the son of Church Growth—and it appears that some in the liberal tradition, and theologians like John Hull, seem not to have forgiven us for it. Critics of Church Planting can fail to realise that it was different in several crucial ways from the Church Growth way of thinking.

Firstly, it represented a shift away from thinking in terms of the Church as an organisation, which is common to both the institutional and the managerial paradigms. It was a significant departure to think of the Church as an organism. It was a shift from pursuing inanimate and structural growth to working with living and biological growth. This was required by the language of 'planting' and it was welcome. It reunited the Church with horticultural images in scripture, such as seeds, vine and vineyard, branch and fruit. It moved to a focus on what was alive, not just what existed.

Secondly, it marked another large shift. It went beyond thinking in terms of growth by addition, embracing a radical shift to growth by multiplication. Both Church Growth and Church Planting were interested in growth, but planting meant creating further churches. To change from more in Church to more churches was a significant move, both mentally and in terms of what people were being asked to do. The same period in the UK saw an attempt to import the DAWN strategy (Discipling A Whole Nation). This movement's thinking focused on an interdenominational 1992 congress. It included an intentional policy of planting one church for every 1000 people, with targets for the year 2000 which were, at best, faith-stretching. Sadly, in retrospect, the targets proved internally disabling and invited external ridicule.

Connected to this second change was a third significant factor, which was to see mission no longer as mainly inwards but as inherently outwards. This change may be connected with the return of Bishop Lesslie Newbigin from India to the UK and his insistence that the West had again become a cross-cultural mission field. Planting people out beyond the existing church would be tactically necessary. Thus, the mathematical symbol for Church Planting is different from its parent, Church Growth: instead of a plus sign, it is a multiplication sign. Additionally, the arrow direction shifts from inwards to outwards.

Christian Schwarz's work *Natural Church Development*, published in 1996, perhaps straddles these two paradigms. It appears fundamentally biological in many of its illustrations and it advocates a shift from what he calls 'technocratic' to 'biotic' principles. Yet ironically, the style is strongly controlling, prescriptive and managerial—biological engineering, one might say, despite his helpful advocacy of what he calls the 'all by itself principle' (which means that once the conditions are right, the plant grows by itself). In addition, although the book is very open to Church Planting, the text is almost always about improving the quality of existing churches. That is not foolishness, because there are a lot of existing churches that need to develop, and many of its insights do apply to young new churches, too. I find that Schwarz's work is used more in Free Churches than within Anglicanism—which is of interest, not a criticism. Perhaps Anglicans always resist definitive solutions. However, in tracking the overall changes of paradigm, for me his book never really gets beyond a cross between the managerial and horticultural.

I am glad that the Church Planting paradigm brought a further, fresh view of the underlying assumption about the kind of thing the Church is. At its heart it is more than an institution: it is alive with all the marks of life, as taught in schools by the 'MRS NERG' abbreviation: Moving, Respiring, Sensing, taking Nutrition, Excreting, Reproducing and Growing. The institutional paradigm does not work with these terms. Church Growth thinking broadly fits with them, but its focus remained on improving what is, not creating what is not yet. In the third paradigm, the Church, the organic creation of God, did not reluctantly embrace the idea that there should be more churches. It profoundly believed that they could and should be planted. Planting was how more churches came into being. In the Anglican story, the notable 30-year history of churches begun from HTB in London may be the best known. For many, this is still where matters have rested.

However, I observed two things unfolding as I watched the Church of England. The first was that, in the 1990s, we were seeing types of Church plant diversify in a way not anticipated. An illustration would be the differences between holding multiple services in one shared venue on a Sunday and beginning an alternative worship community and event. The second change was increased attention to the diverse and cross-cultural missional context of the British Isles. The language of contextualised or inculturated Church became more frequently used.[9]

The problem, then, with 'planting' language and its expectations is that you get exactly what you expect, whereas you may not know what is needed until after you have started. So Frost and Hirsch write, 'We encourage Church-planting missionaries not to assume they know what Church is or what it should look like without first listening to its context very, very carefully.'[10]

In the garden, strawberries invariably produce more strawberries. That is fine, unless you need raspberries or have a demand for runner beans. Thus, some forms of planting were heavily criticised, by both Stuart Murray and me, for their tendency towards cloning. As ever, it is the problems within a paradigm that knock on the door of a necessary reimagination beyond it. It is now ironic that Dulles remarked decades ago, 'Those botanical models, however, have obvious limits, since they evidently fail to account for the distinctively interpersonal and historical phenomena characteristic of the Church as a human community that perdures through the generations.'[11] (For his rare word 'perdure', read 'endure'.)

It was these observations and limitations that made me revise both the terms and a way of seeing that I had welcomed and lived by for 20 years. I needed to search for what should be kept of the best of the past, without being limited by it. I have become convinced that it is both more helpful and truer to reality that we move on again, beyond the horticultural paradigm. We need a more accurate image that is no longer to do with plants but thinks in terms of people. It stays organic, but goes deeper.

The interpersonal paradigm

This shift to thinking about the Church primarily in interpersonal terms assists a necessary change in the way we first see things and then describe them. It also offers appropriate greater flexibility in assessing all expressions of Church, not just newer ones. Of course, as an image it is still an analogy, but it offers further progress.

The first change it brings, compared with the three previous views, is that we should not assume that we are observers who control the Church. This means recognising and accepting that we are involved participants. We should no longer view the Church as outside us— something that belongs to us, which we do something to, make do something, or even treat like a plant. As Brian McLaren says about the Church, 'It is not ours, it is us.'[12] In addition, it is plainly wrong that we control other people. I love my wife and my children, and I hope they won't correct me if I say I have never seriously thought I could control them.

The instinct for control is, of course, strongest in the institutional mindset; it is strong in the Church Growth view, and is still present in Church Planting. But think of how we used to describe a plant as a 'young church', and the picture changes. Guidance and support can be essential, but this young church is embarking on a journey from dependence, quite possibly through a period of independence, into adult interdependence with other churches. What a different but energising viewpoint! You wouldn't get that from the other paradigms.

The further resultant changes of language are also very striking. If we shift to the interpersonal view, then churches are not planted, for they are not vegetables; they are 'born'. They do not merely close; they 'die'. They do not just grow; they should 'mature'. They will not passively 'exist'; they should have the capacity for continued change and adaptation, as 'learners'.

This change of language not only invokes greater personal investment in the process. It also joins the best of pastoral skills to the mission task, and encourages greater responsibility in the process. There is a profound set of differences between the four paradigms, which could be represented by four groups of people respectively: civil servants like Sir Humphrey Appleby of *Yes, Prime Minister* ensuring no change; accountant-led managers planning organisational change; farmers planting crops; and a couple having a baby. None are totally disinterested, but the joys and losses for the fourth are the most profound and life-changing.

Some people, not least those who have been helped by the Church Planting paradigm, resist this change towards thinking in interpersonal human terms, because of the many horticultural images in scripture. They include the parable of the sower in Luke 8, the vine in John 15 and the grafting process in Romans 11. But the task of theology, which needs both courage and humility, is to sift the variety of biblical images and suggest which are controlling ones. Paul Minear did just this: he sifted the 96 images he found and came up with what he called four master images: the people of God, the new creation, the fellowship of faith, and the body of Christ. All of these images include the interpersonal.

None are fundamentally horticultural, let alone mechanistic; much less are they institutional. We should note this view, which scripture reveals, of what the Church is.

There is another deep theological reason for thinking that this change is healthy and a step in the right direction. It is the renewed emphasis on the Eastern view of the Trinity as three persons in one communion with each other. This serves as the best base we have for thinking in interpersonal terms, both about what it is to be human and about the Church. The Church is fundamentally made up of human beings, and we are in the image of God. Moreover, we are having that image restored to fullness by the grace of Christ and cooperating with the gift of the Spirit.

I began to see that this human interpersonal view subverts the previous one—the horticultural. It also made more sense of what I was observing. The young churches were not carbon copies of those that had sent them. They had a strong sense of their own identity. The growth advocated by the interpersonal paradigm is still, mathematically speaking, by multiplication, and the direction of growth still facing outwards. These are enduring features to be honoured and celebrated. However, the interpersonal lens brings changes from the simplistic planting or multiplying image, in several important related ways.

Firstly, growth of further churches is necessarily, rightly and exclusively by non-identical reproduction. It is the dynamic of reproduction that creates multiplication, not the other way round, as Schwarz taught 20 years ago.[13] I think the first person to apply the biological term 'non-identical reproduction' to churches, in published form, was my PhD supervisor, the Methodist leader Martyn Atkins. Maybe his comment arose from our supervision conversations as I worked on the thesis, under him, that such reproduction is a forgotten part of the identity of the Church.[14] Non-identical reproduction is itself the consequence of an equally deep spiritual feature, which I call the two-source or bipartite preference in God's work. Later chapters will develop the spiritual pairs across the following list. It is seen in dust and breath in the creation story; in the divine gift of life to the barren matriarchs Sarah, Rebekah and Rachel; and in the Genesis covenants between divine and human partners. In the New Testament, we see cooperation between the Spirit and Mary, and in Christ's being divine and human. It crops up in Jesus' teaching in John 12 about the seed falling into the ground, by which the ensuing plant is both related to and different from the seed.

The second change is that multiplication is necessarily accompanied by diversity. This is a shift from duplication to diversification. As the persons of the Trinity are three in one, all God yet not identical, we have the deepest reason of all for embracing diversity as intrinsic to a Christian view of unity. There are also missional reasons in making this a principled change, not merely seeking a transient relevance. Context legitimately shapes Church. The simple phrase 'Mission-shaped Church' tried to explain this. Too often, it has been misinterpreted as meaning merely a Church that adds an Oxo cube, with mission flavour, to its existing stew, while remaining essentially the same. Diversity is rooted in many biblical themes: first in the nature of the Trinity, then in creation. It is shown by the two genders, celebrated in the variety of cultures, and demonstrated by the Church as a body of many parts, and diversity will contribute to the colours of heaven. Thus, any view of the Church that cannot cope with diversity, while also seeking unity, has missed a profoundly Christian mark, which is very clear in the interpersonal paradigm of Church but far less obvious in any of the others.

A third gain is that the interpersonal view of Church links naturally and clearly with Christian and Church maturity. The danger for the institutional was that it thought it had arrived. Church Growth thinking was interested in maturity, but it was hardly central. The horticultural could barely cope with the idea: what could it mean to talk about a mature carrot? However, it is entirely natural in the interpersonal image and sits well with the present high interest in discipleship.

Maturity in churches is subtle, and the interpersonal paradigm helps. I suggest that when we are assessing all expressions of Church for maturity, we are not asking what it is to be an adult, for there can be mature eight-year-olds and immature 80-year-olds. Instead, we seek for the Church equivalent of what it is to be human.[15] Subtle maturity cannot be properly computed in the terms beloved by the legal mind or financial brain, nor by the ecclesial pedant or liturgical fundamentalist. To be human, and to be mature, is far more than just having a legal identity, financial security or approved ways of speaking and acting in public.

By likening Church to being human, not adult, a dignity is given to all expressions of Church, whether old or young, large or small. Dignity certainly does not arise from unhelpful words like 'experimental', 'new' and 'provisional'. If Church is akin to what is human, not what is adult, then, for all expressions of Church it becomes appropriate and helpful to search for the complex and often elusive quality of maturity, with generosity and flexibility. We should expect that what has begun will and should develop, both as it grows over time and as it continues to engage with its context.

The interpersonal understanding bears upon another issue. Should there be the same sauce for the fresh expressions goose and the inherited Church gander? I think this would not be very helpful. The criteria for assessing the life and health of a child are, in some respects, different from those we apply to an adult, or to a frail old person. Here, the analogy with being human, thinking in interpersonal categories, instantly opens up generosity and flexibility. I began to think in all these ways some years ago, in my chapter on the topic of the maturity of fresh expressions, within the book edited by Steven Croft, *The Future of the Parish System*.[16]

These are the gains that come from the interpersonal paradigm of Church. There are good theological reasons to think that this way of seeing is closer to the instincts of the New Testament. It is more appropriate to the people who make up churches, and better for understanding the multiplication, with diversity, that we see today. To illustrate the latter, I often use the following sentence: 'We know that our children are ours, but we also know they are not us.'

Bringing the threads together

I've tried to show that we have lived through some big changes of assumption in the last 40 years. I am convinced that each successive paradigm recovers something important about the Church and represents a step forward. The story also shows that the changes have occurred partly because each previous view could not account for all aspects of the reality of the Church.

This book traces connections to be made and limitations to overcome. It is sadly true that within the institutional view of the Church, reproduction terminology makes almost no sense. With Church Growth, it was possible to think of churches as reproducing, but the idea was overshadowed by the drive to improve existing ones. The calling to reproduce could be derived from the horticultural paradigm. Reproducing was specifically named and affirmed, but the process, as it was imagined, was too narrow; what it created was inadequately described; and the diversity of what occurred could not be easily explained. Non-identical reproduction is obvious and natural in the interpersonal paradigm of the Church.

It is not too much to say that the interpersonal way of looking at the Church and the calling and capacity to reproduce non-identically stand and fall together. I suppose the interpersonal view could be held by itself, but it would be odd to think that such a Church was sterile. The capacity to reproduce could be held, through the horticultural paradigm, but our understanding of its dynamics and the path to maturity would be deficient. Reject the interpersonal view, and you will struggle to accept an argument for Church reproduction. Accept it, and reproduction is just what you would expect, even if you've never heard the argument that it is expected by scripture, emerges in the tradition, is underscored by some parts of theology and fits with more recent experience.

New lamps for old?

By tracking this set of changes, I am not suggesting that the interpersonal paradigm now has no need of the images that came before it. The horticultural is good at teaching us the value of longer seasons and rhythms. The managerial encourages responsibility and assessment. The institutional reminds us that traditions and patterns offer welcome stability. However, interpersonal Christian communities are not adequately described by the three previous paradigms, although they have some reliance upon them.

So, how the four are held together, and which is seen as primary, is vital. I nervously acknowledge the gravitational pull of the earlier models, not least the institutional. You might say that 'good' gravity stops you flying off the planet, but 'bad' gravity prevents you from flying at all. I'd prefer something like the analogy of an anchor for the institutional paradigm. There are times to be rooted and held secure, not least in periods of rest, and times when it is good to stay in the harbour. However, it is perfectly normal to haul up the anchor and set the sails; to journey into adventure, knowing how and when to lower sails and anchor again.

Another set of connections across the four paradigms is that we humans share many biological traits, including reproduction, with the rest of the living creation. We have drawn upon mechanical methods ever since the invention of tools, and we organise ourselves in ways that form traditions and institutions. Human beings need blood and breath, our fingers are mechanically wondrous and it is distinctly useful to have a skeletal structure, but none of those elements make up the essence of being human in the image of God.

Imagine two different bishops, two district superintendents, two divisional commanders or two new Church apostolic figures, who each have examples of fresh expressions of Church in their patch. One says, 'We have some interesting experiments.' The other says, 'These are our children.' Is it not clear that these views are utterly different and also which set of young churches is likely to thrive?

Notes

1 A. Dulles, *Models of the Church* (Gill & Macmillan, 1988), p. 198.
2 G. Arbuckle, *Refounding the Church* (Geoffrey Chapman, 1993), p. 4.
3 M. Frost and A. Hirsch, *The Shaping of Things to Come* (Hendrikson, 2003), p. 225.
4 E. Gibbs and I. Coffey, *Church Next* (IVP, 2000), p. 211.
5 B. Jackson, *Hope for the Church* (CHP, 2002) and *The Road to Growth* (CHP, 2005).
6 Some of these began in the large parish of Chester-le-Street, written up in E. Gibbs, *Ten Growing Churches* (MARC Europe, 1984), chapter 7, by a curate there, Kerry Thorpe. They were called Area Family Services, but were described as 'planted'.
7 M. Hill (ed.), *How to Plant Churches* (MARC Europe, 1984).
8 B. Hopkins, *Church Planting: 1 Models for mission in the Church of England* (Grove Books, 1988) and *Church Planting: 2 Some experiences and challenges* (Grove Books, 1989).
9 For example, Frost and Hirsch, *Shaping of Things to Come*, pp. 76ff.
10 Frost and Hirsch, *Shaping of Things to Come*, p. 213.
11 Dulles, *Models of the Church*, p. 25.
12 B. McLaren, *The Church on the Other Side* (Zondervan, 2000), p. 7.
13 C. Schwarz, *Natural Church Development* (BCGA, 1996), p. 68.
14 M. Atkins, *Resourcing Renewal* (Inspire, 2007), pp. 222–23, 241.
15 This was explored in R. Warren, *Being Human, Being Church* (Marshall Pickering, 1995), pp. 114–28.
16 G. Lings, 'Fresh Expressions growing to maturity' in S. Croft (ed.), *The Future of the Parish System* (CHP, 2006), pp. 138ff.

2

Creation and covenant's mandate to reproduce

Approaching the task

This chapter first outlines both the need to be biblical and the way I am looking at scripture. I then explore the connections between the creation accounts and the Church. I also unpack the enduring legacy from the covenant with Abraham. Both creation and covenant are part of the overall story of the salvation that God brings to the world. Both theological themes deal with reproduction.

Being biblical, not literal

Avery Dulles made scripture his first test of any addition to thinking about the Church: 'Basis in Scripture. Nearly all Christians feel more comfortable if they can find a secure biblical basis for a doctrine they wish to defend—the clearer and more explicit the better.'[1]

Of course, the New Testament contains stories of church planting, yet these stories only illustrate the case. We can't just argue that Paul planted churches and thus so should we. Paul also made tents, travelled by foot and ship, and circumcised his assistants when necessary. Understandably, in starting fresh expressions of Church today, none of these features are deemed necessary. We need to enquire more deeply. Is there an overall biblical rationale for the Church to have the calling and capacity to reproduce?

My assumptions in working with the Bible

I have assumed that there is an overall message of scripture. That is a theological view, not textual exploration. Biblical scholars and theologians can fight. The biblical scholar is reluctant to claim more than the text demonstrates. However, the New Testament itself does not operate so precisely. It is cavalier in its use of the Old Testament, which it sees through the lens of Christ. Theologians also operate more widely. Their views about the Trinity, the exact identity of God the Son, the nature of the Spirit, not to mention who can lead in the Church, all show development and sophistication beyond explicit evidence in scripture.

I am drawn to the views of the 17th-century writer Richard Hooker, who is held high on Anglican Church doctrine. He taught that scripture has a unity and purpose. It is ultimately about Christ and how people can be saved.[2] There are others today who agree, like Christopher Wright in *The Mission of God*.[3] Others, like Dan Beeby, want to put right the way that Christendom 'obscured the fact that the Bible from Genesis to Revelation, if taken as a unity, is a handbook of mission'.[4] He likens scripture to a drama with an intended end, which is the view of N.T. Wright. Wright suggests that the Bible is like a five-act play, but it is up to the actors to finish off the last act. This presents scripture as a narrative with unity and authority, yet we have to apply it.[5]

I am persuaded by this approach—a focus on mission and Christ— but I do not expect all biblical scholars to be impressed. For me, it means we can use older texts without saying that they were written with elements in mind that we see in them later. We can draw things from them, particularly features that the New Testament itself draws. Equally, we can suppose some overall unity about the identity of the people of God across the Bible, without pretending that the writers of the Genesis texts originally thought the same.

So I look at the creation story in general, and humans in the image of God in particular, to see what we learn about reproduction. I'll connect this idea with some New Testament texts and images of the Church, and show how they resonate. Similarly, I'll underline the emphasis on the promise of descendants to Abraham, as a source of blessing of the nations. That will be linked to the ways in which the New Testament writers think the Church inherits this story of blessing for others. Overall, there appears to be no significant development of the salvation story without involving the people of God. First, they receive grace; then, they are sent to live out that gift before others.

Those are my assumptions. Now let's see what we learn about reproduction from the creation accounts.

Creation, capacity and calling

The organic level

Firstly, we learn that all living things have a capacity for reproduction embedded in their creation: 'Then God said, "Let the land produce vegetation: seed-bearing plants and trees on the land that bear fruit with seed in it, according to their various kinds"' (Genesis 1:11). Notice the emphasis on seed and fruit-bearing, and that each breeds true to itself. Capacity for reproduction is basic to organic creation. Yet plant life is not the best image for either human or Church reproduction. Genesis helpfully makes theological distinctions between differing levels within creation.

The creation and blessing of the animals

The animals are treated differently. While they share with plants the capacity for reproduction, there is more, as Von Rad writes: 'These living creatures are the recipients of a life-giving, divine power by virtue of which they themselves are capable of passing on the life they have received by means of their own procreation.'[6]

This is rather like a calling. The specific word 'created' is only used three times—in the headline of Genesis 1:1, for the creation of the animals, and for the creation of humans. Genesis distinguishes between the general word 'made' and the specific term 'created'. Animals and humans are 'creatures'. The lights, seas, dry land and plants are only things 'made'.

So God is described as speaking with the creatures in his creation, not merely naming them. They share the gift of receiving the breath of life, as well as the capacity to pass on that life by active participation in the process. This is a blessing and a calling.

There is some evidence, then, not just of a capacity to reproduce, present in all living things, but also of a calling to reproduce where life is sentient. I remember my excitement in coming across this quote from Westermann. He put it in terms that I could not better.

> It is impossible to think of a living being otherwise than a creative being that reproduces itself; the living being is by definition reproductive. One cannot say that the animals were created and then received a blessing over and above; the act of creating living beings includes endowing them with a capacity to reproduce themselves… The living being, be it animal or person, has the capacity to reproduce simply because it is a living being.[7]

That calling, shared by animals and humans, is given further weight by being called 'good'.

The goodness of creation

The refrain 'God saw that it was good' occurs after each stage of the story. Creation and physicality are good, purposeful and beautiful. This positive evaluation includes approval of the calling and capacity for reproduction. In the longer biblical narrative, fruitfulness is seen as blessing[8] and barrenness as a curse. Reproduction is good.

Parents at the birth of their child identify with this goodness. Artists too can identify with the sense of being struck by their art. Part of the wonder and delight is that this baby, or that artistic creation, is both produced by our efforts and yet different from us, and new. Reproducing contains this characteristic mix of the curious presence of both connection with and difference from the source.

Humans created in the image of God

The importance of the step in creating humanity is noted by many. For Von Rad, the fact that the word 'created', *bara,*' 'occurs three times in the one verse' makes it 'clear that here the high point and goal has been reached'.[9] Westermann argues that the image of God is not something that 'has been added to the created person, but explains what a person is'.[10] Christopher Wright thinks the same.[11] Westermann adds that 'humans are created in such a way that their very existence is intended to be their relationship to God'.[12]

Here is evidence that a reproductive capacity and calling are closely bound into the term 'image' and define what it is to be human. Calvin is direct: 'Adam with his wife was formed for the production of offspring.'[13]

In English, the verbs 'to create' and 'to produce' are related. We even have the verb 'to procreate'. Atkinson writes, 'Procreation strictly means creation "on behalf of another"—in this case him who is Love, God himself.'[14] This is not just about the need to continue a species. Here are theological connections between human life and the creativity of God. But how important is the capacity and calling to reproduce for understanding human beings?

Genesis 1:26 connects 'image' to a responsible relationship with the rest of creation. In verse 28 comes the first command given to humankind, heightened by its being a blessing. The Jewish commentator Sarna is clear: '"The image of God"... must be connected with the immediately following divine blessing.'[15] These first words are 'Be fruitful and multiply' (RSV). It is a direct divine call. Image and reproduction are very closely linked by this text. Oddly, very few modern commentators focus on it. Rather, they move to the second command: 'Fill the earth and subdue it.' They either ignore the first clause or make it a minor point.[16] Wenham is an exception: 'The focus in Genesis is on the fulfilment of the blessing of fruitfulness. This command, like others in Scripture, carries with it an implicit promise that God will enable man to fulfil it.'[17]

Avoidance and assertion of the reproductive priority

I can understand the absence of a focus on reproduction in the light of today's ecological emphases. We know the problem of population explosion. We don't want to see humanity detached from creation. We condemn past exploitation of creation and support ecological care. In addition, the big picture, from the creation of all that is to the making of all things new, reminds us not to have a human-centred view. But contemporary distortions are not a justification for absence of comment on what the text says. The absence may also be connected to the welcome emphasis on commitment and love as foundational for marriage, within which childbearing occurs. Maybe the decrease in rates of childbearing in Western societies over the last century plays a part. In addition, about ten percent of couples are unable to have children and no one implies that those people are not fully human.

However, these contemporary concerns do not justify the omission. There is a clear textual link between humans being in the image of God and the capacity and calling to reproduce. Because humans are in God's image, we share, in a limited way, in his creativity. It is intended, blessed and normal that we will also create in our own likeness and image. Of course, being able to create does not make us divine; it only works out part of the meaning of being in God's image. There is further evidence of this pattern in Genesis 5: 'When God created mankind, he made them in the likeness of God... When Adam had lived 130 years, he had a son in his own likeness, in his own image' (vv. 1b, 3). Reproduction is rooted in the intention and pattern found in the creation account.

A characteristic feature of reproduction is emerging: it is the presence of both connection and difference. In humans, this occurs in three ways. Firstly, it is through gender; it takes the two to fully express what is meant by 'image'. Brueggemann understands that 'humankind is a community, male and female'.[18] Secondly, it also takes the twofold partnership of male and female to enable reproduction. It is a loving creative relationship across difference (Genesis 2:22–25). Thirdly, connection and difference in the non-identical reproductive process are expressed because the one who is born is a fresh and different person. This pattern of intentional creative combination of connection and difference also occurs in Genesis 2:7. Humans are made of the dust of the earth and the breath of God.

Connecting creation and the Church

Creation purposes and the people of God

If the creation accounts tell us much about humanity, why should that apply to the Church? The story of Adam and Eve is, in part, the story of God's intentions for humankind. Ideally we exist in relationship with the rest of creation and in glad yet dependent relationship with God. In that sense it begins the story of the people of God. We are intended to be a God-focused community with a mandate to govern the earth with justice, responsible ruling and care. That happens partly as we fulfil the command to be fruitful, increase and fill the earth. Without reproduction, quite literally, life would cease. Only by reproduction can such proper dominion be achieved. From the start, God's human community is to reproduce as part of fulfilling the divine purpose. The Church is one receiver of this inheritance.

Church images borrowed from creation messages

Another response is that the Church is principally made up of people. To think of the Church essentially as an institution is a viewpoint that the New Testament would barely recognise and to which few people today relate positively. My view, and the view of others, sketched in the previous chapter, is that we are living through a significant reimagination of the Church. In it, recovering the human face of the Church is vital. Of course, the Church is not a single person, but we can think of it as interpersonal. If there is any helpful triangulation between the realities of the Trinity, humanity and thinking about the Church, then it is not so difficult to see why what is true of humanity should, with some care, be applied to ecclesiology.

The New Testament suggests theological links. One is that it calls Jesus, the Lord of the Church, the 'second Adam'. This term connects the purposes of human creation and the Church. Romans 5:14 also calls Adam a type, or pattern, for Christ. Both are seen as founder members with consequences for all who follow them. Yet they are also utterly unlike in the results each brings: 'For as in Adam all die, so in Christ all will be made alive' (1 Corinthians 15:22). 1 Corinthians 15:45–49 also uses creation language in calling Christ 'the last Adam', and the surrounding verses echo this creation association by using the terms 'image' (15:49) and 'firstfruits' (15:23).

This link is strengthened in that a new person in Christ is seen as 'a new creation' (2 Corinthians 5:17; Galatians 6:15). John is boldly explicit with his reproductive language through his characteristic term, 'born' of God. You find it in both his Gospel and his letters. A later witness, linking creation and Church, is Paul Minear in his influential work, *Images of the Church in the New Testament*. Let's pick up what he called the four master images. The 'new creation' group covers other lesser images that resonate with the creation accounts: firstfruits, the new humanity, the last Adam, sabbath rest, the name, life, and the tree of life.

Within his cluster of 'new creation' images, the resurrection of Jesus is likened to 'the first fruits of the dead, 1 Corinthians 15:20–23'.[19] Minear continues, 'This new humanity has been created in the event of his death and resurrection.'[20] The verses and sources see the Church as a new humanity. But the connection is even closer: 'So the new creation was the spearhead of transformation which would rapidly come to pervade all things.'[21] How can that happen? Partly, it will be by the grace of God and the impetus of the Spirit, as in the first creation. But now, that grace empowers the capacity and calling of the Church to reproduce.

Those are some connections underlining the idea that a part of the identity of the Church, as the 'new creation', includes the command and blessing to reproduce and so fill the earth, to the glory of God. The interpersonal Church, made of human beings, inherits the creation calling to all living creatures to reproduce 'after its kind'. God's purpose for humanity in creation lends support to the belief that one strand of Church identity is to be the community called to, and capable of, reproducing. Fresh expressions of Church are the normal, natural consequence.

Creation teaches us

The creation accounts teach that all life has the good *capacity* to reproduce. Higher forms of life are furthermore commanded to do so, which constitutes a *calling*. Humans share that gift, and it is part of what being in the image of God means. Fruitfulness is the very first command to human beings. It is not that God reproduces himself in human beings, but that the creative capacity for reproduction is part of the purpose of the human race. This is carried over by the New Testament images into the ongoing life of the Church.

The creation accounts in scripture offer us persuasive convictions about reproductive thinking as being essential and legitimate. Yet Sarna argues that they are 'only introductory to what is its central motif, namely, the Exodus from Egypt'.[22] This makes God's acts in history, forming a people for himself in which his life and love are being reproduced, more central than the creation—which introduces the next section on covenant.

The covenant and reproduction

The importance of Abraham

I examine Abraham because, if the case from creation has any weight, then the more historical sections about covenants, made with founding members of the people of God, should add to it. If not, the biblical case for reproduction is flawed.

The calling and promises to the patriarchs

The covenant with Abraham is mentioned five times across Genesis as a whole, showing its centrality. It includes the promise, 'All nations will be blessed through you.' Chris Wright goes as far as saying, 'From a missiological perspective, the covenant with Abraham is the most significant of all the biblical covenants.'[23] There are, however, notable differences of emphasis across the Genesis texts, which show how central reproduction is.

Abraham

Genesis 12:1–3 commands Abram to go to the land that God will show him, and the command is accompanied by a host of promises: I will make you a great nation; I will make your name great; and you will be a blessing; I will bless/curse those who bless/curse you; all peoples on earth will be blessed through you. The universal scope of the promises to one man is astonishing. Chris Wright argues that 'blessing' is crucial, and unpacks its meaning: 'Blessing must include at least the concept of multiplication, spreading, filling and abundance.'[24] However, there is a problem: the barrenness of Sarai makes readers conscious of a paradox.

Genesis 15 has Abram protesting his childlessness, in contrast to the vision. God then renews three promises. Firstly, Abraham will have a son from his own body (v. 4); thus reproduction is made explicit. Secondly, his offspring will be as numerous as the stars, which is prolific multiplication (v. 5). The third promise links his descendants with the land, but the land plays a minor role.

Genesis 17 confirms the covenant, after the complications surrounding Hagar and Ishmael. God says that he 'will greatly increase your numbers' (v. 2). The reproductive element is strong. 'This is my covenant with you: you will be the father of many nations… Your name will be Abraham… I will make you very fruitful; I will make nations of you, and kings will come from you' (vv. 4–6). This chapter also contains Abram's change of name. Westermann writes, 'The conferring of a new name marks a new era in life.' He sees it as installing Abraham as 'father of Israel'.[25] Wright links the name change to the blessing coming 'to all nations'.[26] The name change underlines a universal outworking of the promise via reproduction.

Sarah, Isaac, Ishmael and election

Genesis 17:5–19 returns to the strong links between covenant, blessing and reproduction. The Sarai–Sarah name change is parallel to the Abram–Abraham change and its meanings. She is described as 'mother' of nations and kings. Yet at the same time, human doubt continues. It will be followed, in Genesis 18, by the visit of the mysterious three, their promise of a son in the following year, Sarah's inner laugh of disbelief, and their challenge to her.

Then a development comes. Our understanding of reproduction is modified by God's choice, or 'election'. Sarna notes that this passage (17:20–21) 'marks the distinction in spiritual destiny between Isaac and Ishmael'.[27] This is the first indicator that reproduction as a sign of blessing is insufficiently diagnostic, taken by itself. Spiritual and moral qualities are important in those chosen for covenant and blessing (18:17–19).

Here are significant implications. The creation endorses a general human capacity and calling for reproduction, but these don't earn election or covenant. In theological terms, creation gifts cannot achieve redemption ends. Similarly, the Church's capacity to reproduce should not become a source of pride or lead to a misplaced sense of achievement. Also, the capacity of the Church to reproduce does not constitute a calling to do so in each and every context. The calling depends on divine election and purpose, which must be revealed and discerned, not assumed.

The fourth reaffirmation of the covenant is Genesis 22:15–18. After the morally perplexing testing of Abraham, with the near sacrifice of Isaac, the promises are reaffirmed. The strand emphasised is the multiplication of descendants, as prolific as the stars in the sky and sand on the shore.

Variations with Isaac and Jacob

The fifth account, Genesis 26:3–4, confirms the promises to Isaac after the death of Abraham. It repeats the language of chapter 22, but it mentions the future gift of the land first. It seems that, because of famine, Isaac was tempted to leave for Egypt. This different order may just be making the practical point that the multiplication of descendants would be essential before the taking of the land would be feasible. The latter could not be done by a small group of aliens.

What the Genesis covenant passages teach

It is clear how prominent fruitfulness is in these five Genesis accounts. If the creation undergirds a *capacity* for reproduction, it is the covenant that underlines a clear *calling*. Wenham sees this: 'Within these promises, that of being fruitful and multiplying is central.'[28] Reproduction is not the whole point, but it is essential. Moreover, it is made explicit and consistent that through reproduction all nations will be blessed. Election is for mission. It also begins to emerge in the Jacob passages that through reproduction the land can be possessed in future.

Thus, a two-way pull is set up between the universal mission and an inward, narrowly territorial perspective, which occurs through the rest of the Old Testament. The covenant could only find its truest fulfilment as the called community was reproduced among the nations, but this idea was usually ignored or subverted into a proselytising call to the nations to join the existing community, focused on Jerusalem and the land.

One danger of stressing reproduction as central to the covenant is the implication that such reproduction is in our own hands. However, important strands around the necessity of grace and election forcibly deny this implication.

Undeserved covenant and call

Covenants in the ancient Near East were unequal partnerships. Sarna draws parallels with Hittite empire records of 'relationships between the great kings and their inferior vassals'.[29]

The covenant with Abraham shows all the signs of what Christians would call grace, or undeserved favour. Election is a cause not for pride, but for surprise and humility. The exodus story underlines this: 'The Lord did not set his affection on you and choose you because you were more numerous than other peoples, for you were the fewest of all peoples' (Deuteronomy 7:7). Nor should his people imagine that virtue earns this grace: 'It is not because of your righteousness or your integrity that you are going in to take possession of their land' (Deuteronomy 9:5).

Similarly, the Church's capacity and calling to reproduce should never overstep these boundaries. Rather, we should have a humble response and gratitude for a calling that is a gift. Newbigin comments, 'When the Church faces out towards the world, it knows that it only exists as the first-fruits and the instrument of that reconciling work of Christ.'[30] Grace and election come before the existence of the Church, and, within that process, reproduction is only one intended consequence, not a self-justifying feature.

Barren and few

The capacity and calling are shown in Genesis to be very dependent on grace. A repeating pattern is the necessary divine interventions that mark the birth of Isaac, his twins Esau and Jacob, and Joseph. All three generations of the mothers to the children of promise—Sarai, Rebekah and Rachel—are described as barren (Genesis 11:30; 25:21; 29:31). Indeed, if the Abraham story is of greatest significance, then his and Sarah's infertility problem is the longest-lasting, biologically least likely to be resolved, and most convoluted by unprofitable human attempts to resolve it.

Here are themes of personal weakness, understandable human foolishness and dependence on grace. Let those convinced by the argument for reproduction, as part of Church identity, note these dynamics. When we talk of capacity, it is more like potential, not ability, much less power. Without divine involvement, the calling for it is not likely to be fulfilled. Grace will be needed throughout.

Another factor emphasising the need of grace is the motif 'from the few to the many'. 'The few' naturally underlines weakness and dependence, but still is a basis for hope. Let one example suffice. Isaiah 51:1–3 invites the exiles to look to Abraham and Sarah, their father and mother figures. We might expect that covenant promises would be quoted, but which is selected? None is cited directly, but the reproductive element is used allusively: 'When I called him he was only one man, and I blessed him and made him many' (v. 2).

These dynamics of grace also exhibit the bipartite process character-istic of Church reproduction. There is a divine and human partnership in a covenant. There is divine intervention and human cooperation in the unlikely birth of the three generations of promised sons to barren couples. A similar pattern of grace and dependence about reproduction is seen with the parents of John the Baptist at the beginning of the New Testament.[31] The very next story, of Mary, is not of infertility, but is still of dependence and necessary divine intervention. Paul's dependence is expressed in his comment about the gospel and the Church: 'I planted the seed, Apollos watered it, but God has been making it grow' (1 Corinthians 3:6). Reproduction in the Church is profoundly and intimately connected to grace and election.

Linking the Genesis covenants and the Church

Abraham has vast significance as the first patriarch. The Old Testament is full of references to the promises to him. His founder status is without question. Jewish identification with him was instinctive. One designation of being Jewish was being called children of Abraham. What is true for Abraham has important significance for his descendants, but who are they?

The New Testament changes the answer. John the Baptist opens the possibility that God can raise up children of Abraham from other sources (see Matthew 3:9 and Luke 3:8). Jesus, in the controversies described in John 8, continues to drive in a wedge that physical descent from Abraham is not diagnostic. It confers neither spiritual identity nor true freedom. They come as gifts of the Son and are followed by behaviour honouring the Son.[32]

These beginnings are developed in Paul's letters. In Romans 4 is an echo of Genesis 15:6 and the case of faith credited to Abraham as righteousness, prior to circumcision. This connects Abraham with Gentile believers. Romans 9:6–29 contrasts children of promise and human descendants as different within 'God's purpose in election' (v. 11). In Galatians 3:7, Paul argues that people of faith in Christ are sons of Abraham. Consistent with this argument against those who insist on circumcision, he concludes the letter with words in which the people of 'the new creation' are called the Israel of God (Galatians 6:15–16). Abraham is thus not just a character in the story. Wright explains how Paul argues that the Gentile mission is a fulfilment of scripture and the promise to Abraham. Patterns set for Abraham pass on to those now entitled to call themselves the people of God. Giles, concluding his book, writes that across New Testament authors, 'the Christian community, the Church, is "true Israel"'.[33]

The covenant material shows that the Abraham story makes fruitfulness, or biological reproduction, and God's enabling of its outworking one core element. Indeed, without it, the story would both end and fail. An objection could be that this only demonstrates the desire for, and necessity of, physical descendants. While some exilic texts begin to open the understanding of covenant as a spiritual not biological interpretation, it is the New Testament which completes that transformation. It legitimises the step of taking what is originally intended as physical and social language and applying it to spiritual reproduction, beyond physical Israel. To belong to the Messiah by faith was to belong to Israel. 'To belong to Israel was to be a true child of Abraham, no matter what a person's ethnicity.'[34]

If we accept that the unity of scripture requires a Christ-centred and salvation-focused view, then this reapplication of the Genesis narratives is consistent. However, without that interpretative key, the door to a spiritual application of these covenant passages remains only ajar. It could be argued that the strong universal blessing theme in Genesis only required the energetic post-exilic Jewish proselytising, with its requirement for circumcision among those added to the existing covenant people. But the New Testament ushers in a disturbance of past patterns, brought by Jesus and in the early Church. They make covenant blessing and fruitfulness a matter of the Spirit, grace and faith, not of the law or past ancestry.

There is nothing anti-Semitic in this. I went to a London school that included many Jews, and some became good friends. I take serious notice of anything said by Rabbi Jonathan Sachs. I learn from Jewish spirituality. Yet the centrality and uniqueness of Jesus remains a problematic issue.

Paul, in Romans 11, also struggles with the implication of this change for his own people, and the 'grafting in of new shoots' image used there embodies the idea of an insertion and a breaking off. This picture conveys both continuity and an as-yet-unresolved long-term hope for the Jewish people. Paul argues in 11:17–21 that such dynamics of grace and faith preclude pride and arrogance. But the shift to reproduction, seen spiritually, is unmistakable. Minear is clear: 'The apostolic writings of the New Testament… express the conviction that in the new community in Christ, God has truly fulfilled his promise to Abraham.'[35]

I've shown why the covenant with Abraham is highly relevant to the understanding of the Church, and its mission over succeeding generations. The host of images that Minear examines under another master image, 'the people of God', all work from the assumption that the Church rightly inherits these Old Testament images. He holds no brief for my viewpoint, but even more starkly he continues, 'In the resurrection of Christ, God has raised up children to Abraham in fulfilment of his promise.'[36] This quote explicitly opens up connections between Christian identity in Christ and spiritual reproduction, but that is work for my chapters on the New Testament.

The New Testament treatment of who are the spiritual children of Abraham makes it secure for me to argue that the Church inherits the calling to Abraham to reproduce. Now, this calling must be understood and applied spiritually. But I am clear that such thinking is seen through the lenses of Christ and his salvation. It can't be read off directly from the Genesis texts.

Notes

1 A. Dulles, *Models of the Church* (Gill & Macmillan, 1988), p. 191.
2 R. Hooker, *Of the Laws of Ecclesiastical Polity* (CUP, 2002), pp. 112–16.
3 C.J.H. Wright, *The Mission of God* (IVP, 2006).
4 D. Beeby, *Canon and Mission* (Trinity Press, 1999), p. 3.
5 N.T. Wright, *The New Testament and the People of God* (SPCK, 1992), pp. 140–43.
6 Gerhard Von Rad, *Genesis* (SCM, 1973), p. 56.
7 Claus Westermann, *Genesis 1—11* (SPCK, 1984), pp. 138–39.
8 Gordon J. Wenham, *Genesis 1—15* (CUP, 1965), comments, 'God's blessing is most obviously visible in the gift of children, as this is often coupled with "being fruitful and multiplying"' (p. 24).
9 Von Rad, *Genesis*, p. 57 (re Genesis 1:26); Nahum M. Sarna, *Understanding Genesis* (Schocken Books, 1972), p. 15.
10 Westermann, *Genesis 1—11*, p. 157.

11 Wright, *The Mission of God*, p. 421: 'The image of God is not so much something we possess, *as what we are*.'

12 Westermann, *Genesis 1—11*, p. 158.

13 John Calvin, *Genesis*, p. 97. This attitude is reflected in the language about the purposes of marriage in the Book of Common Prayer wedding text, which has since been rightly revised to place love before procreation.

14 David Atkinson, *The Message of Genesis* (IVP, 1990), p. 41.

15 Sarna, *Understanding Genesis*, p. 15.

16 Atkinson, *The Message of Genesis*, p. 41, gives two closing paragraphs in a six-page discussion. Wright, *The Mission*, pp. 421–28, has only two separate sentences, one that production of children needs male–female cooperation (p. 427). His emphases fall on creation care and relationality reflecting God's image.

17 Wenham, *Genesis 1—15*, p. 33.

18 Walter Brueggemann, *Genesis Interpretation* (John Knox Press, 1982), p. 34. Westermann, *Genesis 1—11*, p. 160, agrees.

19 P.S. Minear, *Images of the Church in the New Testament*, 2nd edition (Westminster Press, 2004), p. 112.

20 Minear, *Images of the Church*, p. 115.

21 Minear, *Images of the Church*, p. 113.

22 Sarna, *Understanding Genesis*, p. 8.

23 Wright, *The Mission of God*, p. 327.

24 Wright, *The Mission of God*, p. 209.

25 Claus Westermann, *Genesis 12—36* (SPCK, 1985), p. 261.

26 Wright, *The Mission of God*, pp. 204–205.

27 Sarna, *Understanding Genesis*, p. 132.

28 Wenham, *Genesis 1—15*, p. 24.

29 Sarna, *Understanding Genesis*, p. 126.

30 L. Newbigin, *The Household of God* (SCM, 1953), p. 11.

31 Westermann, *Genesis 12—36*, p. 141, notes this connection.

32 John 8:31–59 and especially vv. 34–41. Minear, *Images of the Church*, p. 74, agrees (re John 6:31).

33 K. Giles, *What on Earth is the Church? A biblical and theological inquiry* (SPCK, 1995), pp. 184–85. He explores the variables of Israel restored (pp. 89–92).

34 Wright, *The Mission of God*, p. 194.

35 Minear, *Images of the Church*, p. 109.

36 Minear, *Images of the Church*, p. 109.

3

The reproductive strand in the kingdom and the Gospels

How do the Gospels contribute to the Church's calling and capacity to reproduce? One significant source is the intriguing number of kingdom parables that are about reproductive growth. However, this immediately raises an objection. Can we apply kingdom texts to the Church?

Connecting kingdom and Church

The long-running debate over the relationship between kingdom and Church includes incompatible views. Some see polar opposites, while others offer reasons for overlap. I shall now evaluate the range of views.

At one extreme is the claim that Church and kingdom are like two identical circles. This tended to be the Western medieval Church view: 'Christendom promoted the notion that… the Church was held to be the visible expression of the Kingdom of God. Functionally, Church and kingdom were treated as one.'[1] Tom Wright refuses that view: 'To equate the kingdom and the Church is at best putting the cart before the horse, and at worst a complete anachronism.'[2]

The opposite view is of two disconnected circles. It claims that Jesus preached the kingdom but the Church distorted his radical simplicity and created an organisational hierarchy. It argues that Jesus never intended to found a Church. The word is rare in the Gospels and the few examples, it is argued, were added back by the early Church. The Catholic reformer Loisy, a century ago, is quoted: 'Jesus proclaimed the kingdom of God and what came was the Church.'[3] Scholars argue over whether Loisy thought that was a mistake or a good natural progression. Both the ecumenist Eric Jay and the Catholic encyclopaedia support the positive view.[4]

Different images of connection

If we reject total overlap and total separation, then reasons for connection need exploring. One element is Jesus' choice of twelve disciples. Against a background in which disciples usually chose their rabbi, the fact that Jesus turned the process upside down is significant. Matthew makes a clear connection with the twelve tribes (Matthew 19:28),[5] and this choice of the Twelve reflects a new Israel. James begins his letter, 'To the twelve tribes scattered among the nations: Greetings.'

Moreover, to separate the kingdom from the people of Israel is impossible. As Wright says of Jesus and the kingdom, the latter 'must instead be thought of as *his agenda for Israel*'.[6] Jesus did subvert what kingdom was held to mean, basing it upon himself and his followers. Wright concludes, 'There is a sense in which the community of Jesus' people was part of the overall meaning of his announcement of the kingdom.'[7]

Another connection between the kingdom and the Church is the rapid emergence of a community dedicated to the spreading of the story of Jesus and the resurrection. Newbigin points out that the kingdom had been proclaimed by the prophets and John the Baptist. 'What is new is that in Jesus the kingdom is present. That is why the first generation of Christian preachers used a different language… He spoke about the kingdom, they spoke about Jesus.'[8]

It is also significant that kingdom language occurs only eight times in Acts. In all cases it involves some Jewish listeners.[9] This suggests that the kingdom is a cultural term. It resonated with Jewish hearers who were expecting its coming, but it is virtually unused by the apostles among Romans and Greeks.[10] Newbigin says, 'The phrase "kingdom of God" in the ears of a pagan Greek would be almost meaningless.'[11] Both Jesus and Paul are accused of creating political conflict with talk of kingdoms. This adaptation to context is more convincing than the suggestion that the kingdom was Jesus' plan and that the Church was substituted by his followers.[12]

The New Testament letters do use 'kingdom' 18 times. Most cases urge moral and spiritual qualities consistent with the kingdom and it is assumed that members of the body of Christ will want those qualities. Connection between kingdom and Church is explicit. A typical example reads, 'Lead a life worthy of God who calls you into his own kingdom' (1 Thessalonians 2:12, RSV). The Church, a community centred in Christ, is connected to the process of the kingdom continuing to come.

The Church is not an end in itself. Take Newbigin's words: 'Jesus manifestly did not intend to leave behind him simply a body of teaching... What he did was to prepare a community chosen to be the bearer of the secret of the kingdom.'[13] The kingdom is related to the mission of God; the mission helps express the rule of God; but the kingdom needs embodying in the people of God. The subsequent tarnished history of the Church remains a vexed problem of credibility in linking the Church positively to the kingdom, but that does not undo an intended connection. Let's now explore the words that express a relationship—that the Church is an 'instrument', 'agent', 'sign' or 'foretaste' of the kingdom.

Instrument

'Instrument' is the least satisfactory. Something I hold in my hand is not me. If the Church has only a functional connection with the kingdom, there need not be any overlap between them. Newbigin rejects an instrumental view on two grounds. Firstly, the Church is both the means and the end because it is a foretaste of that which it proclaims. Because of its grafting into Christ and the giving of the Spirit, the Church has 'a real participation in the life of God'.[14] Secondly, he argues that the way salvation is proclaimed must fit with the nature of salvation. If that message is reconciliation, then it is best communicated by those who have been reconciled with God. 'The Church can be instrumental… because she is much more than instrumental—because she is in fact herself the body of Christ.'[15]

Agent

John Hull's critique of *Mission-shaped Church* values the term 'agent': 'The flowering of the mission is the kingdom; Church is merely an agent.'[16] Hull is correct that the report is inconsistent, sometimes using the term and occasionally repudiating it.[17] As the writer, hesitant about the term 'agent', I can comment further.

On the positive side, 'agent' suggests more involvement than 'instrument'. It implies human participation. However, it is limited because we need modesty about what the Church can achieve. Newbigin makes the crucial objection: 'The Church is not so much the agent of the mission as the locus of the mission.'[18] He argues that it is the Spirit who does mighty works, creates signs and draws people to Christ.

Although the Church is called to carry and embody the message, it is presumption to call the Church the agent of either the mission or the kingdom. We cannot confer on others what God has done in us. We live, with the life of Christ within, but we can't transfer that life to others. The role of agent belongs to the Holy Spirit. In terms taken from Romans 11, we are only branches that have been grafted into the trunk; we are not the trunk that sends up the sap. As Jesus said, in the vine parable, 'Apart from me you can do nothing' (John 15:5). So 'agent' won't do.

Sign

'Sign' is helpful because it points beyond itself to what is fuller and greater, but 'sign' only does some of the work needed to unpack the relationship between church and kingdom. It helpfully reinforces the idea that the Church is less than the kingdom. I am not surprised that the kingdom is more impressive than the Church, but the Church needs to point in the right direction. The Church will always be an imperfect sign of the kingdom, not least because we, its members, are fallen. We have a flawed corporate life and are not fully effective in mission. This fits with the eschatological framework to the kingdom: it is already advancing but not yet completed.

'Sign' also sits well with the Church's role of witness. Signs point to what they signify. The Spirit enables that witness. 'Signs' in Acts and the epistles marked the influence of the Spirit within the early life of the Church,[19] and the presence of the kingdom.[20] The term 'sign' suggests that the kingdom acts more like the *direction* for the Church than a *description* of the Church. It articulates what the Church faces, not what its face looks like. There is always some distance between a sign and what it points to. However, the report *Eucharistic Presidency* then picks up a problem: 'The Church does more than merely point to a reality other than itself.'[21] That takes us to the key word 'foretaste'.

Foretaste

The term 'foretaste' Is a distinct contribution offered by Newbigin. Without the word 'foretaste', the connection between kingdom and Church is not just incomplete but is robbed of its most intimate and most overlapping feature. Throughout Newbigin's book *The Household of God*, we meet 'foretaste'. Its two closing chapters focus on the now and not-yet nature of the Church, which fits perfectly with the term 'foretaste', and then on mission. In the mission chapter, he ties 'instrument' and 'sign' to the deeper reality of 'foretaste', arguing that without it the other two terms become empty. Newbigin also connects 'sign' with the witness of the Church and 'foretaste' with its life.[22] Unless the foretaste is real, the witness will be hollow. This underlines his famous statement: 'I am suggesting that the only answer, the only hermeneutic of the gospel, is a congregation of men and women who believe it and live by it.'[23] Yet throughout, the overlap is partial, which is implied by the very word 'foretaste'. 'The presence of the kingdom in the Church is the presence of its foretaste, its firstfruit, its pledge in the Spirit.'[24] It is the gift which is genuine, but it is partial.

This partial nature of the gift is important to notice and work with. Those who are convinced that the Church is called to reproduce, and that kingdom and Church do overlap, need to acknowledge that kingdom is more dynamic than Church. It is helpful to be reminded that the kingdom is an activity, by which God extends his rule, whereas the Church is but a community. This helps the Church to resist becoming static and to recognise how provisional it is. Kingdom values are often more radical than Church readily allows, and this keeps justice and social issues prominent, while pietism domesticates them. The kingdom is ahead of the Church and the Church is always catching up with God at work in individuals, communities and the levers shaping history. God the King is free to work within, outside, beyond and even without the Church. We join his mission; we should not invite him to join ours.[25] It is the kingdom that should define the Church and the way we understand the scope of God's mission, not the other way round. That fits with the broad pattern in the New Testament. First, we see Jesus declaring the coming of the kingdom, then we see his sending of others in mission, within which we see the forming of the Church.

Another part of the modesty required is provided by the framework of a now and not-yet kingdom. This should lead us to expect a now and not-yet Church to which a 'foretaste' points. We can think in that way because we see the same in related areas. The 'now and not-yet' dynamic applies to the three tenses of salvation used in the New Testament. We can say: I *have* been saved from the penalty of sin, I *am* being saved from the power of sin and I *will be* saved from the presence of sin. There is a similar path in the quest for spirituality. I *have* been called into life with Christ and embarked on the journey to become more like him. Yet in my experience, and that of all spiritual masters, I *am* aware of how much further there is to go. Nevertheless, the prospect that I *will* finally be united with Christ is before me.

Regarding holiness, I applaud the Sermon on the Mount, yet I find it troubling because only Jesus has yet managed to live it out. I *have* accepted its values; they are foundational for all disciples and monastic movements. But I *am* painfully aware of my inner thoughts. I am aware that I do not fully live the values. Here is my own 'not-yet'. However, I *will* one day be whole in mind. I shall be like Jesus, for I shall see him as he is. If this framework affects so much of Christian doctrine and living, and if it is true personally, surely it is also true corporately and applies to what we think of the Church? If 'now and not-yet' is true of salvation and spirituality, why not of our ecclesiology too? Foretaste language is both hopeful and modest.

Yet, with 'foretaste', genuine overlap occurs. The partial occurs now, and 'foretaste' expresses the 'already' dimension of the now and not-yet kingdom and the kingdom / Church relationship. Moreover, only the language of foretaste enshrines an overlap, not just a link. The biblically rooted experience of foretaste, by the Spirit, undergirds a meaningful overlapping connection between the kingdom and the Church.

So *Eucharistic Presidency* says of the Church, 'By virtue of its participation in the life of God, it is not only a sign and instrument, but also a genuine foretaste of God's kingdom.'[26] This fits with Dulles' observation that scholars 'cannot find anywhere in the New Testament the idea that there are people called to the Kingdom without also being called to the Church'.[27]

Kingdom and Church do connect

I have shown why I believe we can look at kingdom texts and apply them, with modesty, to the purpose and nature of the Church. Through 'foretaste' language we can take kingdom texts and have them contribute to the Church's identity and purpose, including how they bear on the strand of reproduction. If the kingdom dynamic includes the strand of reproduction, so should the Church, adding it to its ecclesiology but holding it modestly.

Evidence of reproduction from the parables

The parables are a major source for discerning the dynamics of the kingdom. The Gospels contain around 38 parables, most of which are intentionally unexplained. About one-third of them are not directly about the kingdom but address the highly specific contexts that prompted them. Thus, I shall set them aside.

There are a further 14 in number, clustering around a notable kingdom theme of who is included and who is rejected. Another feature shared by the majority (ten out of 14) of these parables is that they are focused more on the future completed kingdom, not on its start. The parables that deal with the completion of the kingdom cannot be expected to yield much on whether the kingdom, before its completion, should favour the reproduction of subjects of the kingdom. To use a farming picture, when the harvest is in the barn and the chaff is outside, it is not the best time to discuss the essential and mysterious generative power of the seed.

The parables about kingdom growth

This leaves a final one-third of the parables that seem to be about the nature of the kingdom, not a specific issue. When the coming kingdom is illustrated in these parables, a dominant theme is biological growth, within which reproduction has a natural and necessary role. In the Gospel of Luke, who is sometimes called a theologian of the missionary Holy Spirit,[28] we can consider the following: trees that bear fruit (6:43), the seed and four soils (8:5), the spreading branches of the mustard seed tree (13:19), the yeast that works through the dough (13:21), and the talents (19:13). Matthew echoes all of these and adds the story of the seeds and weeds (13:24–30), plus two parables about lack of growth: the unreproductive fig tree (21:18–22) and the vineyard taken away from its tenants (21:33–44). Mark completes the catalogue with the story of the mysterious growing seed (4:26–29). Within all these, the kingdom has reproduction as one strand of its nature. I began to notice that these very parables, which are generic not specific, share a reproductive theme. This shapes our expectations of the incoming kingdom and the Church.

We should not be deflected by the argument that Jesus operated in an agricultural context and thus would inevitably use this kind of parable. He also selected material from political, military, economic, legal, ecclesial and interpersonal stories. The question arises: why are the growth parables told in this way? Intention rather than coincidence is plausible. Alison Morgan writes in stronger terms, citing C.H. Dodd, that Jesus' use of the created world arises 'from a conviction that there is no mere analogy, but an inward affinity, between the natural order and the spiritual order'.[29] Then such growth of the kingdom can be regarded as not just normal, but even normative. The growth comes usually from tiny beginnings, typified by seeds. Is this an echo of the Abraham stories, where the call to reproduce is strong but the capacity to do so is often feeble and those called to it are few?

There is a mystery here, as the Mark 4:26 parable of the seed makes explicit. Tiny, fragile beginnings make for a remarkable and particular story of reproduction and multiplication. This is borne out in the 30- to 100-fold increase at the end of the sowing parable. The same point is made strikingly with the parable of yeast inserted into a remarkable volume of 22 litres of dough,[30] and the mustard seed that becomes the 'largest of garden plants'. All these parables are grouped in Matthew 13. At the heart of Jesus' teaching on the kingdom, the reproductive strand is not only discernible, but prominent.

It would be an overstatement to argue that the only good growth of the kingdom, or the Church, is by reproduction and multiplication. Jesus' parables also promote growth by addition, as in the case of the talents. They also acknowledge growth by restoration, as in the cases of the lost coin, lost sheep and lost son. All I am saying is that the reproductive aspect is the most frequent component of the growth that is natural to the kingdom. If it is there in kingdom understanding, and the link between kingdom and Church is sound, then this strand does belong in ecclesiology too. It is intended for the Church, as both the new creation of God and the ingrafted branch of the kingdom-based, covenanted people.

The acts of Jesus and reproduction

The miracles

The miracles, in part, demonstrate the presence and character of the kingdom. The exorcisms and healings are connected to the incoming of the kingdom, which at times will involve conflict. One could say that these deeds have their own meaning and do not connect to the theme of reproduction. Is this a problem?

I suggest they can be linked to reproduction, but in a different way. As part of the overall kingdom process, Jesus called, trained and sent others. Evidence is found in the initial callings of the disciples. They are to emulate his fishing skills but apply them to human beings. Also, the sending out of the twelve in Matthew 10, or the 72 in Luke 10, is explicitly for preaching and demonstration of the imminent coming of the kingdom (Matthew 10:7; Luke 10:9). What they are sent to do, bringing kingdom healing and exorcism, in a limited sense reproduces what Jesus has been doing. It is the similarity to his pattern that is to be reproduced.

Some commentators take from this only the continued need for mission. While I'd include that element, it is possible to miss the point that Jesus' roles in the coming of the kingdom are being reproduced more widely in other people. Penney sees this broad pattern across Luke and Acts: 'The pattern of mission experienced by Jesus is also experienced by the early Church.'[31] Is this more than obedient imitation? Mike Moynagh has taken my kind of thinking on board at the functional level. In a section on good practice, he writes, 'Reproduction is fundamental to the life of the Church. At the end of Matthew's Gospel, Jesus told his disciples to reproduce what he had done.'[32] If the generic kingdom parables are diagnostic, then we could see here a wider reproductive process. Reproduction is not limited to the birth of Christian communities. Its wider application includes the birth of Christians and the emergence of gifts and ministries, because all these are within the nature of the Church as reproductive.

It is then significant that another theme, associated with reproduction, appears again. In both the calling and sending stories, the weakness and vulnerability of those called by Jesus comes out. Luke 10:3 speaks of their being sent as 'lambs among wolves'. Furthermore, this kingdom value fits with the first and last beatitudes, where it is said of the poor in spirit and the persecuted that 'theirs is the kingdom of heaven' (Matthew 5:3, 10). This language of vulnerable weakness is in keeping with what we saw in the story of the patriarchs. Once again the *calling* to reproduce is not accompanied by a sense of self-sufficient *capacity* to do so.

The 'shape' in the feeding of the 5000

Commentators agree that one mighty deed is present in all four Gospels—the feeding of the 5000. Cranfield wrote, 'The early Church regarded the feeding(s) as being among the greatest and most luminous for faith.'[33] How might it connect with reproduction? Others have noticed, in Matthew, Mark and Luke, that the feeding of the 5000 has a similar 'shape' to the account of the Last Supper. Cranfield makes a table of the closely related but not identical Greek words, italicised here in the New Revised Standard translation.[34]

Taking the five loaves and the two fish, he looked up to heaven, and *blessed* and *broke* the loaves, and *gave* them to his disciples to set before the people; and he divided the two fish among them all (Mark 6:41).

While they were eating, he *took* a loaf of bread, and after *blessing* it he *broke* it, *gave* it to them, and said, 'Take; this is my body' (Mark 14:22).

The common shape is seen in four actions: taking, blessing, breaking and giving. Is the shape suggestive for all Christian ministry? Henry Nouwen's book *Life of the Beloved*, written to introduce the Christian faith to a secular Jewish friend, uses this very shape.[35] I suggest that it can be taken even further.

The identical shape of the action in Holy Communion and the feeding of the 5000 is evidence that we should not drive a wedge between worship and compassionate mission. A divine foundation lies beneath both. The fourfold shape reflects the broad pattern of Jesus' own ministry.

- He *took* the very nature of a servant, being made in human likeness, and that led eventually to taking his own blood into the Most Holy Place.[36] Metaphorically, between those poles, he took people as he found them, not least children, to himself.
- He was *blessed*, notably at his baptism, and he pronounced others blessed by his work or by following his ways. The beatitudes bear witness to this.
- He *broke* with Jewish legalism and literalistic conventions, and broke open understanding beyond it.
- He *gave* himself in life to others. The wording in the New Testament letters centres this on his self-giving death.[37]

One way to describe the result is to say that this shape and process led to multiplication of his life in his new people. Here, in Christ's patterns, is a case for a shape to all ministry. The connection occurred to Augustine of Hippo: 'You are to be taken, blessed, broken, and distributed, that the work of the incarnation may go forward.'[38]

The fourfold shape then applies elegantly to the creation of fresh expressions of Church.

- They too are *taken*. God takes a group of Christians, calling them as they are but sometimes with little idea of what they may be taken to, in terms of mission or its costliness.
- It is essential that they have been *blessed*, in the sense shown in Jesus' baptism. Unless those taken are already blessed by their encounter with God, they have no life to commend to others. We can only give away what we receive.
- In the process of sending people out, *breaking* is involved. There is some break-up of the old congregation and also a breaking away

from previous ways of doing things, which the process of meeting another culture involves. Establishing new Christian communities means that, to borrow language from Jesus, the new wine goes into new wineskins.

• Finally, in this parallel, the essence of planting fresh expressions of Church is a matter of *giving*; it involves giving away. The sending church gives resources of people, time and money for the sake of others. Then, in turn, the young sent church gives its own life to those surrounding it. It is costly, outward and, in that sense, apostolic.

By the grace of God, the result can be the multiplication of the life of Christ in a further group of people, both to embody and to serve the kingdom, as befits the kingdom–Church connections exemplified in the words 'foretaste' and 'sign'.

Evidence of the reproductive strand in John

Children of Abraham

John 8 chronicles a debate about who are the true children of Abraham. This issue surfaces as the test of who are truly his children: 'If you were… you would do what Abraham did' (v. 39). John underlines that the followers of Jesus are spiritually linked to Abraham, and this makes the reproductive call into a mandate that the Church inherits.

The vine in John 15

Minear recognises that the vine analogy for the Church only occurs in John 15, yet he calls it 'so important'. He stresses the strong and intimate theological links between Christ and the Church: 'It is characteristic of many images, but never more succinctly expressed than here, that Christological reality is absolutely basic to the ecclesiological reality… The decisive "you are" can be said to the Church only by the decisive "I am" of the Christ.'[39]

I emphasise that this passage in John 15 is decisive for the nature of the Church. The vine analogy does at least two pieces of work, which would have resonated with an early Jewish reader, and expresses the connection between Christ and his Church. The vine is a plain reference to the people of God. Psalm 80 describes a vine planted out of Egypt, which spread remarkably and yet has later been judged by God and is in desperate need of restoration (Psalm 80:8–19). This is further evidence of the Church's early instinct to see itself as the new Israel. They have inherited the mantle of the vine, with its expectations and demands. Secondly, the same passage explicitly links the vine and a 'son of man' figure, with C.H. Dodd calling them 'equivalent concepts'.[40] Hence, Jesus' claim to be the 'true vine' is not surprising.

If Christ and his Church are linked here, what characterises this union? It is identity with and in Christ. The chapter does not call Christ the stem and Christians the branches. Christ is the whole vine, just as, in Paul sometimes, Christ is the whole body.[41] The interdependence of vine and branch is profound and mutually essential. Vines without branches would be purposeless, and branches without the vine are lifeless. We see again the theme of the profound dependence of those called to produce fruit, first noted in the patriarchs, and the vulnerability of those whom Jesus sent out. Jesus puts it starkly: 'Apart from me you can do nothing' (John 15:5). What is essential for the branches is, then, both to remain in the vine and to be fruitful. To be outside the vine is literally to be dead wood. To be fruitless is no better, for it means being cut off. Even the branches that do bear fruit are pruned for greater fruitfulness.

Minear summarises: 'It is made unmistakably clear that the continuing purpose of the whole vine, stock and branches, is the bearing of fruit.'[42] John 15 strongly commends various well-recognised Christian virtues and disciplines as part of 'remaining in Christ'. They include staying in the word, prayer, love and obedience. But if those things are understood as the remaining, what is the fruit? What is the purpose of remaining in Christ as the vine? It is to be united in love and obedience with Jesus most certainly, but also to bear fruit which is to the Father's glory and shows that we are his disciples.

The meanings of fruit

John 15 has an intriguing progression: no fruit (v. 2); fruit (v. 4); much fruit (v. 8); fruit that will last (v. 16). The exponential verse numbers are merely amusingly coincidental. However, intention is forcefully present. The condition of 'no fruit' leads to removal of the branch. 'Fruit' is appreciated, but it leads to pruning for more fruit. 'Much fruit' shows who are his disciples. Jesus chose them to go and bear fruit that will last. The key questions are: 'What is this fruit?' and 'What is it for?'

The commentators do not agree. Some assume a search for holiness, and so fasten on the obedience theme, seeing fruit as virtues. For example, Bridger makes the link to Galatians 5 and the fruit of the Spirit, citing qualities like love, joy and peace.[43]

But might fruit mean 'more Christians'? This viewpoint is taken by Marsh. He argues that 'Israel should have borne fruit already by the conversion of the Gentiles' and adds that Jesus' cleansing of the temple exposes the Jewish hoarding of spiritual treasures. He understands fruit to mean that 'the Church would and could and must evangelise. The world must come to know that the Son loves the Father, and the Father the world.'[44] I can see that some case could be made from other instances of the term 'fruit' in John. 'He who reaps receives wages, and gathers fruit for eternal life, so that sower and reaper may rejoice together' (John 4:36, RSV). Newbigin belongs to this group but takes it wider: 'They are chosen… to be the bearers of the secret of his saving work for the sake of all. They are chosen to go and bear fruit… To be elect in Christ Jesus… means to be incorporated into his mission to the world.'[45] Historically, this has included not just converts but the creation of churches.

However, I want to take it further. While fruit is meant to nourish and to be enjoyed, well known in the example of grapes, leading to wine, there could be yet another view. Is it totally accidental that fruit also implies the biological method of reproduction? The language of fruit and fruitfulness in scripture even has an explicit connection with human reproduction—for example, in the phrase for a child in Old and New Testaments, 'the fruit of the womb'.[46] Fruit in John 15 seems to me to fit with, and even suggest, the notion that the ability to reproduce spiritually is part of how God intends his people, the Church, to be. Seen in that light, is it far-fetched to see here some foreshadowing of the Church as the community containing, in its being, the strand of a calling and capacity to reproduce?

I am not saying that this is the only meaning, but can it be confidently excluded? Could our assumptions about fruit have excluded what is there within Jesus' teaching in the Gospels as a whole, and in this evidently ecclesial passage? A number of commentators make positive supporting connections. William Temple comments on the vine as Israel: 'Its origin is recorded in the call of Abraham, in whom all families of the earth should be blessed.'[47]

However, the starting point in reproduction goes even further back. Dodd writes, 'At every point the unity of Father and Son is reproduced, in the unity of Christ and believers.'[48] Nor is this an isolated case. 'Christ's love for His "friends", reproducing the love of the Father, and issuing in loving obedience on the part of the disciples, is the "fruit" the branches bear.'[49] Others pick up this connection. Marsh sees it: 'This manner of bearing fruit repeats in the life of the members of the new Israel that relationship of love between Father and Son.'[50] Westcott talks about the union 'revealed in the absolute type of union, the relation of the Son to the Father'.[51] This is where the reproductive strand has its deepest root.

Where we've got to

The chapter shows how and why, mainly through 'foretaste' language, kingdom texts can be responsibly applied as a beckoning device to the Church. The one-third of the parables that are the most general about the character of the kingdom work predominantly through the image of reproduction, often from vulnerable sources. Reproduction of the ministry of Jesus himself was demonstrated in various ways: in the sending out of the twelve and the 72, and through the shape common to both the feeding of the 5000 and the Last Supper. That shape itself undergirds the same broad pattern in Jesus' own mission.

Links in John's Gospel work through the 'children of Abraham' passages, which connect with the reproductive elements of the covenant. The link is most focused in the clearly ecclesial John 15 vine passage. There, reproduction occurs in the cascading outwards of the loving dynamics between the Father and Son; it is also manifested through the meaning of fruit. It is possible to interpret this to include the birth of more churches. The reproductive element is only a strand of Church identity, so it is not always dominant, but this examination of the Gospels has shown the ways in which it is present, inherent and so to be expected in the Church.

The biblical themes of creation, covenant and kingdom, and the links in the Gospels between Christ and his Church, all bear witness to this capacity and calling. That is the clear and explicit case, which claims that it meets Dulles' test of sufficient biblical evidence.

It is time to move from a concentration on biblical texts to theological thinking, and Dulles' tests of any fresh way of thinking have demands to make there too.

Notes

1 W. Shenk and D. Parker, 'The realities of the changing expressions of the Church', *Lausanne Occasional Paper* 43 (2005), p. 7.

2 N.T. Wright, *Jesus and the Victory of God* (SPCK, 1996), p. 222.

3 A. Loisy, *The Gospel and the Church* (Picard, 1902), p. 111.

4 E.G. Jay, The Church: *Its changing image through twenty centuries*, Vol. 2: '1700 to the present day' (SPCK, 1978), p. 20. *Catholic Encyclopaedia*, in its article on the Church, subsection 4, 'The Organisation by the Apostles': www.catholic.org/encyclopedia/view.php?id=2950, accessed 14 November 2016.

5 P.S. Minear, *Images of the Church in the New Testament*, 2nd edition (Westminster Press, 2004), p. 74, links this to their place at the wedding feast and the Twelve as foundation of the holy city in Revelation.

6 Wright, *Jesus and the Victory of God*, pp. 173–74 (italics in original).

7 Wright, *Jesus and the Victory of God*, p. 222.

8 L. Newbigin, *The Open Secret* (SPCK, 1995), pp. 40–44.

9 Acts 1:3 and 1:6 are discourses with the (Jewish) apostles; 8:12 is by Philip to the Samaritans, who shared some thinking with Jews; 14:22 is Paul on the return towards Antioch, visiting young churches, where preaching always started in synagogues; 19:8 is in the Ephesian synagogue; and 20:25 to the Ephesian elders. The final pair are 28:23 to the synagogue in Rome, and 28:31 as a tailpiece to the volume.

10 A. Walls, *The Missionary Movement in Christian History* (T&T Clark, 1996), p. xvii, sees this absence not as regrettable but rather as a positive sign of cross-cultural mission.

11 Newbigin, *The Open Secret*, p. 40.

12 Atkins notes that power, geography and nationalistic problems of 'kingdom' language remain. 'What is the Essence of Church?' in S. Croft (ed.), *Mission-shaped Questions* (CHP, 2008), p. 19. Kirk concurs: 'Kingship sounds masculine, hierarchical, dominating and constraining', *What Is Mission?* (DLT, 1999), p. 29.

13 L. Newbigin, *The Gospel in a Pluralist Society* (SPCK, 1989), p. 133.

14 L. Newbigin, *The Household of God* (SCM, 1953), p. 199.

15 Newbigin, *The Household of God*, p. 200.

16 J. Hull, *Mission-shaped Church—A Response* (SCM, 2005), p. 2.

17 G. Cray (ed.), *Mission-shaped Church* (CHP, 2009), p. 34, rejects 'agent', while p. 85 affirms the positive use of 'agent'.

18 Newbigin, *The Gospel in a Pluralist Society*, p. 119.

19 As noted by Newbigin, *The Household of God*, p. 186, in 1952, long before the ministry of John Wimber.

20 Acts 4:30; 5:12; 14:3; 15.12; Romans 15:19; 2 Corinthians 12:12; Hebrews 2:4.

21 House of Bishops, *Eucharistic Presidency* (CUP, 1997), p.16, para. 2.12.

22 Newbigin, *The Household of God*, p. 196.

23 Newbigin, *The Gospel in a Pluralist Society*, p. 227.

24 Newbigin, *The Gospel in a Pluralist Society*, pp. 119–120.

25 S. Murray, *Church Planting: Laying foundations* (Paternoster, 1998), pp. 40–41.

26 House of Bishops, *Eucharistic Presidency*, p. 16, para. 2.12.

27 A. Dulles, *Models of the Church* (Gill & Macmillan, 1988), p. 101.

28 J.M. Penney, *Lukan Pneumatology* (Sheffield Academic Press, 1997), p. 15, would be an example of this view.

29 A. Morgan, 'What does the gift of the Spirit mean for the shape of the Church?' in Croft (ed.), *Mission-shaped Questions*, p. 150, from C.H. Dodd, *The Parables of the Kingdom* (Fontana/Collins, 1961), p. 20.

30 B. Hopkins, 'Institutional and local change through Church plants' in M. Mills-Powell (ed.), *Setting the Church of England Free* (John Hunt, 2003), p. 139.

31 Penney, *Lukan Pneumatology*, p. 16. He speaks of the parallels as the Spirit anointing, followed by miracles, increasing opposition, trial and consummation and the role of the Spirit as the Lord of mission, p. 84.

32 M. Moynagh, 'Good practice is not what it used to be' in S. Croft (ed.), *The Future of the Parish System*, p. 119.

33 C. Cranfield, *The Gospel According to St Mark* (CUP, 1959), p. 216.

34 C.E.B. Cranfield, *The Gospel According to St Mark* (CUP, 1966), p. 222: 'Mark also surely has the Last Supper... in mind.'

35 H. Nouwen, *Life of the Beloved* (Hodder and Stoughton, 2002).

36 Philippians 2:7; Hebrews 9:12. John's Gospel uses 'take' four times in the crucifixion narratives. Jesus is taken to be scourged, and to Golgotha; the garments are taken and, eventually, so is the body (John 19:1, 16, 23, 40).

37 The phrase 'he gave himself' occurs in Galatians 1:4; 2:20; Ephesians 5:2, 25; 1 Timothy 2:6; Titus 2:14. 'He gave up his spirit,' John 19:30.

38 I met this sentence in a liturgy devised in 2007 by the Provost of Derby Cathedral, but both of us, through internet searches, have only found further contemporary sermon citations, not the source document.

39 Minear, *Images of the Church*, p. 42.

40 C.H. Dodd, *The Interpretation of the Fourth Gospel* (CUP, 1970), p. 411, and A.M. Hunter, *According to John* (SCM, 1972), p. 87: 'The vine of God, Israel, is actually called "the son of man".'

41 W. Temple, *Readings in John's Gospel* (Macmillan, 1952), p. 259; B.F. Westcott, *Gospel of John* (John Murray, 1902), p. 217.

42 Minear, *Images of the Church*, p. 42.

43 G. Bridger, *The Man From Outside* (IVP, 1969), p. 143.

44 J. Marsh, *Saint John* (Penguin, 1968), p. 520.

45 Newbigin, *The Gospel in a Pluralist Society*, pp. 86-87.

46 Psalm 127:3; Isaiah 13:18; Luke 1:42 (all NRSV).

47 Temple, *Readings in John's Gospel*, p. 253.

48 Dodd, *The Interpretation of the Fourth Gospel*, p. 195.

49 Dodd, *The Interpretation of the Fourth Gospel*, p. 412.

50 Marsh, *Saint John*, pp. 520–21.

51 Westcott, *Gospel of John*, p. 219.

4

The Trinity and the Church seen as community-in-mission

It comes as a surprise to some that the way we understand the Church comes from other parts of theology—so it is called a derived doctrine. Two of those parts of theology are the Trinity and the mission of God, or *missio Dei*. In this chapter I set down what we learn from both sources about the Church and what is being reproduced from them.

This chapter also tackles a second task, however. It is about showing how the reproductive strand of Church identity provides some 'theological fruitfulness'. Any idea that better connects parts of theological thinking suggests its own truth as well as being useful. Dulles' sixth test reads:

> *Theological fruitfulness.* One criterion for the selection of new paradigms is their ability to solve problems that proved intractable by appeal to older models, or to synthesise doctrines that previously appeared to be unrelated.[1]

The Trinity seen corporately as 'communion' and *missio Dei* have been two important rediscoveries in the last century. Yet for a long time the two remained largely disconnected, until the last few years. This chapter offers one bridge across that gap by describing the Trinity as 'community-in-mission'. From there I explore in what senses the Trinity also reproduce and how these factors apply to the Church.

Two important but disconnected recent themes

Until recently, I had noticed an odd lack of links between two important but relatively recent rediscoveries: Eastern trinitarian thought and *missio Dei* thinking.

The Trinity as communion

Giles dates the recovery of a connection between Trinity and ecclesiology to 1961, in an ecumenical definition of the Church as grounded in the Trinity rather than just in Christ. The connection between Trinity and Church is put by the Orthodox theologian Zizioulas: 'The mystery of the Church… is deeply bound… to the very being of God.'[2]

The very word 'Trinity' may create fear that this chapter will be too technical and remote from life, so let me explain why it matters. The way you view the Trinity affects the way you see the Church. There is a tendency in Western Christian thought to focus on the unity, oneness and 'substance' of God. That leads to an emphasis on the exclusive oneness of the Church and a hierarchical view of it. But in the East there is more emphasis on the communion between the three persons.[3] This holds together the divine unity and diversity through the profound linkage of the three persons with one another. The latter's technical term is *perichoresis*. Perhaps the nearest we have in human experience to that reality is the relationship between a mother and a foetus. Each affects the other intimately and automatically. This Eastern view makes room for two vital things in Church life. We see ultimate reality as fundamentally relational, and with genuine diversity within unity. Giles affirms this connection between Trinity and Church: 'The term *communio* (*koinonia* / community) is not simply a way of describing what should be the hallmark of our life together in Christ, but what defines it.'[4] He then suggests that the best equivalent of *ecclesia* today is the term 'community'.[5]

This Eastern thinking stems from the fourth-century Cappadocian Fathers, but it became prominent in the West relatively recently. From it we are more confident to say that the nature of the Church is relational, diverse and communal. That's what is being reproduced from the Trinity. 'Community' is one plausible shorthand term to express those values.

Missio Dei

The other helpful rediscovery in the 20th century has been *missio Dei* thinking. Bosch is one writer who traces it back to the 1930s.[6] He summarises its view: 'Mission is not primarily an activity of the Church, but an attribute of God.'[7] The source and legitimacy of mission are in God. So we can then say, as did Vatican II, 'The Church is missionary by its very nature, since it has its origin in the mission of the Son and the Holy Spirit.'[8] Here is the Church deriving its being from God. Notice that the word 'origin' suggests that some of God's attributes are being reproduced in the Church.

But there has been little connection across these two influential streams, and no good way to combine them. The reason why this gap has existed includes the Orthodox view that mission is mainly the search for unity. That makes purity of Church doctrine and internal agreement the focus. Another factor has been its focus on eucharistic worship.[9] Zizioulas admits that 'her worship has tended to paralyse missionary activity to an alarming degree'.[10] The gap also shows up in that the word 'Trinity' is not in the index of Dulles' Roman Catholic book on the Church, nor is there a chapter on the Trinity. Among Anglicans, Paul Avis surveyed literature contributions to doctrines of the Church in 2002. His summaries contain nothing on the Trinity, from them or from him.[11] One notable exception is the Bishops' report *Eucharistic Presidency*, which in four dense pages underlines a vision of the Church as communion, based on the Trinity.[12] In 2012, Mike Moynagh did write about this gap and offered reconnections, arguing that mission belongs at the heart of the Trinity. He uses the analogy of mission as a first, second or eternal 'step' for God.[13]

On the other side of the divide, many mission thinkers are sceptical about making the Church too central. A stark example is Hoekendijk, who described the Church as 'unnecessary for the *missio Dei*'.[14] They are also still addressing internal divisions between social and evangelistic aspects of mission. Even those writing theology to assist British church planters, such as Robinson and Murray, focus on *missio Dei* and the kingdom to give breadth and depth to the mission needed,[15] but they don't discuss the Trinity, much less connect it to ecclesiology. Years ago, Volf noted that 'the idea of correspondence between Church and Trinity has remained largely alien to the Free Church tradition'.[16] Even the theological chapter of *Mission-shaped Church* only listed the Trinity and *missio Dei*, in that order, but failed to explicitly join them up.[17]

A recent exception is Moynagh's *Church for Every Context*. He writes on the identity and purpose of the Church, first as seen through the lens of the kingdom, then as marked by four interconnecting relationships. We both map the latter on to the words 'one, holy, catholic and apostolic'. We both refuse to prioritise public worship over mission and see the need for the worship to express 'that the Church is being drawn into God's missional life of self-giving to the world'.[18] Moynagh reiterates the division I began to point up some years before, and argues the case that mission and communion are equally in the very being of the Trinity.[19] He goes on, 'Mission as giving provides a theological starting point for understanding ecclesial reproduction.' While self-giving is a good metaphor, it is but one element within reproduction. His book quite often refers to Church reproduction, but more to assume it than justify it, and the subject index includes the term 'multiplication' but not 'reproduction'.[20] What might be a further step forward?

The Trinity, community and mission

The Church Army's Research Unit's qualitative research into fresh expressions of Church, since 1997,[21] has highlighted how community is vital not only in the identity of the Church, but also in the process of mission today. Our observation of their practice suggested profound links between community and mission. That very link straddles the two historically estranged disciplines, missiology and ecclesiology. Both have exponents persuaded of the priority of their own discipline and yet both deriving support from the Trinity. Mission writers tend to be weak on the communal and inner life of the Trinity. An example would be how Newbigin's emphases fall on what the Trinity do.[22] By contrast, Volf, writing on the Trinity and Church, does not even index the word 'mission'. These tendencies show the need to connect community and mission at the deepest level. To do this, I introduce my phrase: 'God as community-in-mission', coined in 2004.[23]

Most other writers use the term 'communion' rather than 'community' for the Trinity. Mike Moynagh prefers it, though knowing my rival term, arguing that 'communities' vary too widely and there is a danger of tritheism—that is, having three Gods.[24] He reserves the phrase 'community-in-mission' for the Church. This raises a host of issues. It links to a much wider debate than I can cover, let alone plumb. It relates to whether we opt for the Western or Eastern view of the Trinity. It depends on whether we are more alarmed by the heresies of monism, where nothing is outside God, or tritheism. It connects with whether, for the three in the Trinity, we use the term 'persons' rather than more abstract language like 'pure relationality' (Ratzinger) or 'movements of relationship' (Fiddes).[25] Frankly, theologians vary across all these spectrums.

The language of persons

I'm paddling here in the shallow end of a deep pool, but I throw in a few stones to add ripples showing my preferences and limitations. I am convinced by Tom Smail's writing connecting Trinity and humanity. He works with what we take from their diversity. He repudiates the charge that this approach means thinking that the three within God act in three modes—creation, salvation and transformation (the heresy of modalism). I share his view, doubting that tritheism is seriously being advocated. Rather, the word is used by opponents of diversity as a theological bogey monster. I think Rowan Williams is right to distinguish between the terms 'individual' and 'person'. He points out that the former is never used of the members of the Trinity and the term 'person' is, by definition, formed by connection with others.[26] I have appreciated the emphasis on the three persons in the spiritual writings influenced by what is deemed Celtic. I notice that most liturgy, hymnody and modern songs operate in practice with, and thus nurture, the 'persons' approach. Spiritual devotion, for the majority of us who operate below the level of pure wordless or imageless contemplation, is through the language of persons. The New Testament and its earlier Hebrew roots deal, without embarrassment, in the analogy of persons for God. John's Gospel, in particular, makes much of the terms 'Father' and 'Son', which push us toward relationship and personhood. This also fits with the way the term 'image' links God and human beings. I wonder if the retreat from biblical 'person' language has more to do with the encounter with Greek philosophy.

The existence on earth of Jesus the God/man was undoubtedly personal. Link that to Luther's comment, 'There is now a man in heaven', and it raises the stakes about dismissing the language of persons. I also value the Eastern and charismatic view that the Holy Spirit is not to be reduced below person level, to a force, energy or even the love between the Father and Son. That approach leads, in terms of persons, to a two-way, or binitarian, view of Trinity.

I know we use analogies to speak of God and that the reality is greater and beyond them all, but for the time being, the least worst analogy will do. I have no difficulty in believing that God the Trinity are more than persons, without having much idea what that means in reality. My difficulty is to believe that they are less than persons. The emphasis on *perichoresis* is helpful in taking forward the mystery by which the three are one. I live more easily with that mystery than with the abstract terms for the three that seem to me to be subpersonal. I hold a view of revelation that God is gracious and humble enough to cope with my feeble understanding, and one simple enough to commend to others.

For these reasons I adopt what I hope is a humble and human use of the term 'persons'. I find that 'community' has stronger resonances with interpersonal categories, which seem to me to flow from the Trinity and to describe what the Church is. By contrast, I find that 'communion' is rather static and abstract. It is too tightly linked to, and unduly influenced by, a very high view of the Eucharist that is only the view of some.[27] This language is ethereal to all but trained theologians.

The rest of this chapter does not stand or fall by this disagreement. Behind both terms 'community' and 'communion' are the sense of being communal and the assertion that God, and thus humans and also the Church, share this sort of being, which is based on relations. My present understanding is that the analogy of persons will do for the time being.

Mistaken views of how community and mission in God relate

Some commentators seem to suggest that the being of God is prior to the acts of God, that the Trinity are communal before they are missional. That is only true chronologically, as in the statement 'Mission comes from the Father, through the Son in the power of the Spirit.'[28] Here, the words 'Mission comes' remind us that it comes from something else. If it comes from something else, it cannot *by itself* be the starting point.

This is a useful corrective to the thrust of some books by mission-minded people. Take the view of the widely read and respected Eddie Gibbs: 'The Church must re-establish the priority of the Great Commission. It is the Lord's mandate that *defines* the Church as people who follow Christ… with a local and global vision for Christ's reign on earth.[29]

I agree with Gibbs about past Church failure and ineptitude in mission, but this should not make us overbalance in the other direction and make mission the exclusive definition of Church identity. The Trinity teach us that mission does not, *by itself*, define the Church, though it is part of the Church's identity. I'd even say that the communal view of the Trinity means that *doing* mission is not the true start, for it is the same in the being of God. Missional activity flows out of how God is, for the Trinity are community-in-mission. This creates surprises for pioneers and fresh expressions of Church practitioners. They want to be creating mission-shaped churches, but to discover the best way means that they do not start with *doing* mission. In the Trinity, the *activity* of mission is not the starting point. God's mission proceeds from the inner missional and loving community life of the Trinity.

There is value in stating that the being of God is prior to the activity of God. Similarly, it is a mistake to derive our identity from our activity. Being busy is not purpose. Even being purposeful does not explain who we are. Who we are determines what we should do. This is true of being human and of being Church. We are wise to take those categories chronologically in that order. The danger, then, is to think that, in God, community is to do with being, but that the missional is only a subsequent activity. I agree with Moynagh that this should be resisted.

God the Trinity as community-in-mission

The chronological view of community and mission is flawed because it is imprecise about the being of God—what we call ontology. Moreover, we should not divide the inner life of the Trinity from the outer activity of the Trinity. This invites the kind of unacceptable description that God was content with being only communal, either until the desire to create arose or until the fall regrettably occurred, at which point the Trinity invented being missional as a remedy. The House of Bishops' report *Eucharistic Presidency* connects the two: 'The communion of persons of the Trinity is not to be understood as closed in on itself, but rather open in an outgoing movement of generosity. Creation and redemption are the overflow of God's triune life.'[30]

'Overflow' is a helpful picture. It suggests generosity and abundance, but also continuity. What overflows is the same as its source. However, both *Mission-shaped Church* and *Eucharistic Presidency* stop short of the organic union of terms that I propose. The Trinity understood as 'community-in-mission' is one way to create a permanent bridge across the unwelcome gap between the inner and outer understandings, known as the immanent and the economic Trinity. Both community and mission are in the ontology of God. As a working term, it embodies one way in which the hitherto disconnected passions of trinitarian communion thinkers and *missio Dei* exponents can be joined together.

Progress to date

This chapter is presenting evidence to meet Dulles' test of theological fruitfulness and is also showing how the Trinity affects our view of Church. For nearly 20 years, I have watched missional and ecclesial reproduction occurring in fresh expressions of Church. From this I came to my suggestion of a fruitful combination of two largely separate schools: Trinity seen as communion, and Trinity as *missio Dei*. Describing the Trinity as 'community-in-mission' refuses to separate or privilege one over the other. Zizioulas considers such a process valid. He writes without embarrassment that 'St Irenaeus and later St Athanasius approached the being of God through the experience of the ecclesial community, of *ecclesial being*.'[31] For me, reflecting on fresh expressions of Church, as themselves exhibiting and reproducing community-in-mission, led me to offer that phrase to combine Eastern trinitarian thinking and Western *missio Dei* thought, which most literature has, until recently, treated as unrelated. This connection is precisely the value prized by Dulles in his sixth test.

Trinity as reproducing

Let's now unpack a kind of reproduction at work in both streams of thought. Those interested in trinitarian being and those championing *missio Dei* both teach that the Church derives its identity from these sources respectively. That is a kind of reproduction. Zizioulas argues, 'The Church… must herself be an image of the way in which God exists.'[32] The *missio Dei* proponents similarly argue that the Church is missional because God is missional. Martyn Atkins goes further:

'Whatever God is perceived to be like, the Church, if it is true and faithful, will embody and emulate.' I agree, but my interest is in how that occurs. Both sources have stepped towards saying that part of God's nature is being reproduced in his Church. If we put the two sources together, we can reasonably expect that the divine community-in-mission will seek to reproduce these dynamics, of community-in-mission, in the identity of the Church. Moynagh uses my kind of vocabulary at one point: 'Eternal self-giving within the Trinity is reproduced in the life and death of Jesus. This life and death, this self-donation, gives birth to the Church.'[33]

This chapter raises theological support for the legitimacy of the reproductive strand within Church identity. It is not just that the people of God, in both Testaments, are called to reproduce. Alone, this evidence could be reduced to divinely ordained functionality. Connection with the Trinity raises the bar to the level of being or ontology. It begins to look as if God the Trinity, as community-in-mission, themselves reproduce something of this identity in the being of the Church. Church life is, in turn, communal, relational, giving, creative and missional. This is not just imitation of God from below. It is what was intended and bestowed, as is true too of humanity in God's image. Because this strand is part of its identity, the Church will also have the propensity to reproduce that dynamic in future generations of Church. I shall now explore this idea further. (The following subsection is the most technical, and some readers may want to skip on to the next.)

The theologian Cunningham explores the theme of what and how God the Trinity 'produce'.[34] He draws on the biblical account of the mission of Christ and the experience of the Spirit, using the historic term 'the two processions' within God. Admittedly his chosen verb is to 'produce', not to reproduce. Yet for the birth of the Word, he begins by choosing the obviously apt reproductive analogy of a mother and child. Cunningham then finds the analogy inadequate on the grounds that it focuses on persons as identities rather than 'subsistent relations', which he thinks leads to the dreaded tritheism.[35]

By 'subsistent' he means distinct, and not dependent on something else. He calls three relations 'initiation, fruition and emergence'.[36] He then employs a water analogy and likens them to 'Source, Wellspring and Living Water'.[37] I like the two-way connection across the three pairs and the strong bonding between the three. The weakness, to me, is that the identities and connections in the water image are all subpersonal. This analogy is poor as a way of expressing Trinity as relational, or a community of persons. Thus, it can't be applied to the interpersonal categories within humanity or the Church.

Smail raises another difficulty, reviewing trinitarian thought in East and West. He highlights that in the West there is reliance on Augustine's metaphor as the self-awareness and understanding of the *one* human being. He finds a typical Western case of privileging the one over the three. His criticism is that 'the actual relationships that are the basis of a biblically-founded doctrine of the Trinity are expressed in specific inter-personal categories'.[38] He then rejects the tritheism charge.[39]

It seems there are real difficulties attached to all analogies. I agree with Smail that to retreat from the interpersonal is an overreaction. His earlier book, *The Forgotten Father*, is worded throughout in relational terms. He comments that the Old Testament reserve about talking of God as Father, for fear of pagan associations, is broken in the New Testament with the coming of the Son, who calls the Father 'Abba'.[40]

Cunningham does affirm that God 'produces' the world. He sees the connection as having the sort of loving sustenance and gift of freedom that we see between a parent and child, and includes the restoration of spoilt relationships. That last point enables him to connect with the redemptive work of the Trinity. However, I find it odd that there is no atonement theology; nor does he mention the resurrection. Cunningham believes that he argues what is mirrored in the Nicene Creed. God produces God eternally, produces the world and draws it back to himself.

All of this shows another person thinking through ideas about God 'producing', although the limits of any analogy when working with the Trinity emerge. There are further limits that we should respect.

Care and boldness in what is reproduced from the Trinity

To speak of the Trinity producing, let alone reproducing, their qualities in the Church needs guarding. There are three major caveats. Firstly, the Church is not divine, reproducing the being of the Trinity. Secondly, the Church does not save; salvation is complete in the work of the Trinity. Thirdly, the Church's mission, continuing Christ's mission by the Spirit, is not to reproduce another Trinity.

However, I am intrigued that this careful work by Cunningham twice gravitates to reproductive analogies in order to try to express something which doubtless goes way beyond them, to express the connections between Trinity and Church. It seems that some aspects of the qualities we prize in God are being reproduced. These include relational community, mutual love, and a missional instinct to share that love. These are expected to be in the nature of the Church. In that sense, this identity and these virtues are intentionally being reproduced.

And it is not the case that they are merely being *imitated* by the Church, for the connection is by grace and the operation of the Spirit (Romans 8:15; Galatians 4:6), not human effort. The Church has been given her identity and calling before she is called to live it out. Some might say that grace is simply by transfer, not reproduction. But terms like being 'in Christ', being made a new creation, being born again, and receiving a foretaste of the age to come suggest more than just changes of status and receiving a gift. They all suggest elements of something beyond us being created, or reproduced, within us. We therefore participate in these changes, not only imitate them. At the same time, I know we should not 'simply project onto God our preconceived images of "father", "son", "begetting" and "generating", derived from our particular experiences'.[41]

However, scripture, being neither systematic theology nor remedial feminist insight, nor philosophy of linguistics, seems less embarrassed by this kind of bold connection. The writings of John are especially full of terms connected to reproductive processes, like 'children of God' (John 1:12; 11:52; 1 John 3:1, 10; 4:4; 5:2), and 'born of God' or 'of the Spirit' (John 1:13; 3:3, 5, 7–8). John 1.13 is especially bold in saying, 'not of natural descent, nor of human decision or a husband's will, but born of God'. The language in 1 John is also bold, with variants on the theme. It includes some attributes of God that are reproduced in his children: 'Everyone who does what is right has been born of him' (1 John 2:29); 'God's seed remains in them… they have been born of God' (1 John 3:9); 'Everyone who loves has been born of God' (1 John 4:7); 'If we love one another, God lives in us and his love is made complete in us' (1 John 4:12); 'born of God' (1 John 5:1, 4). Also striking in its links between Christ and his Church is this: 'Anyone born of God does not continue to sin; the One who was born of God keeps them safe' (1 John 5:18).

However, with Smail, we should note a crucial difference. In John, Jesus alone is *Huios*, 'son'; we are only *tekna*, 'children'. It is also true that there is the model of adoption, the metaphor more commonly used by Paul.[42] Yet Peter has his own similar birth terms, as does Paul (1 Peter 1:3, 1:23 and Romans 8:12–17). James, too, joins the chorus: 'He chose to give us birth through the word of truth, that we might be a kind of firstfruits of all he created' (James 1:18). All these texts are innocent of literalistic suggestions of divine or human sexuality. Unless dismissed as entirely meaningless, the vocabulary suggests that something that was inherent in God, and from God, is now reproduced and manifest in us.

The invitation to *theosis*

This transformation from God has an exalted long-term goal, as further texts suggest: 'Be perfect, therefore, as your heavenly Father is perfect' (Matthew 5:48); 'become mature, attaining to the whole measure of the fullness of Christ' (Ephesians 4:13); 'so that… you may participate in the divine nature' (2 Peter 1:4); 'we shall be like him, for we shall see him as he is' (1 John 3:2).

In the early Church there was understood to be a call from the divine, but, more remarkably, it was a call to become in some senses divine, a process known as *theosis*. Note its striking language.

- Irenaeus of Lyons: God 'became what we are in order to make us what he is himself'.
- Clement of Alexandria: 'He who obeys the Lord and follows the prophecy given through him… becomes a god while still moving about in the flesh.'
- Athanasius: 'God became man so that men might become gods.'
- Cyril of Alexandria: we 'are called "temples of God" and indeed "gods", and so we are.'
- Basil the Great stated that 'becoming a god' is the highest goal of all.
- Gregory of Nazianzus implores us, 'Become gods for [God's] sake, since [God] became man for our sake.'

None of the Fathers were saying that humans can aspire to omnipotence, omniscience or omnipresence, but they were saying that in character and virtue we are supposed to become far more like God. This occurs as the divine spark in all of us is restored, strengthened and released. It happens through the interaction of grace from Christ and spiritual disciplines. Central to the disciplines is the renouncing of our thoughts, across John Cassian's classic eightfold list,[43] and learning to have them replaced by virtues, grown of prayer and practice. More recently, Tom Wright in *Virtue Reborn* links the necessity of growing such a virtuous character with the call for the active and responsible roles we shall play in the new heaven and new earth. *Theosis* raises the bar about what of God is to be reproduced in Christians, who bear his image.

Master images of the Church and the reproductive strand

Minear's four foundational New Testament images of Church all fit naturally with the reproductive strand and help connect the biblical and theological sections of this book. Firstly, his grouping of images around 'the people of God' supports and interprets the calling to reproduce, which Chapter 2 showed was core to the covenant. Secondly, in the same chapter, the 'new creation' image of Church underscored the capacity to reproduce, which comes from the creation narrative.

Thirdly, 'the fellowship in faith' contains a set of images which expects that the life of God, with a focus on Christ, is being formed in the Church. Reviewing this section, Minear speaks of the link 'between Christ the Holy One and the Church as holy ones'[44] and of 'the faithful whose trust is in the faithful one',[45] and says that 'the supreme ambition for the disciple is simply to be like his teacher'.[46] There is a repeated sense that roles and attributes of Jesus are taken into the Church and what identifies it. Minear himself connects up all the first three major groups, partly through the obviously reproductive image of the Church as sons of God.

> To early Christians nothing was more distinctive of their common life than their existence as sons of God. As sons they had been born again into the new creation; they were moulded on the pattern of Jesus Christ, the new humanity; they were sons of the Day and sons of the Kingdom.[47]

Minear's fourth image, 'the body of Christ', has a different sort of linkage to reproduction. This is in the sense that the life of Christ is reproduced in his Church, rather than the idea that there should be further bodies. The latter would be foreign to the way the 'body' image is used. Its consistent application is about holding a diversity of parts within the unity of the one body. Overall, then, his work lends weight to the legitimacy of the reproductive image, because it connects across the whole of his fourfold scheme.

So, I would argue that unless and until Church is deeply and effectively community-in-mission, we shall neither follow the example of the three persons of the one Trinity nor connect well with God's world and make much impression upon it. To live out being community-in-mission, with an identity reproduced from the Trinity, in limited human imitation of them, is the primary call of the Church. This connects with the reason why Jesus, in the great commandment, speaks of the centrality of loving God, others and oneself. Any insistence that the great commission eclipses the great commandment, or vice versa, distorts the relationship between being and doing. It will rob the commission of its heart, its authenticity and its best message. That is why Paul writes 1 Corinthians 13 on love and why John's epistles make love the hallmark of the Church. Without it, the Church is not the silver behind the mirror that God intends. It becomes dull and cannot reflect the communal love of God the Trinity. The Trinity began the whole of creation and salvation, called the Church into being, and work ceaselessly for transformation, when eventually the community of the new heaven and earth will be disclosed. The mission story starts in the community of God, and the closing shots are of the wider community of the people of God restored.

Applications of Trinity as reproducing

Church is relational too

The first key element of the Trinity being reproduced in the Church echoes the dynamics of being community-in-mission.[48] This includes a process whereby relational, moral and spiritual qualities, vital for interconnecting and interpenetrating persons, are being reproduced. Daring New Testament language about this, of the Church as sons of God, the body of Christ and those indwelt by the Holy Spirit, is not to be dismissed as flowery imagery. Reproduction supports a high doctrine of the Church. This needs balancing by a repentant realism over how it shows as missional in practice, and how poorly this identity is lived out both as community and in effective mission. However, those failures do not destroy this identity.

Infant Church is possible

'When does something become Church?' is a current question.[49] A second application re-evaluates what happens when a church sends out members to begin another expression of Church. My approach sheds new light on when such a group becomes a church. From a trinitarian way of thinking, this group are Church even as they are sent out, not just when they have won further disciples and gather with them to publicly express their identity as Church. To think they become Church later, via achievement, would be a distortion equivalent to adoptionism—that is, the heresy that the human Jesus became the divine Son only at his baptism. The source and the intention are diagnostic, not the performance. They are Church from the start, although there is a difference between public recognition and inner identity. The latter comes first, and it may be secret for a time.

Avoiding replication

A third application supports the subtleties of reproduction, as opposed to the crudity of replication. The Athanasian Creed wanted to avoid both 'Sabellians, who denied the real distinction of Persons, and Arians, who divided the substance of the Godhead by making the Son a creature'.[50] It says that the Son shares the one substance of Godhood, yet is not the person of the Father. The Son is truly God, but also truly himself. In faithful ecclesial reproduction, there are similar dynamics. The newly created expression is Church, and yet is rightly distinct from the other part of Church that sent it out. Replication or cloning thus earns the just criticism of having Sabellian tendencies.

Hints of a DNA of Church

Reproductive thinking leads naturally to another analogy—that the Church has a spiritual DNA received from the Trinity, and therefore reproduces it. I use 'DNA' not as a precise scientific term but as an analogy to talk about two factors.[51] One is naming something of the essence of Church. The second is the means by which that enduring identity, but not the totality of the parent body, is transmitted into future expressions of Church. This DNA will include the realities required by the four classic marks, as tests of its authenticity. Within the analogy I could suggest that the central twin features of community and mission act like the famous double helix. They intertwine and it is disastrous to separate them. The DNA analogy supports holding together the oneness of community-in-mission as the key identity of both Trinity and Church. However, I am not suggesting here that we can map the whole ecclesial genome. I gladly accept the language of Dulles and Vatican II that the Church's identity is bound in mystery, because of 'the most important thing about the Church: the presence in it of the God who called the members to himself'.[52]

But maybe one part of this mystery can be likened to a gene which we might call 'a calling and capacity for reproduction'. Within the ecclesial DNA, it carries this message faithfully and continues to reproduce it in all as-yet-unborn expressions of the Church. Thus, something rather small, which does not claim to explain everything else, is nevertheless rather significant, both for the Church's continued existence and for its self-identity.

Summing up

I have shown in what ways the theory of the reproductive strand to Church identity fulfils Dulles' sixth test of helping other bits of theology connect better. From observing fresh expressions of Church, I have found a way to connect two very important major theological themes, *missio Dei* thinking and the trinitarian basis for the Church. This is to approach the Trinity as 'community-in-mission'. It offers to disarm the argument over the relative priorities of missiology and ecclesiology by insisting on their inherent unity, just as the inner/immanent and the active/economic Trinity should be kept together.

This examination strengthens the case for the reproductive strand. It argues that its deepest basis is that the life of the Trinity is, in meaningful but limited senses, being reproduced in the Church. This helps amend the way we see the being of the Church and goes a bit further than previous ecclesial models. As such it is fulfilling part of what Dulles' sixth test requires: the ability to offer solutions to problems that were intractable in previous models.

In addition, the sendings of the Son and the Spirit affirm the prior Church identity of the group sent out, in starting a fresh expression of Church. This view also critiques replication's distortion of reproduction for its Sabellian tendencies. It also creates theological space for planted expressions of Church to have their own distinct identity and yet be authentically Church. In turn, the trinitarian-based reproductive analogy welcomes the use of a DNA analogy, which continues to bind Christian community and mission to one another.

The reproductive strand brings theological fruitfulness in the relations between Trinity, Church and mission. The next chapters explore links between Christ and his Church.

Notes

1 A. Dulles, *Models of the Church* (Gill & Macmillan, 1988), p. 192.
2 J.D. Zizioulas, *Being as Communion* (SVS Press, 1997), p. 15.
3 M. Volf, *After Our Likeness* (Eerdmans, 1998), pp. 75–81.
4 K. Giles, *What on Earth is the Church? A biblical and theological inquiry* (SPCK, 1995), p. 228.
5 Giles, *What on Earth is the Church?*, p. 243
6 David Bosch, *Transforming Mission* (Orbis, 1991), pp. 389–93.
7 Bosch, *Transforming Mission*, p. 390
8 Bosch, *Transforming Mission*, p. 391.
9 Volf, *After Our Likeness*, p. 73.
10 Zizioulas, *Being as Communion*, pp. 181–82.
11 P. Avis, *Anglicanism and the Christian Church* (T&T Clark, 2002), pp. 321–54.
12 House of Bishops, *Eucharistic Presidency* (CUP, 1997), pp. 14–18, paragraph 2.4.
13 M. Moynagh, *Church for Every Context* (SCM, 2012), p. 106, and his own approach of a way forward in pp. 120–34.
14 Bosch, *Transforming Mission*, p. 392, on the influence of Hoekendijk.

15 Murray deals with these at greater length and includes incarnation as another principle: S. Murray, *Church Planting: Laying foundations* (Paternoster, 1998), pp. 27–61.
16 Volf, *After Our Likeness*, p. 196.
17 G. Cray (ed.), *Mission-shaped Church* (CHP, 2009), pp. 84–85.
18 Moynagh, *Church for Every Context*, p. 132.
19 Moynagh, *Church for Every Context*, p. 99–114 and 120–34.
20 Moynagh, *Church for Every Context*, p. 27, of Paul's example; p. 128 referring to Church history; pp. 418–20 regarding multiplication.
21 This is published through the *Encounters on the Edge* series from 1999 to 2012, lectures, book chapters and articles.
22 L. Newbigin, *The Open Secret* (SPCK, 1995), chapters 3–6, or his earlier *Trinitarian Doctrine for Today's Mission* (Wipf & Stock, 2006), chapters 4 and 8.
23 G. Lings and B. Hopkins, 'Mission-shaped Church: the inside and outside view', *Encounters on the Edge* 22 (Church Army, 2004), p. 13.
24 Moynagh, *Church for Every Context*, p. 141.
25 Volf, *After Our Likeness*, p. 67, and P. Fiddes in Pete Ward (ed.), *Perspectives on Ecclesiology and Ethnography* (Eerdmans, 2012), p. 25.
26 R. Williams, *Silence and Honey Cakes* (Lion, 2003), pp. 52–53.
27 Volf, *After Our Likeness*, p. 73
28 Cray, *Mission-shaped Church*, p. 85.
29 E. Gibbs, *Leadership Next* (IVP, 2005), p. 89 (his italics).
30 House of Bishops, *Eucharistic Presidency*, p. 15, para. 2.7. It is also cited in Cray, *Mission-shaped Church*, p. 85.
31 Zizioulas, *Being as Communion*, p. 16.
32 Zizioulas, *Being as Communion*, p. 15.
33 Moynagh, *Church for Every Context*, p. 128.
34 D. Cunningham, *These Three Are One* (Blackwell, 1998: 2002), pp. 55–88.
35 Cunningham, *These Three Are One*, pp. 60–64.
36 Cunningham, *These Three Are One*, p. 73.
37 Cunningham, *These Three Are One*, p. 72. He suggests this as only technical, not liturgical, language.
38 T. Smail, *Like Father, Like Son* (Paternoster, 2005), p. 84.
39 Smail, *Like Father, Like Son*, pp. 77 and 95–99, where he explores Basil's rejection of the tritheist charge and the later use of *perichoresis* to nuance the one unity and distinctness of the three persons.
40 T. Smail, *The Forgotten Father* (Hodder, 1980), pp. 36–37.
41 S. Grenz, *The Social God and the Relational Self* (WJKP, 2007), p. 7, citing J.B. Torrance 'The doctrine of the Trinity in our contemporary situation'

from A.I.C. Heron (ed.), *The Forgotten Trinity* (BCC/CCBI, 1989), p. 4.

42 Smail, *The Forgotten Father*, pp. 131–33.

43 The list is (physical) food, sex, things, (mental) anger, dejection, (spiritual) listlessness, vainglory and pride.

44 P.S. Minear, *Images of the Church in the New Testament*, 2nd edition (Westminster Press, 2004), p. 137.

45 Minear, *Images of the Church*, p. 140.

46 Minear, *Images of the Church*, p. 148.

47 Minear, *Images of the Church*, p. 167.

48 'Echo' is a sound-based analogy, just as 'reproduce' is a biological one. R. Greenwood, *Transforming Priesthood*, p. 109, uses the term 'echoing' for the transmission of 'relationality' as central to the inheritance between the Trinity and the Church. So does Giles, *What on Earth is the Church?*, p. 222.

49 Even those within the Anglican and Methodist fresh expressions movement do not agree on whether a venture begins as Church or becomes it. My own contribution began in G. Lings, 'Joining the Club or Changing the Rules?', *Encounters on the Edge* 5 (Church Army, 2000).

50 Joseph Lienhard SJ, 'Athanasian Creed' in Trevor A. Hart (ed.), *Dictionary of Historical Theology* (Paternoster, 2000), p. 40.

51 See G. Lings, 'Unravelling the DNA of Church: How can we know that what is emerging is Church?', *The International Journal for the Study of the Christian Church* 6.1 (2006), pp. 104–16.

52 Dulles, *Models of the Church*, pp. 16–17.

5

Looking to Jesus the pioneer

Let what we see of Jesus Christ shape the Church

I am convinced that several factors within what we believe about Christ should shape what we think about his Church. After all, one biblical image of the Church is 'the body of Christ'. Theologians compress this idea to say that Christology shapes ecclesiology; in other words, features connected to Christ apply also to his Church. They would also rightly insist that the way we think about the Church is drawn from aspects of the Trinity, the mission of God and the values of the kingdom.

What do we learn about the reproductive nature of the Church from our founder? For some years I have been teaching that if we want to know what being mission-shaped means, we should learn from Christ, the divine missioner. Going further, if we want to know if fresh *expressions* of Church are theologically possible, it is helpful to explore our understanding of Christ, who is the definitive *expression* of God on earth. Jesus himself said, 'Anyone who has seen me has seen the Father' (John 14:9). Hebrews 1:3 calls the Son 'the exact representation of [God's] being'.

This chapter and the next one put the case that three features—how God the Son came to this world, how Jesus lived, and the pattern of his dying to live—all make a difference to how we understand his Church. Jesus was serious when, immediately after the resurrection, he said, '*As* the Father has sent me, *so* I send you' (John 20:21, NRSV). Those little words 'as' and 'so' pack a punch. He intended that his patterns would be for us. At the same time, we must preserve what is unique about Christ—being God the eternal Son, saving the world by reconciling us to the Father, and promising the Holy Spirit. That still leaves a lot for us to do and be.

This bears on some quite basic questions. Some people ask, 'Can Church be freshly expressed and remain authentic? If we know what the Church is, how can that change? Surely any change is necessarily for the worse?' So the secretary of an Anglo-Catholic priest's society emailed me a few years ago with an entertainingly worded invitation: 'New ways of being Church is, we realise, just jargon from a Catholic point of view—could you talk about Church ways of being new?' It was this delightfully worded invitation that got me thinking more about the patterns we see in Christ and how they apply to the Church.

I agreed with his group that there are no new ways of being Church. Either something is Church or it isn't. There might be 'renewed old ways of being Church' but that is rather clumsy language. So in writing *Mission-shaped Church* I was part of the decision that we should reject the term 'new ways of being Church' because there aren't any. We recommended adopting an invented term, 'fresh expressions of Church'. In writing the report, we wanted to hold that Church is Church, but to explore how Church, expressed freshly, can change in a principled fashion. That all connects to what we see in Jesus.

So let's explore the dynamics of this way of thinking in relation to the three features. I'll unpack the original incarnation, delve more into Jesus' earthly ministry and, in the next chapter, tease out more about his predicted dying and rising. In all of them we discover elements of Christ's definitive example that connect to the Church's reproduction.

Learning from the incarnation of God the Son

'Incarnation' is a much-used word. I frequently hear it used to justify a pastorally based style of ministry which comes alongside people, seeking to identify with them in everyday life and work with their issues. The word 'in-carnation' has a Latin root, literally meaning 'enfleshed'. It is not found within the New Testament, although widespread sources support it. One Christmas reading includes the phrase 'The Word became flesh and made his dwelling among us' (John 1:14).[1] What does this doctrine teach us about the reproductive process of creating Church, done in the cause of mission and the kingdom? What features of the incarnation apply to the Church?

The incarnation involved a birth

I begin with the obvious: the incarnation involved a birth. Matthew emphasises Joseph's part and Luke brings out Mary's roles. A male baby was born, soon named Jesus, to a young woman called Mary. Birth is one high point in overall human reproduction; it fulfils a longer process which ideally is both loving and creative. It is undeniable, then, that a fresh life has come into the world. Reproduction of the species has occurred.

In Jesus' case, do not confuse the incarnation with whatever is meant in the Creed when it refers to the 'begetting' of the Son. The incarnation is nothing to do with the mystery of the beginnings of God the Son. It is about the enfleshing of the unique divine person, now worshipped as the God/man known, too, as Jesus of Nazareth.

To work out why a birth matters, consider some alternatives. Unacceptable ones include the idea that Jesus only appeared to be human. This is a heresy called docetism; in Greek, *dokein* means 'to seem'. A figure appears who 'seems' to be human but is actually divine, not human. We rightly refuse such thinking. The epistles of John are strong on that. We refuse it because it is not true, and also because of the way we understand the atonement. The heart of the argument says, 'What is not fully entered and identified with cannot be healed or saved.' This principle applies both to substitutionary models of the atonement and to the lofty concept called *theosis*, which teaches that the divine Son became human so that we may become, in some sense, divine.[2] If Jesus was not truly human, all of that breaks down.

However, these twin principles of true substitution for humanity and eventual human inclusion into the divine are loose, not exact. Jesus was not female, and he was Jewish. Yet no one thinks that the incarnation leading to salvation applies only to male Jews. So why need God the Son be born? Why not make his first entrance as an adult? Even Mark is untroubled by starting his Gospel with Jesus as an adult.

Some say that Christ had every kind of human experience, from birth to death. Hebrews 4:15 argues that Christ was tempted in every way, but without succumbing to sin. Yet we know that there are pastoral situations Christ did not face, occupational professions he did not experience and world views he did not meet. Once again we see that the principle of identification is loose, not tight. Jesus' humanity is representative but not strictly inclusive of all human experiences.

So why was a human birth important? I suggest three factors. Firstly, his mother was the prime witness to the genuine humanity of Christ. A first appearance as an adult could never have shown that humanity. Two pieces of evidence towards this are Luke's emphasis on her role, and the tradition linking John and Mary at the crucifixion and, later, in Ephesus. It is intriguing, then, that John's letters most explicitly make the humanity of Christ a test of orthodox belief.

Secondly, a birth shows that God in Christ *affirms* reproduction by undergoing it himself. This underlines the suggestion that the calling for humans to reproduce is not so spoilt by the fall that it cannot be part of the process chosen by God to redeem humanity. The incarnation, as a birth, affirms the continuing place of reproduction, both in the story of humanity and the story of salvation. We could say that if a birth was essential and welcomed for God the Son, then the birth of his churches is made honourable and even diagnostic.

Thirdly, Jesus the God/man, being conceived and born, shows God *experiencing* reproduction. We can think this without compromising the virginal conception and without involving sexual imagery or experience. At this point we enter mystery and debate. Some theologians affirm that in the incarnation God the Son remained fundamentally unchanged. Others happily discuss what changes the process of 'emptying himself' (a phrase in Philippians 2:7, RSV), technically called *kenosis*, might involve. In orthodox understanding, which abilities God the Son put down in the incarnation, and whether they do involve change for God, are complex questions. Within orthodoxy no one denies that the human person Jesus of Nazareth came into being. God in Christ, in the supreme disclosure of the divine, chose to submit to reproductive processes in his mission, which makes the calling and capacity of Christ's Church to do the same, in the mission entrusted to it, more compelling.

One key is a bipartite process

We say it takes two to tango. The word 'bipartite' means there are two partners. Please notice that this is God's characteristic way of working. We see it in the creation, with humans fashioned from dust and breath. We meet it in the covenants, with their divine and human partners. We find it also in the Genesis story, in which the barren wives, Sarah, Rebekah and Rachel, are made fruitful to bear children by divine intervention.

Luke's annunciation story is also bipartite. It shows the creative initiative of God but also the necessity of Mary's willing cooperation. She chooses to hear the call of God and cooperates with God. She declares God's praises (in the Magnificat) and both bears God and shows God to others. Yet she is neither compelled nor bypassed.

Another witness to this characteristic bipartite process is the pair of New Testament terms 'Son of God' and its much less frequent partner, 'Son of Mary'.[3] The Creeds also teach us that both terms used together safeguard Christ's unique identity. The Lukan genealogy acknowledges this dual source. Luke 3:23 says, 'He was the son, so it was thought, of Joseph', while verse 38 ends with the phrase 'the son of God'. This refers to Adam, but also acts as a bookend to the genealogy and thus refers back to Jesus, echoing what verse 22 proclaimed: 'You are my Son, whom I love.' The identity of Jesus thus rests on a deliberate bipartite process.

Let's push this further. To borrow Church planting terms, the incarnation was not a transplanting of the eternal Son. The founder figure in Christianity took part of his identity and inheritance from Mary. Some people do not realise that Jesus of Nazareth did not exist in heaven beforehand. They may never have thought that God the Son inherited Mary's DNA. This is a most intriguing pattern. God the Son comes from outside as a separate source, but this involves intimate engagement with Mary as the context, receiving from her.

If the incarnation works like this, then creating further churches through mission should neither be an unchanged imposition from outside nor be sourced from just the Church. Nor should these churches be derived solely from context. Genuine creation of churches by reproduction is always bipartite, never a single-sourced cloning.

The incarnation, continuity and change

Publicity given to 'fresh expressions of Church' raises the debated question of whether this is theologically responsible language. Can Church be new and still really be Church?

The incarnation has a significant contribution to make. If we ask whether genuinely fresh expressions of Church are theologically possible, the example of Christ turns out to be highly relevant. I've hinted that a promising place to start is Philippians 2. It celebrates glorious and sacrificial changes. Out of a divine love, which the passage calls us to emulate in spirit, enormous changes occurred. He who was in the form of God, and equal with God, emptied himself, taking the form of a slave; he who was in nature God was found in human likeness; he who is eternal became obedient to a shameful death.

I might be the first person to put it in this way, but the incarnation leading to the life of Jesus the God/man was, I suggest, a fresh expression of the second person of the Trinity. To drive home the point, Jesus of Nazareth did not come down from heaven. God the Son came to earth, in a bipartite process between the Spirit and Mary. Jesus came to birth on earth in an existence different from that experienced by God the Son prior to the birth. Central to my point are two things. In the incarnation, the continuity is that the divine identity of the Son was not damaged in any way; nevertheless this incarnation had not been seen before. It was not only change; it was novel. It was not a change that destroyed or distorted God the Son's identity but, rather, freshly expressed it.

I could show you three pictures. They would all be images of what we call water. None of them is not of water, yet one is of steam, the second of a flowing brook and the third of ice. Both the steam and the ice look, feel, and even behave differently from the stream because of the change of localised climate in which they exist, but they all remain H_2O. What endures is H_2O; what changes is the form. They are all expressions of water. Who can say which is more real? This illustrates that continuity of H_2O and change of form can belong together.

After the birth, the story of Jesus continues for some 30 years. I now see that the life he lived is presented by the Gospel writers as containing two contrasting factors. On the one hand is continuity. We see it in his strong sense of call, sharply focused in events such as his baptism. It is also exhibited in patterns like his intentional moving on to proclaim the kingdom despite apparent success (Luke 4:42–44). It is emphasised by his resolutely setting out for Jerusalem (Luke 9:51). It is underlined by his insistence that all these things had to be so, as he told the two disciples on the road to Emmaus, in Luke 24:13–27.

On the other hand, Jesus seems to live the reality that life is not all preplanned. John's Gospel shows him actively seeking and responsively following what the Father is doing and authorising him to say (John 5:19–36; 12:49–50). Jesus experiences changes during his ministry. He appears limited by the lack of faith in Nazareth, disappointed from time to time with his disciples, surprised and delighted by the faith of the Roman centurion. His suffering and struggle in Gethsemane and during the crucifixion are presented as real, not pretended. Throughout the crucifixion narratives, his understated suffering is clear and real. All these features show experiences of change.

Early on, the Christians had to counter the docetic claim that Christ only seemed human. Today this view would suggest that Jesus was like Clark Kent, who is really Superman and only appears to be human. The reality of Jesus' suffering was part of the evidence by which they could say 'no' to the idea of divinity merely posing as human. Jesus was truly human and so things happened to him; he was not insulated from them.

Then come a pair of supreme changes. The paradox of one is captured by the lines of the hymn 'And can it be' by Charles Wesley: ''Tis mystery all, the immortal dies.' Moreover, the pattern of change continues in that Jesus is raised from the dead by God the Father. In 90 per cent of the New Testament texts, the language is passive: 'he was raised', not 'he rose'.

Across the narrower and broader senses of incarnation, both continuity and change are at work. The *continuities* include Christ's divine identity, his relationship to Father and Spirit, his moral perfection, and his commitment to the mission of the Trinity and to the disciples. The *changes* are in whatever was set aside by his becoming enfleshed, in the ups and downs of where the mission took him and, notably, through his own predicted process of dying to live.

Here is a precedent and a pattern to follow. The identity and practice of Jesus, using the incarnation to mean both the founding story and his earthly ministry, show that continuity and change are held together. How we handle holding change and continuity together is a key issue behind the creation of a fresh expression of Church. Can it really be Church and be freshly expressed? Are both together possible? The incarnation says, 'Yes.'

The incarnation is also crucial in claiming that mission should shape Church. It was so for the divine missioner. His mission shaped him. Why cannot that principle be applied to the Church he founded and with his patterns? This point about the applicable patterns is part of his own post-resurrection teaching: 'As the Father has sent me, so I send you.' Jesus is not just acknowledging the sending action of the Father; he is telling us that the process of continuity and change, which he exhibited in his mission, will be ours as well. So continuity and change can be held together. Jesus is theologically the best and utterly sufficient example of this. Creating fresh expressions of Church by non-identical reproduction, involving continuity and change, is consistent with it. You might even expect it.

So any communities of people starting churches are called to do two things simultaneously: hold on to an essential Church and gospel identity, and follow in the steps of Christ, becoming incarnated in appropriate ways into the cultures to which they are sent. They should not be, as it were, photocopied and distributed by central office. The right process will be two-sourced, just as was true for Jesus. The incarnation opens up the possibility of embracing principled change while keeping essential continuity. Non-identical reproduction of fresh expressions of Church is about holding on to both. The call is to be truly Church and truly changed, shaped by being the mission to a particular place or culture. But the changes may be as far-reaching and surprising as was the incarnation. Like the translator J.B. Phillips who, 40 years ago, wrote an article called 'The visited planet', I occasionally speculate on what it was like in the counsels of heaven when the angels were first told what the Trinity had in mind. 'It hasn't been done before,' might have been an objection even then. I imagine the Father replying, 'That is true, but it is not the point.'

Imitation of the life of Christ—reproduced in the Church

If the principles and patterns relating to Christ shape the way we think about his Church, it would be unbalanced to root all of this in just the birth story. That would fail to address the priorities in the ministry of Jesus and what should be reproduced in his Church from them.

John Webster writes on principles of Church doctrine, or ecclesiology. He names three elements in the overall work of the Son that affect the Church. These are the work of the pre-existent Eternal Son, his earthly mission of reconciliation, and the work of the Son in heaven.[4] He uses this scheme to criticise any ecclesiology narrowly founded on the incarnation alone. I agree, and I want to ask what we learn and reproduce from Jesus' ministry, and from his death and resurrection. However, we cannot reproduce anything from the pre-existent Christ or the ascended Son of God. We are blessed by these but only receive from them. However, we are called by the teaching of Jesus to follow some parts of what Webster calls Jesus' 'temporal mission'. I go back to his words, 'As the Father has sent me, so I send you.'

Knowing that there are some parts of his example that we do not follow, nevertheless there is to be an intentional reproduction of Jesus' example in ministry. Here, by 'reproducing' I mean both conscious imitation and a receiving from him, taking his lead into ourselves. It is spiritual, not biological, reproduction. People use different terms for this linkage, to commend it. Dulles uses words close to mine: 'the Church must replicate the works of Jesus'.[5] I think 'replicate' is too tight; it ignores the need for translation when engaging with a context. A Free Church author commending the instinct to reproduce Christ's patterns is Nigel Wright: 'Christ is the prototype of all faithful mission.'[6] The Anglican Stephen Cherry talks about discipleship not as following behind Jesus, but as 'emulating his way of travelling'.[7] I welcome all these varied calls to imitation. Today we use the word 'reproduction' in a variety of ways. One application is about making classic-looking furniture; another is copying original photographs or duplicating ancient artefacts. Reproductions are both like and unlike their originals. So it is here with Christ, both in how far we can truly copy what he did and in preserving to him alone all that is rightly uniquely his.

What is to be reproduced from his example comes in two diagnostic and interconnected ways. Firstly, the ministry of Jesus progresses from an incarnational to a counter-cultural stance. By this I mean that he began with a loving and sacrificial entry into human culture, identifying with it. (Some call this incarnational ministry.) He then brought critical engagement with that same culture. Secondly, his priorities within that progression turn out to be the very means by which the first change from the incarnational to the counter-cultural takes place. We are called to see both of them reproduced in the Church.

The progression from incarnational to counter-cultural

The Jewishness of Jesus is one demonstration of his starting with cultural identification, typical of the incarnational instinct. Another is his striking acceptance of obviously fallen and socially disregarded human beings. By contrast, his counter-cultural stance comes out in several ways. He proclaimed a kingdom different from either the Roman Empire or the Jewish state. This shows in his retort, 'But I say to you…', which occurs six times in Matthew's presentation of the Sermon on the Mount, and through his growing conflict with the Jewish authorities. We could say that his costly identification with humanity reached its summit in his submission to a sacrificial death at its hands. The counter-cultural stance was supremely disclosed by the resurrection, which bursts human categories.

Thus, the two strands are not a neat progression across time but they intertwine. What we need to notice and follow is that the first strand marks the entry point to a culture, but over time the second one tends to trump the first. This shape was demonstrated by the earliest Christians. They came from, and stayed within, their first-century cultures, yet became known for their assertion that 'Jesus is Lord' (Romans 10:9; 1 Corinthians 12:3) and their refusal to acknowledge Caesar as Lord.

This process helps us get beyond arguments between those who emphasise incarnational ministry and those who emphasise counter-cultural mission, with the often-related rival languages of 'presence' and 'proclamation' respectively. The two contrasts do not necessarily pair neatly. Counter-cultural presence is an option, as is passionate proclamation of incarnational virtues. To notice both in the ministry of Christ powerfully suggests that neither option alone is sufficient. Dangerous distortions occur when one option dominates. Stuart Murray comments, 'Silent presence does not accurately describe the mission or ministry of Jesus, whose words unsettled, challenged and disturbed his hearers.'[8] Similarly, the counter-cultural by itself, or an over-emphasis on proclamation, tends towards insular sectarian attitudes. Murray balances his earlier comment by remarking, 'The language of proclamation is regarded as problematic and potentially confrontational.'[9] So we learn from Jesus' patterns that both are needed but that they should occur in the broad order in which he lived them: first incarnational, only then counter-cultural. That is the overall pattern to be reproduced.

Such discussion also fruitfully feeds into a continued evaluation of the theologian H. Richard Niebuhr's classic analysis in his book *Christ and Culture*. It acts as a further critique of his preferred fifth option, that Christians should be transforming culture. That hope looks increasingly unrealistic, not least as we see the emergence of a view he did not anticipate—'Culture against Christ'. The re-evaluation of the role of the Church in society is becoming more necessary as Western Christendom continues to dissolve. What we see is the identities of the Church and the state going in diverging directions, raising the profile of the counter-cultural identity of the Church. Twenty years ago, Robert Warren wrote, 'Christianity has adapted its role in society. Before Constantine, it was a subversive counter-culture operation. Since then it has had an authenticating role. The time has come for the Church to become counter-culture, prophetic, developing a theology of resistance / insistence.'[10]

It has become increasingly clear that the Church is an alternative source of authority and identity to Western society. Therefore, the questions surrounding the way it reproduces in such a context have increasing importance. Jesus' journey, interweaving the incarnational and counter-cultural, is the pattern to be reproduced in our missionary engagement with the cultures of today's diverse society. This reproduction will be similar but not identical to Christ's distinctive patterns. That is partly because we have our own cultures to engage with, which affects the timing by which we will shift from identifying to challenging. We will also need to discern which of today's cultural issues fit with the Christian faith, and which are contrary to it. In addition, we should not assume we can critique society with the clarity and perception possessed uniquely by Christ. We have neither the spiritual discernment nor the divine identity to be as penetrating or accurate. But those limitations are an invitation to humility, not a disqualification from the task of reproducing the example of Christ's shape to the divine mission.

In moving from incarnation to the counter-cultural, Jesus had twin priorities—firstly, demonstrating and proclaiming the kingdom of God, and secondly, investing in the creation and development of his disciples. These priorities run alongside his movement from the incarnational towards the counter-cultural, and represent the very way in which that transition moves. The change towards the counter-cultural can only occur as the Church reproduces the life and values of the kingdom, with disciple-making being central to that process.

Focus on the kingdom of God

The kingdom is fundamentally counter-cultural, as the breaking in of another authority, power and reality. It ushers in values that challenge the society into which it comes. Brueggemann roots this idea in his Old Testament study of the people of God as being 'always in the shadow of the empire'.[11] In the New Testament the empire was Roman. Some of his conclusions are that a community living 'in jeopardy in relation to its context' and being a community of resistance to an empire will 'require intentional and rigorous disciplines, so intentional and rigorous that outsiders may view them as excessively demanding'.[12] Note how this language stresses counter-cultural discipleship. Yet if we are to create further churches, then they can only breed true by sticking to such kingdom values, and this will make them counter-cultural communities. The priority of the kingdom in the ministry of Jesus then gives the Church a set of values and priorities beyond itself. This in turn shapes its inner life and inspires its outer mission and service to others. That includes campaigning for justice and living its existence counter-culturally.

Some people want to make the kingdom even more crucial than I have laid out here. They suggest that the kingdom is the central feature. It may not be popular or fashionable to say so, but I doubt it. I want to show why the role of Christ is even more foundational than the kingdom for determining what the Church is and how it conducts its life and mission (although it is inspired by the kingdom). Why do I think like that?

Firstly, without the person of Christ there would not have been the New Testament kingdom message, which goes beyond the Old Testament understanding. Without the King, the kingdom is vacuous. Secondly, without Christ's incarnation, atonement and the spiritual transformation brought by an encounter with him, kingdom language is in danger of becoming powerless idealism.

Thirdly, Acts and the epistles move away from the predominance of kingdom language to the centrality of Jesus and his resurrection. The early Church made this move. Fourthly, although the kingdom is sometimes mentioned in Acts and the epistles, it is virtually always in a context involving Jews. To anyone else, the term sounded like seditious political revolution. So, fifthly, this evidence shows that the kingdom is not a universal metaphor. It is culturally limited. Today, in the post-imperial UK, in republics and representative democracies, and in ministry to women, kingdom language sounds patriarchal and imperial. That shows its limitations.

I have become convinced that our thoughts about what the Church should be like are best derived from Christ. The list of reasons is important. Firstly, he is its founder; his view is foundational. Secondly, the Church belongs to Christ; it is the Christian Church. Thirdly, the Church is shaped by many of the dynamics of his identity and ministry.

Focus on the disciples

If the kingdom and the counter-cultural are linked, and both are expressed by communities living these values, it is not surprising that the other priority of Jesus was the time given to making disciples. This is the private development of the dynamics that make public the kingdom values. Hence, the tiny Jesus communities are themselves signs and foretastes of the kingdom, like salt and yeast, or like lamps lit in dark places. In examining this second priority, there are several thoughts to hold together.

Disciples and the counter-cultural

Firstly, there is a clear link between being a disciple and being counter-cultural. Paul Minear argues that 'disciple' is a diagnostic word for the Church. He argues that the stories of the disciples 'were normally understood as archetypes of the dilemmas and opportunities that later Christians experienced'.[13] He notes that the commission at the end of Matthew's Gospel commands the making of disciples. He sees the dynamic of discipleship in the epistles. They urge believers to '*learn* from Christ'.[14] What is the result? They have loyalties to one another, seeing each other 'as the Lord incognito'. They take on mutual obligations that cut across normal social expectations, becoming 'a community of servants'. By this they become 'an entirely new kind of human society'. The Church seen as a community of disciples has a strongly counter-cultural flavour.

Disciples and the new Israel

Secondly, the formation of the disciples is seen as the new Israel. Rodney Clapp has written on the early Church and notes, 'Exactly twelve disciples, one for each of the tribes of ancient Israel, are chosen. This was but one sign that the Church saw itself as Israel's seed restored.'[15] Note in passing that the little word 'seed' picks up the reproductive theme.

Newborn Christians do disturb

Disturbance from within is the counter-cultural effect brought by Jesus-centred, kingdom-inspired communities-in-mission. This is brought out clearly by the theologian Miroslav Volf. He notes the shocking reality of the language used for Christians. It is not that they are outsiders who either try to impose external values or form ghetto communities as resident aliens: 'Notice the significance of the new birth for Christian social identity... Christians are insiders who have diverted from their culture by being born again. They are by definition those who are not what they used to be, those who do not live as they used to live.'[16]

This is counter-cultural language. We might say that Christians are traitors to their past identity. Certainly they have changed sides. Volf is clear that the source of this change is the new birth. Just as Jesus was born new, so Christians and Church need to be born anew. As I would now expect, that bipartite process which is human and divine, as well as eternal and contextual, involves both continuity and change. Volf himself sees, in 1 Peter, these dynamics of continuity and change. His word for the dynamic of change is 'distance'.

> The new birth, whose subject is the merciful and electing God (1:2), creates a two-fold distance. First, it is a new birth. It distances one from the old way of life, inherited from one's ancestors (1:18)... Second, it is a birth into a living hope. It distances one from the transitoriness of the present world, in which all human efforts ultimately end in death.[17]

Does counter-cultural necessarily mean 'sect'?
This emphasis on a deliberate and inevitable journey towards the counter-cultural, exhibited by Jesus and embodied in both the kingdom and in being disciples of Jesus, raises for some people a spectre of sectarian identity. Some think that to be a sect is an unacceptable deviation from being Church. Writing as an Anglican, I know that the word 'sect' is anathema to my own denomination. Any writing which suggests that the counter-cultural became dominant in Jesus' practice and priorities, and that the Church should follow in his steps, will need defending.

Volf re-examines H. Richard Niebuhr's classification in *Christ and Culture*, as well as Ernst Troeltsch's classification, which sharply differentiated sects from the Church. Volf draws on the first letter of Peter, a text that Niebuhr mysteriously ignored as he looked at other New Testament authors. Volf finds Peter to be 'a creative thinker in his own right, capable of integrating the social features which Troeltsch tells us we should find clearly separated and assigned to different social types of religious communities'.[18]

Yes, Peter affirms that Christians have a distance from society, but it is not about withdrawal into a private world. Rather, it is only social difference from the ways 'handed down' by their ancestors (1 Peter 1:18). Also, there is distance from the transitory nature of life because of the living hope through Christ. This distance is rooted in an invitation to a new journey to our eternal home, while still living in the world. Moreover, there is distance because Christians are insiders who have changed sides. They have become part of 'a chosen people… a holy nation, God's special possession' (1 Peter 2:9).

However, this does not lead Christians into aggressive stances against society or a wish for totalitarian power to change it. Their difference is not rooted in a negative spiteful difference for its own sake, or repudiation of the lives of their neighbours. The difference comes positively from the call to follow the example of holiness found in God (1 Peter 1:15) and the sufferings of Christ (2:21), and the call not to be like the people they themselves were (1:14). Volf finds evidence of a strong difference that leads to engagement, not to detachment: 'Instead of leading to isolation, this distance is a presupposition of mission. Without distance, churches can only give speeches that others have written for them and only go places where others lead them. To make a difference, one must be different.'[19]

This difference springs out of positive self-identity through Christ. It operates in gentleness, together with speaking out the very truth that has generated the difference. Thus, Volf coins the term 'soft difference'.

People who are secure in themselves—more accurately, who are secure in their God—are able to live the soft difference without fear. They have no need either to subordinate or damn others, but can allow others space to be themselves. For people who live the soft difference, mission fundamentally takes the form of witness and invitation.[20]

He proves that 1 Peter overflows the neat categories of Niebuhr and overturns the assertion that the counter-cultural must be sectarian.

Dulles, evaluating his sixth model of the Church, the community of disciples, was aware of Troeltsch and that being a sect is not being the Church Catholic. He therefore makes this the first critique to which he responds: 'The discipleship model has the advantage of calling attention to the radical break with worldly values that is required for fidelity to Jesus. A certain tension between Church and world seems inevitable.'[21] It 'always depends upon a prior call or vocation from Christ'.[22] This perception is rooted in John 15:16: 'You did not choose me, but I chose you.' Dulles was convinced that the community of disciples is a model that helpfully recovers the sense of 'a contrast society', particularly necessary when 'the general culture gives little support to Christian values'.[23] He also found that the sectarian charge did not stick.

Those born again in Christ are different and reproduce his values, but this identity does not make them sectarian, antagonistic and withdrawn. Being a counter-cultural disciple can be positive.

Disciples and their teacher

In arguing that the ministry patterns of Christ should shape the Church, the dynamics around being a disciple are very helpful. Minear gives us the core: 'The supreme ambition for the disciple is simply to be like his teacher.'[24] Christ expects us to become like him. This connects to the argument that the life of Christ is supposed to be reproduced in the Church. We can use the word 'reproduced' in this spiritual and metaphorical way. It need not always be understood biologically. I value the term 'reproductive' because it is more subtle than the cruder language of imitation. We know that reproduction across the generations includes inheritance, similarity and difference. It allows for faithfulness and creativity. It naturally has a bipartite process. This includes partnerships between God and the Christian, which in turn embraces the bipartite mix of grace and effort. The divine and the human work together so that disciples and churches continue to reproduce with contextual differences.

This mixture of continuity and change even applies to cases where Jesus taught that he is our example. They need contextualisation. Take the foot-washing command in John 13. In reproducing this attitude, not simply obeying by copying it, it may no longer be either necessary or culturally intelligible to literally wash someone's feet. It might be translated into washing their car, cleaning their shoes, or doing their ironing or laundry. In another culture the result might be different again. Thinking in a non-identical reproductive way shows that it can and should be different. The same applies to other cases. I think of Jesus' sending of the 72 in Luke 10. Here, there are elements of going out in a vulnerable way, finding those people of peace who are open, and in such cases bringing healing and proclaiming the kingdom. All these elements will need translation when being reproduced. But at the heart of being a disciple is to have the values and attitudes of Jesus reproduced in our lives. He stresses the two-way link in Luke 10 before the departure of the disciples on mission, saying that acceptance or rejection of them is acceptance or rejection of him (v. 16).

Paul advocates imitation, which includes the handing on of patterns from the Last Supper, but is summed up in his wider instruction, 'Be imitators of me, as I am of Christ' (1 Corinthians 11:1, NRSV). But why does Paul imitate Christ? Is it admiration, command, or something deeper than both? If we look at his uses of the word 'imitate', we spot a more specific link. Take this comment to the Corinthian Christians: 'In Christ Jesus I became your *father* through the gospel. Therefore I urge you to imitate me' (1 Corinthians 4:15–16, my italics). The Ephesians are urged, 'Be imitators of God, as beloved *children*' (Ephesians 5:1, NRSV). It is being and belonging *as children of a father* that is the basis of subsequent imitation. The phrase in English, 'like father, like son', gives a sense of this connection. It looks as though there are parts of scripture that create close connections between spiritual reproduction—being children of God—and imitation in discipleship. It looks as though spiritual reproduction, or being born anew, is followed by moral, social and ethical reproduction. Thus, we become more like Jesus, but we need to apply his example contextually as well as seriously.

What we learn from our founder

The Church is called to reproduce some of the dynamics of the incarnation in the characteristic way that fresh expressions of Church come to birth. We have seen that a birth is honourable and diagnostic, and found that it happens through a bipartite process. We can now have confidence, from Christ's own pattern in the incarnation and his earthly life, that *continuity* with the essence of Church and *change* in terms of how Church appears in context will both be present. This is entirely normal because they are all Christological features, as God the Son was freshly expressed as Jesus, the baby at Bethlehem and man of Nazareth.

Following that, the Church is called to reproduce what it sees Christ doing, through the priorities of living the kingdom and making disciples. These are first-order Church tasks. Moreover, reproducing those dynamics will put into practice an overlapping transition, and be the very means of its taking place. It is the journey from being incarnational to being counter-cultural, free of sectarian slurs, as modelled by Jesus himself.

That leaves what we inherit from Jesus' understanding of his death and resurrection, which comes in the next chapter.

Notes

1 Other citations include Romans 8:3, '… sending his own Son in the likeness of sinful flesh'; 1 Timothy 3:16, 'He appeared in the flesh'; and 1 John 4:2, 'Every spirit that acknowledges that Jesus Christ has come in the flesh is from God.'

2 G. Cray (ed.), *Mission-shaped Church* (CHP, 2009), p. 88, gives Irenaeus as one among many patristic sources: 'Christ became what we are, in order that we might become what he is.'

3 The only direct citation is Mark 6:3, though there are several more cases that refer to Mary as his mother.

4 J. Webster, 'In the society of God: some principles of ecclesiology' in Pete Ward (ed.), *Perspectives on Ecclesiology and Ethnography* (Eerdmans, 2012), p. 200 onwards.

5 A. Dulles, *Models of the Church* (Gill & Macmillan, 1988), p. 221.

6 N.G. Wright, *Disavowing Constantine* (Paternoster, 2000), p. 10.

7 S. Cherry, *Barefoot Disciple: Walking the way of passionate humility* (Continuum, 2011), p. 10.

8 S. Murray, *Church Planting: Laying foundations* (Paternoster, 1998), p. 36.

9 Murray, *Church Planting*, p. 36.

10 R. Warren, 'Towards an Anglican Theology of Change', a private paper to a House of Bishops Study Day (December 1997), p. 3.

11 W. Brueggemann, in M. Budde and R. Brimlow (eds), *The Church as Counterculture* (SUNY, 2000), p. 39.

12 Brueggemann, in Budde and Brimlow, *The Church as Counterculture*, p. 54.

13 P.S. Minear, *Images of the Church in the New Testament*, 2nd edition (Westminster Press, 2004), p. 146.

14 Minear, *Images of the Church*, p. 146 (his italics).

15 R. Clapp, in Budde and Brimlow (eds), *The Church as Counterculture*, p. 26.

16 M. Volf, *Soft Difference: Theological reflections on the relation between church and culture in 1 Peter*: www.pas.rochester.edu/~tim/study/Miroslav%20Volf%201%20Peter.pdf, 1994, pp. 18–19.

17 Volf, *Soft Difference*, p. 18.

18 Volf, *Soft Difference*, p. 17.

19 Volf, *Soft Difference*, p. 24.

20 Volf, *Soft Difference*, p. 24.

21 Dulles, *Models of the Church*, p. 224.

22 Dulles, *Models of the Church*, p. 225.

23 Dulles, *Models of the Church*, p. 222.

24 Minear, *Images of the Church*, p. 148.

6

Following Jesus in dying to live

This chapter moves on from what we learn from the incarnation and the priorities of Jesus' ministry, and what it is called to reproduce. I want to start by facing a genuine question: what is the very heart of the link between Christ and his people, or the Church?

Limits to incarnation-based thinking

The incarnation is a rich seam for mining material to understand better what a church goes through if it is mission-minded and is healthily reproducing. However, there is only so much we can take from the incarnation.

Many Christians know that the New Testament talks about the relationship between Christ and his people in a wide variety of ways, all of which imply a close relationship. Head and body, branches and vine, bridegroom and bride are some of them. Granted this variety, what is the most central feature of our union with Christ? Fundamentally, is it based on the incarnation or on his death and resurrection? Bishop Lesslie Newbigin faced this question back in 1953, and he showed that biblical evidence and liturgical practice favour the second answer.[1]

This does not mean dividing the incarnation from the passion. The process by which God the Son took flesh and became human is essential to understanding how the atonement works. It is always folly to divide incarnation from death and resurrection. However, which of these two is given as *the* pattern for our union with Christ? Which bit of the whole process are we most called to identify with and to emulate?

Newbigin shows that the evidence points in one direction. Romans 6 is about our union with Christ. It describes that relationship as our entry into his death and resurrection. So people are baptised not into the incarnation, but into Christ's death and resurrected life. This is underlined by what the baptism service describes and its symbolism, particularly regarding immersion. Holy Communion, too, centres on Christ's death and the spiritual life he now offers; the incarnation is only mentioned as a necessary part of the salvation process.

Furthermore, the Christian sign has never been the stable; it is the cross. And the sign of the final victory we hope for, which at present is still hidden, is the resurrection. That was the supreme breaking in of the future, or the first fruits of the kingdom. So Paul, speaking about his life and identity in Galatians 2:20, does not write, 'I have been incarnated with Christ.' Rather, he says, 'I have been crucified with Christ and I no longer live, but Christ lives in me.'

There are further factors to persuade us. Firstly, Newbigin points out that the New Testament knows of no extension of the incarnation; Jesus returns to the Father. Indeed, Jesus taught that it was necessary for him to go away. Christ's incarnation on earth ended.

Secondly, there is no command that the incarnation should be continued in us. Martin Davie was one theologian asked to comment on our first draft of *Mission-shaped Church*. He wrote:

> The references to 'the Anglican incarnational principle' and 'incarnational mission' should be dropped. The incarnation, God becoming Man, was a unique and unrepeatable event. There can therefore be no 'incarnational principle' or 'incarnational mission'. God becoming Man is not a principle and the mission of the Church does not involve God taking human nature upon himself.[2]

Thirdly, being human already and covered in flesh, we could not take that road even if we wished. Whatever some people mean by the term 'incarnational', when applying it to their work or themselves, is not the main meaning of the original sense. Much of what is called 'incarnational' is actually only a lesser theological feature. Technically, it could be called having 'kenotic' attitudes. That means gladly giving up our privileges and preferences for the sake of others and of mission. That's good to do in mission, but it is not the basic meaning of the incarnation, just part of its style.

Some people argue back that talking of the Church as 'the body of Christ' does mean the extension of the incarnation. I disagree, because the body of Christ identified with is not the incarnated body but the risen body of Christ. Moreover, the Church dispersed through the world fits better with the episodic resurrection appearances than with Christ's pre-resurrection ministry, in which he was limited to being in one place and at one time. Furthermore, because baptism initiates us into the risen body of Christ, not the incarnated one, it would be odd to reverse that symbolism.

It looks as if being drawn into Christ's death and resurrection, and what *Mission-shaped Church* called 'dying to live', is truly central. That process applies to Christ's own story and how we understand him. It describes the nature of our union with Christ. So it should determine how we understand the Church in mission and the dynamics surrounding the process of churches reproducing.

Let's now tease out two texts that help us understand and apply the 'dying to live' instinct that Christ taught.

Jesus and seeds: the 'dying to live' principle

There are three elements in the life and ministry of Christ that affect the identity and practice of the Church. The previous chapter dealt with what the Church, in its patterns of reproducing, can take, firstly, from the incarnation and, secondly, from Jesus' ministry priorities—that is, his emphasis on the kingdom and on the time he spent on the disciples.

Yet I have just shown how and why the death and resurrection of Christ are central and shape our understanding of the nature of the Church's union with him. This section weaves together two sources that deal with death and life in Christ and how they speak to the Church. The first and controlling example is Jesus' words in John 12 and the second comes from Paul in 1 Corinthians 15.

Embracing lessons from both death and life

To fail to include both death and life would bring a distortion. It would suggest that we are only to follow the lessons of Jesus' life and not his death. John 12 and other passages show that he did not leave us that option. This develops the connection between Christ and his Church. It has been often assumed that the way we understand the Church is modelled mostly on the resurrected life of Christ in the Church. The dominant image of 'the body of Christ' understandably makes that connection.

The language of death has been applied to Christians individually—say, in their baptism, or at the ending of the old life in the convert—or, more literally, to the rightly celebrated suffering of the martyrs.[3] It has not been usual to welcome the death of Church. This has been taken to mean the regrettable closure of a local congregation. 'Dead' has been the judgemental assertion by some people about the absence of faith, or heretical views, among other Christian groups. It has been linked to fears of the ending of a denomination. But here we are given a seldom-considered way to talk about the cost and style of the way the Church is to reproduce. It is through dying to live, which is rooted in Christ's example and command. So, once more, the patterns and teaching we find in Christ, both in his living and in his dying, can be applied to the Church.

Jesus gave this message to us through an analogy with seeds. So first we need to identity what people thought about seeds in the first century.

Death leading to life is normal and characteristic

Both John 12 and 1 Corinthians 15 are about people facing issues of
death and beyond. To do this, they use the analogy provided by the
familiar picture of seeds being sown and new life emerging from this
process. First-century readers knew about that. The passages speak of
the process in similar ways. Paul starts with a no-nonsense statement:
'What you sow does not come to life unless it dies' (1 Corinthians 15:36).
Jesus begins also with an emphasis: 'Very truly I tell you, unless a grain
of wheat falls to the ground and dies, it remains only a single seed. But
if it dies, it produces many seeds' (John 12:24).

I have learnt that different Greek words are used to distinguish between
the general word 'seed' and the more specific term 'grain'. Grains were
always seen as small and especially as vulnerable. That is the word
employed by 1 Corinthians 15 and used in John 12 by Jesus about
himself and his death. If these patterns in Christ do apply to the Church,
then triumphalism, or easy believing, in churches about going through
a dying-to-live process and having the life of Christ reproduced in them
is out of order.

I therefore regret the publicity that can accompany either larger or more
adversarial church planting stories. I regret even more that these stories
have been taken as typical. Here is a biblical basis for repudiating that
view. Where it is justifiable to send a large team, then it becomes all the
more necessary to emulate the style of vulnerability and readiness to
die that we find in the grain. Our own recent Church Army research has
confirmed that across the Church of England, sending a starting group
of three to twelve people is the usual, and more vulnerable, choice in
beginning the wide variety of fresh expressions of Church.[4]

The cost in the process should be emphasised

The vulnerability is linked to the cost. The costliness in the analogy is
very apparent in John 12. Immediately after the seed parable, Jesus
exclaims, 'Now my soul is troubled' (v. 27). His imminent trial, crucifixion

and death make this abundantly clear. So, if this pattern of dying to live applies to churches, then the cost should not be trivialised. In the West, it will not be as extreme as it was for Christ, but practitioners should not imagine an easy, cheap or painless process to Church reproduction. Please excuse the phrase, but dying is not dead easy.

The cost can be helpfully underlined by applying the analogy of planting seeds. Jesus speaks of the seed falling '*into* the ground'.[5] The point is that the seed is, to use a Latin-based word, interred. It is *buried* in the ground. That is a picture of death, which is about endings. To be buried is entirely in keeping with what the process conveys. As William Temple put it, a seed 'must lose its own identity that the new plant may spring up'.[6] One might almost say that the sowing is the funeral of the seed. It goes into the ground and is not seen again.

This intentional connection is made explicit in Paul. 2 Corinthians 9:10 teaches that God's provision of seeds is for those who sow. Sometimes, to state the obvious helps to make the point. Death to their existence is a significant part of the point of their existence. Jesus teaches something similar in John 12:24: 'Unless a grain of wheat falls into the earth and dies, it remains alone' (RSV). This aloneness is an imperfect state, contrasted with the much fruit that will follow its death. Commentator Raymond Brown saw the point: 'We should note that the contrast to dying and bearing fruit is one of not dying and thus remaining unproductive… the parable is concerned not with the fate of the grain but with its productivity.'[7]

Those called to be part of the birth of young churches need to expect some dying. There is some loss of relationship with people in the parent church. There is a willingness to put down their own preferred ways of being Church, in order to find, with those they are sent to, what it should look like in the new place. They may also need to die to being in charge of the whole process, for it will have its own energy and emergence. A parallel is that new parents do not choose what their offspring will be, and they say goodbye to the stage of life of being just a couple. These are some of the costliness links between the reproductive image and seed thinking. But there are more connections.

Seed and plants are different but related

This difference and connection is yet another example of continuity and change. In 1 Corinthians 15:37, Paul points out the obvious: we do not sow the resultant body, but the grain. It is clear that they are related but also that they are different. This is what every farmer knows: a seed looks and is very different from what comes up later, but leads directly to it. Jesus, in another parable, taught the same about the mustard grain. Both Jesus and Paul knew that this diagnostic mixture—continuity and change—is true of seeds and their resultant plants. Here is further evidence that in all non-identical reproduction, continuity and change, held together, are characteristic. We see it in plants and in childbirth. The same applies to church-birth.

The resurrection appearances of Jesus also demonstrate continuity and change. Take John 20. The continuity includes the fact that, in his appearances to the disciples, his body was recognisable as his. His crucifixion wounds remained, permanently emphasising the cost involved. Yet in the same chapter, Mary Magdalene does not immediately recognise him. Nor, in Luke 24, do the two going to Emmaus. Moreover, he can appear and disappear at will, which is a marked change.

Jesus' birth, the teaching about his death and his resurrection all share this continuity-and-change feature. In sowing a seed that leads to Church reproduction, the cost can be related to the reality of change, and it will be felt by those that are sent, as they face an element of 'dying to' their inherited cultural preferences and the way they liked Church to be. Yet their hope is founded in the continuities, including the God whose reputation is bringing related but different life from the dead. The dying is in order to live.

With sowing, we do not know the results first

Paul says, 'When you sow, you do not plant the body that will be' (15:37). The cost, then, also includes uncertainty and lack of control. That too comes in Jesus' parable about the corn that grows from seed sown, but the farmer 'does not know how' (Mark 4:27). Some might argue at this point: surely, if you sow barley seed, you will get barley? I reply that the parable of the sower shows that the results can vary enormously—from getting nothing to receiving one hundredfold. Sometimes weeds get sown among the crop, and that too changes the situation. There is a sense in which each field is different. Even individual stalks and ears may be of different height and fruitfulness.

Mission-shaped Church advocated this move away from certainty. It urged a change from precise advance planning to discernment in context.[8] We can't know it all at the start. The report commended 'double listening' as a 'process that enables something to evolve as its context changes'.[9] Its chief section on dying to live[10] also thinks in these terms. The sense of willingness to let the seed die and wait for what will emerge also lies within the crafted definition of church planting given in *Mission-shaped Church*:

> Church planting is the process by which a seed of the life and message of Jesus embodied by a community of Christians is immersed for mission reasons in a particular cultural or geographic context. The intended consequence is that it roots there, coming to life as a new indigenous body of Christian disciples well-suited to continue in mission.[11]

A similar conviction is found within the very term 'emerging Church' and in the thinking of the groups who embrace it. The term 'emerging' assumes that the end is not known at the beginning, and people may even be glad of that. The phrase leans towards the virtues of discovery, the necessity of fitting with context and not being bound by inherited views of the existing Church.

Soil and seed demonstrate a bipartite relationship

Throughout this book I have insisted that the reproductive strand in the identity of Church has always had two partners—a bipartite element. The seed analogy fits this pattern. The seed provides the continuity by carrying the inheritance. This offers one answer to how and why we can face radical change in the missionary journey—being secure in the continuity that comes from the seed. The famous missionary Vincent Donovan exhibited this sense of confident risk. 'I had to plant the seed in the Masai culture, and let it grow wild.'[12] The soil is the context for the seed. The interaction between the two is what provokes the change, including the large change by which the seed dies.

This pattern might be only of some biological interest, were it not for the fact that Jesus chooses such an image to describe his impending death. By this he contemplates both cost and hope. He seems increasingly aware of the change, which will be his own costly death. But he embraces the continuity, which rests on his loving relationship with Father and Spirit and the determination to see through their joint mission, which, in hope, will lead to resurrection. This bipartite process applies in the two-way relationship between gospel and culture. This is boldly expressed by Donovan: 'If we would be consistent I think we would see that the field of culture is theirs, ours is the gospel… The incarnation of the gospel, the flesh and blood that must grow up on the gospel, is up to the people of the culture.'[13]

The seed's dying, and thereby leading to the living of a related but different plant, is not just a useful analogy. We need to take seriously the fact that Jesus used it of himself, and Paul applied it to Christians coming to terms with death. They are elements of the overall case that seeds are a good way to approach the bringing of both gospel and Church to a new context. John 12 (supplemented by 1 Corinthians 15) is helpful and diagnostic in revealing the dynamics that should apply in the non-identical reproduction of churches. This all leads to the next crucial question.

Do Jesus' patterns in John 12 and 20 apply to the Church?

Did Jesus intend to apply this teaching to his followers? Weigh this text.

> The hour has come for the Son of man to be glorified. Truly, truly, I say to you, unless a grain of wheat falls into the earth and dies, it remains alone; but if it dies, it bears much fruit. He who loves his life loses it, and he who hates his life in this world will keep it for eternal life. If anyone serves me, he must follow me; and where I am, there shall my servant be also; if any one serves me, the Father will honour him. (John 12:23–26, RSV)

Consider the flow of Jesus' words. The immediate shift from the seeds parable to wider comment suggests that he intended a link. The choice between the two paths, loving or hating one's own life, is characteristic of Jesus' response to those who are considering following him. The presence of a choice implies a call. If there is a call, Jesus expects that the pattern will apply.

That necessary choice is accompanied by some degree of compulsion: 'If anyone serves me, he must follow me.' 'Must' leaves little wriggle room. The use of the term 'servant' is also further evidence of an intended connection. Minear calls it a characteristic image of the Church: 'Every disciple and believer was *ipso facto* (necessarily) a servant.'[14] Lest there be any reasonable doubt, Jesus adds, 'and where I am, there shall my servant be also'. All these features demonstrate that Christ did make explicit that his patterns are to be ours. The self-denying style and cost of reproduction of the Church, here called 'dying to live', is properly anchored in Jesus' teaching about the pattern of his own death and its resultant fruitfulness.

What might John 20:21 add?

The commission of John 20:21

John 20:21, 'As the Father has sent me, even so I send you' (RSV), could be conclusive as to whether Christ's patterns are to be reproduced in his followers, the Church. I want to tease out what these words meant in their context. To begin, we should note that they have enormous significance, for four reasons.

Firstly, this is the first appearance of the risen Jesus to the shut-away disciples. Secondly, he shows them his hands and his side. The figure appears as the very person who was crucified. A week later, that is emphasised to Thomas. The principle of suffering and dying is tied into the subsequent sending. There is no option only to follow the pre-crucifixion Jesus. The cost in 'dying to live' is not glossed over. 'These will be the authentic marks of the body of Christ until the end. His mission is to be their mission.'[15]

Thirdly, his following words are missionary in flavour, for the concept of being sent is central. We could say that, here, apostolic identity is conferred on the Church. Fourth comes the immediate bestowal of the Spirit on this group. Paul Fiddes, unpacking the sending of the Son within the mission of the Trinity, rightly calls this verse 'the key thought'.[16]

My own transliteration of John 20:21 is '*Even as* the Father has sent me, I also am sending you.' How close is the parallel between how Jesus was sent and what therefore transfers to and continues in us? The word chosen and translated 'even as' helps answer the question. Wenham explains that there are three words for 'as' in Greek.[17] I combine his description of the differences with an example of an equivalent contemporary English statement. *ōs* meaning 'as' is very commonly used. Today we might say, 'It's as simple *as* falling off a log.' *Kathōs* means 'as, even as' and is stronger in feeling. For example, 'They lost the match, *even as* I predicted'. '*ōsper* means 'just as, even as'. This term has more force, as in the comment, 'That worked because you did it *just as* I told you.'

In John 20, the word is *kathōs*. If Wenham is right, this middle choice tells us something. Of course, we cannot follow 'just as' Jesus went. We are so different. His divinity, grace and salvific effect are unrepeatable, as are the things he has done for the Church and for the world. Yet the word chosen is stronger than simply 'as'. The 'even as' choice suggests an intention for close following, without creating impossible or heretical implications. It is clear that following a pattern is expected by the risen Christ in this sending.

We could then expand his meaning. '*Even as* I was sent, as God's sent one, so I send you. Even as I was sent on a journey from incarnational identification with culture, to disclosure of my Lordship endorsing counter-cultural engagement, so I send you. Even as I entered a process to become like those I was sent to, yet be faithful, so I send you. Even as I knew continuity and change, so I send you. Even as I, the seed, died in the ground and have now emerged both similar and different, so I send you, to follow similar fruitful patterns of dying to live.'

Christ was well aware of his unique identity. He alone was the 'only Son' (John 1:14, 18), who can draw all people to himself when he is lifted up (John 12:32–33). If he was aware of this, then why does John 12 include the sayings clearly showing that what was true of him was intended to be applied to his followers? John 12 and 20 suggest the answer. His followers are to have a similar *attitude*, not seeking emulation of his identity, deity or salvific power. Brown is clear: 'The saying about following Jesus is a call for a *willingness* to imitate Jesus in suffering and death.'[18] Yet that attitude may hope for a proper resultant fruitfulness, because that is what dying seeds lead to.

Where this takes us

The last two chapters have examined the incarnation, Christ's patterns of ministry and one key descriptor of his death and fruitful resurrection. Dying to live is not just true of spirituality and individuals. It applies also in the costly, vulnerable, non-identical reproduction from churches seen as 'grains'. In a bipartite way, characteristic of reproduction, these seeds interact with the soil and become related but different new plants.

We can now see how and why, in every stage of the life and death of Jesus, there are diagnostic patterns that should be taken in Church theory, life and practice. We are meant to reproduce them all. The very way that the Church is intended to function, and to grow via non-identical reproduction, is modelled by the overall life of Christ. That's a high and noble calling and gives fresh meaning to the image of the Church as the body of Christ.

Notes

1 L. Newbigin, *The Household of God* (SCM, 1953), pp. 147–55.
2 M. Davie, private paper, 'Response to the *Mission-shaped Church* draft' (June 2003), p. 1.
3 D. Bonhoeffer, *The Cost of Discipleship* (originally translated 1937; SCM, 1971), p. 80, notes that Luther called suffering a mark of the true Church. Bonhoeffer speaks of suffering as 'the highest joy', p. 81. A. Dulles, *Models of the Church* (Gill & Macmillan, 1988), gives it as the seventh mark of Luther's 1539 treatise *On the Councils and Churches, Models of the Church*, p. 125.
4 G. Lings, 'An analysis of fresh expressions of Church and Church plants begun in the period 1992–2012' (Church Commissioners and Church Army, 2013), Table 4, p. 26.
5 R. Brown, *The Gospel According to John I—XII* (Anchor Bible) (Chapman, 1975), p. 471, resists allegorising the parable and thereby making the term 'falling' into code for the incarnation.
6 W. Temple, *Readings in John's Gospel* (Macmillan, 1952), p. 195.
7 Brown, *The Gospel According to John*, pp. 471–72.
8 G. Cray (ed.), *Mission-shaped Church* (CHP, 2004), p. 24.
9 Cray, *Mission-shaped Church*, p. 105.
10 Cray, *Mission-shaped Church*, pp. 30–31.
11 Cray, *Mission-shaped Church*, p. 32.
12 V. Donovan, *Christianity Rediscovered* (SCM, 1982), p. 77.
13 Donovan, *Christianity Rediscovered*, pp. 30–31.
14 P.S. Minear, *Images of the Church in the New Testament*, 2nd edition (Westminster Press, 2004), p. 160.

15 L. Newbigin, *The Open Secret* (SPCK, 1995), p. 48.
16 P. Fiddes, 'Ecclesiology and ethnography: two disciplines, two worlds?' in Pete Ward (ed.), *Perspectives on Ecclesiology and Ethnography* (Eerdmans, 2012), p. 17.
17 J.W. Wenham, *The Elements of New Testament Greek* (CUP, 1965), p. 208.
18 Brown, *The Gospel According to John*, p. 475 (my italics).

7

The Holy Spirit and the surprises in reproduction

We've looked at how patterns from Jesus apply to his Church. What comes next? I'm following the lead of Lesslie Newbigin: 'We shall look first at those once-for-all events on which our redemption rests, and then at their *reproduction* in the life of the believing Church.'[1] That takes us to the role of the Holy Spirit to aid what is reproduced in the Church. One writer playfully expressing that link between the Spirit and reproduction was John Taylor in his book *The Go-Between God*. The titles of the first six chapters are Annunciation, Conception, Gestation, Labour, Birth, and Breath.[2] Yet, almost immediately, do we hit a problem?

The emergence of the reproductive strand

Does the book of Acts show a specific mission story of Spirit-led 'non-identical reproduction' of churches? At the start, no it doesn't. It is initially missing because the earliest disciples of Jesus were Jews with an inward-facing view of mission. This limited growth to the addition of new people to the existing community. They did not grasp true reproduction, because it includes welcoming difference and diversity. The overcoming of this resistance is played out in Acts, which is why it is important to tell that story. The early disciples had their minds changed about how mission worked and who could be Church. It came from missionary experiences, through surprising interventions of the creative Spirit.

The early community grew only by addition in just one city until Acts 8. You could say that it remained a Jewish subgroup until Acts 13.[3] Only after the events at Antioch can we really talk about *church* planting rather than adding to a Jewish renewal movement. Until then the story is about changes for individuals (and their households) like Cornelius, or for groups, but without calling them new churches, as in Samaria. Acts 13 covers Paul's visit to Cyprus and Pisidian Antioch. The initial strategy was to find the synagogues and proclaim the message. When the apostles met jealousy and resistance among the Jews, a turning point was reached. Having spoken to the Jews first, Paul considered himself free to turn to the Gentiles.

This was a tipping point. The mission journey was no longer solely geographical, aimed at Jews dispersed throughout the Roman Empire. It became a cultural and theological journey, going beyond the historic people of God, who had rejected the revelation in Jesus and the universal thrust it included.

At this point, creating more and different communities became necessary. The non-identical reproduction of churches was the consequence partly of travel to diverse places, and partly of the variable response of first-century Jews. John Taylor shows that a characteristic work of the Spirit is highlighting choice.[4] These Jews had to choose, and so did Paul. It was a significant choice to shift from the 'attractional'[5] model of mission, dominant in Acts 1—12. An outward thrust had finally arrived as the dominant, but not the sole, force.

Evidence implying that reproduction was non-identical

One obvious feature of Acts (for that reason, sometimes passed over) is the start of the diverse churches created during Paul's journeys. They were the result of the mission and its surprises. Acts is the clearest account of how these diverse churches were created; it is not a story of addition to one original place and its community. Although Acts does not use this language, that diversity points towards a non-identical reproduction process.

Newbigin comments that starting further churches is an integral part of the Acts mission. In Romans 15, Paul explains that he is moving on.

> What, exactly, has he done? Certainly not converted all the populations of these regions. Certainly not solved their social and economic problems. He has, in his own words, 'fully preached the gospel' and left behind communities of men and women who believe the gospel and live by it.[6]

Newbigin argues that Paul's view would surprise advocates of mass evangelism, proponents of Church Growth and supporters of social regeneration. Paul has planted Church, and those churches are trusted to continue the work by planting further churches throughout their own region. This is the reproductive instinct at work, although this term is not used in Acts. Newbigin asserts that the creation of churches that will continue to repeat the process is core to Paul's essence of mission. Earlier, the Anglo-Catholic missionary Roland Allen endorsed this view. He uses a parallel term to 'reproductive', saying that church people should learn the gospel 'in such a way that they can *propagate* it'.[7]

Let's now follow the early Church's struggles over what emerged because of its Spirit-led, surprising experiences in mission, which prompted revision of its Church doctrine. New Testament scholar Loveday Alexander notes the necessity for change in Acts. She calls it 'a story that is packed full of different ways of being Church' as an untidy but appropriate response of trust to the wind of the Spirit.[8] Taylor comments, in his chapter on the Spirit as breath, 'We cannot command the wind.' He is entertained by the freedom and irregularity brought by the Spirit: 'The Holy Spirit does not appear to have read the rubrics.'[9]

Newbigin returned to the UK after a lifetime of overseas mission and participation in international Church gatherings, and comments on a disturbance which creates a progression: 'The Spirit… is Lord over the Church, guiding the Church from its limited, partial and distorted understanding of, and embodiment of the truth, into the fullness of the truth in Jesus.'[10]

This is what is happening in Acts and why it is a crucial New Testament book to study.

The importance of surprises in the Acts story

In Acts 1:8, Jesus links the continuing outpouring of the Spirit to a trend of witnesses moving out from Jerusalem, to all Judea, to Samaria and to the ends of the earth. As we have seen, there were reasons why this radical expansion was domesticated. But then, chapters 6—13 disclose how resistance to non-identical reproduction of the Church was overcome gradually, even reluctantly, through Spirit-led surprises. They underline the crucial place of mission experience in shaping an evolving understanding. The young Church was taken from what was little more than a Jewish sect.[11] The story then shifted its focus to Antioch. From there the Holy Spirit called, and its Church sent, the first intentional cross-cultural missionaries. The Church as a whole was changed by being thrust into rather unwelcome aspects of mission. Its calling, which included the reproduction of diverse churches, not replication of further Jewish groups, was a surprise.

Some commentators imagine a narrow charismatic interpretation of the call in Acts 13:1-3. They attribute it to a combination of intense worship at Antioch and the prophetic intervention of the Spirit. However, the earlier chapters of Acts disclose a longer and more disturbing work of that same Spirit. The events recorded at the outset of Acts 13 are better seen as the tip of the iceberg. The vast volume of the rest is more hidden and is the story of the missionary Spirit preparing them by stages for this call.

Acts 8:1-4: Persecution unintentionally spreads the Church

Persecution followed the uncompromising witness of the newly appointed deacon, Stephen. The effect was the scattering of the Church across Judea and Samaria. The early Church did not seek persecution;

however, if we are searching for signs of the outward-facing work of the Spirit, we can think that God used, but did not send, this experience to widen the spread of the Church. Tertullian later wrote, 'The blood of the martyrs is the seed of the Church.' Seed has a reproductive ring to it. It was also clear that this sudden and unlooked-for mission outside Jerusalem was not carried out by authorised leaders.

Acts 8:5–25: Samaritans become Christians

Most unusually, Philip went to a Samaritan city and proclaimed Christ. We need to remember the mutual contempt and hatred between Jews and Samaritans. There, Philip saw both the power of the Spirit demonstrated and a wide response to the message about Jesus, leading to baptisms. Somehow, news of this reached the Jewish leadership in Jerusalem and they sent two prominent apostles, Peter and John, to inspect the work.

Many commenters agree that this was significant. Lampe speaks of it as follows:

> [It was] a crucial moment in the first advance of Christianity… The leaders of the Church's mission… incorporate [the first Samaritan converts] into the apostolic (i.e. missionary) Church with the result that there occurs a Samaritan 'Pentecost'… This event is meant to demonstrate that a new nucleus of the missionary Church has been established… Luke's readers are intended to infer that the Gospel proceeded to radiate outwards from this new centre of the Spirit's mission.[12]

Please take on board two facts about this episode. Firstly, there was no suggestion that the converts in Samaria should go to Jerusalem to have their religious experience validated. The apostles came to them. Secondly, they were not told to join the Jerusalem community or its worship. This is the first recorded Christian community beyond Jerusalem and the first indicator of a shift of centre, challenging the previous exclusive 'come to us' view. Marks of healthy contemporary church reproduction are exhibited here. There is an outward journey, without the assumption that converts will be sucked back into the sending church. Moreover, a further church comes into existence that previously did not exist. I know this is not the language of Acts, but Samaria represents the first case of reproduction or a fresh expression of Church, by contrast to replication of the Jerusalem expression of Church.

Moreover, Peter and John, on their way back, followed the example of Philip and preached in 'many Samaritan villages' (v. 25). This was both unusual Jewish behaviour and a poignant reversal of John's previous attitude. He had once wished Jesus to call down fire on a Samaritan village (Luke 9:54). This unlooked-for experience of the Spirit was changing them, by exposing them to a mission initiated by the Spirit, containing big surprises.

Acts 8:26–40: Philip and the Ethiopian

Philip's encounter with the eunuch shares features with the previous story. The Spirit's initiative and a communication of Christ are central. Belief, by a person similarly excluded from the temple,[13] is again immediately followed by baptism. Once more, there is no pull back to Jerusalem; rather the eunuch 'went on his way rejoicing' (v. 39). There was a speculative view in the early Church that 'he became a missionary among his people'.[14] Thus, Philip was the first to be involved in the reproduction of churches. He was, in effect, a very short-stay church planter in Samaria, and the impetus for another one in Africa. The account does not explicitly say that the events of Acts 8 began to change the mind of the young Church, but it is significant that Luke tells these stories, closely modelling what Jesus had commanded in Acts 1:8, which until this time had been lacking. They became the first signs of the disturbance that would become more noticed in Acts 10 and explicit by Acts 15.

Acts 9:1–30: The calling of Saul

Saul's unsought encounter with the risen Christ is the foundation of his self-understanding and call. Ananias is told, 'Go! This man is my chosen instrument to proclaim my name to the Gentiles and their kings and to the people of Israel' (Acts 9:15). The direction, of being sent to the Gentiles, is undeniable, as is the change in the man. These were big surprises for Saul; what was equally surprising, and even unconvincing, to the Jerusalem church was God's choice of an ardent persecutor. The overall theme of surprise is very clear: God surprises both Saul and the church. Here once again is an indicator that past boundaries are being challenged. A key player is being called, who will later drive through the gaps made. Saul is then sent to Tarsus and the focus moves to Peter.

Acts 10—11:18: The Cornelius story

In Acts 10, Peter often seems taken by surprise by the Spirit. He arrives in Joppa to pray for fellow disciple Dorcas, who has recently died. Her resuscitation leads others to believe, so he stays longer. He has no idea or plan that this will involve the Roman, Cornelius. Yet even at Joppa, is a change starting?[15] Peter is staying with a tanner. Harnack remarks that 'tanning was an uncleanly trade'. Bruce comments that it was 'a mark of his increasing emancipation from ceremonial traditions'.[16]

An angel from God, unknown to Peter, had spoken to the Roman NCO, Cornelius. While his servants were coming to find Peter, God sent Peter an unpleasant dream, containing an illegitimate command to kill and eat an unclean animal. Mike Riddell, an Australian exponent of emerging Church, points out this clash between two ways of knowing what is true—convincing experience and long-established tradition.[17] But if the message was clear, the application was obscure. Both Cornelius and Peter, in their parallel visions and the unfolding story, were kept dependent on the Spirit for the next stage.

The story of God's intervention continues. The Roman threesome arrived as the dream finished with a further message from the Spirit:

'Get up and go downstairs. Do not hesitate to go with them, for I have sent them' (Acts 10:20). The verse suggests that Peter instinctively did feel hesitation, which he expresses later, in Caesarea (Acts 10:28). However, having heard the story of his 'foreign' guests, he unlawfully invited them in; worse, they stayed the night and then they all took a day's journey together, back to Caesarea.

On arrival, Peter admitted that he was surprised, religiously compromised, yet challenged by the vision, and asked why he had been summoned. Cornelius retold his vision at greater length and invited Peter to speak. I imagine a faltering start: 'I now realise how true it is that God does not show favouritism but accepts from every nation the one who fears him and does what is right' (Acts 10:34).

He began to explain the good news, but could not finish the talk. 'While Peter was still speaking these words, the Holy Spirit came on all who heard the message. The circumcised believers who had come with Peter were astonished that the gift of the Holy Spirit had been poured out even on Gentiles' (Acts 10:44–45).[18] These Roman hearers were not circumcised; they had given no indication of accepting the message about Jesus.[19] The level of surprise is considerable. Newbigin says, 'The fruit of the telling is an action of the Spirit which takes matters out of Peter's hands.'[20] The 'matters' include the big question of who can be in Christ, for that is what the giving of the Spirit meant,[21] and the smaller question of the right order in which preaching, deciding for Christ and signs of the coming of the Spirit normally best happen.

The story is of great significance, as Luke gives us a long, intimately described narrative. It shows how the Spirit propelled the early Church beyond its inherited instinct for what we could call 'mono-ethnic replication', into 'cross-cultural reproduction'. This meant changes to their inherited view of mission, about who are the people of God and even how we know what is true. As Newbigin comments, 'The fulfilment of the mission of the Church thus requires that the Church itself be changed and learn new things.'[22]

These new things included the fact that the first Church needed to grow in new ways, characterised by non-identical reproduction rather than replication. Simply adding more of the same only reinforces a preference for numerical expansion. That is not the message of Acts 10. There is a profound meeting with surprising and diverging difference. Yet, as we have seen with the life of Jesus, holding on to both continuity and difference is a hallmark of the reproductive process. This text is persuasive evidence of the non-identical reproductive strand being part of the Church's identity. Moreover, the change to thinking in that way was Spirit-led, not the result of human innovation.

This emphasis on the Spirit was central to Peter's case back in Jerusalem, when his actions were questioned. He retold the unlooked-for vision. He noted the elegance of the timing: 'Right then three men who had been sent to me from Caesarea stopped at the house' (11:11). He recalled the urging of the Spirit to overcome his natural hesitations and the visible early intervention of the coming of the Spirit 'as he had come on us at the beginning' (v. 15). He concluded, 'Who was I to think that I could stand in God's way?' (v. 17).

Acts 11:19—12:25: The moves to Antioch

Some of those who were scattered by the persecution only understood half the journey. The journey was not just outwards, to bring people back to one way of doing things; it was about legitimate diversity. Those who spoke only to Jews (11:19) were still trapped inside the view that Jesus the Messiah had come and it was time to tell other Jews around the Roman Empire. For them, there was still only one way to be the people of God; one way to join, which involved circumcision; one group with whom to eat, that is, other Jews; and one set of laws about what could be eaten—one way, one initiation, one group, one diet. True, it did not involve all being drawn to one place, Jerusalem, although that was the one pilgrimage venue. All this was about to explode into a diversity that was difficult for them to comprehend.

Others from Cyprus and Cyrene, scattered by the persecution, spoke also to Greeks in Antioch.[23] The response was noteworthy and the news reached Jerusalem (11:19–22).[24] James Dunn calls it 'a truly astonishing break with the past'.[25] Moreover, Bruce notes that they did not talk of Jesus as Messiah, but used the terms 'Lord and Saviour… widely current in the religious world of the eastern Mediterranean'.[26] So it was not just *whom* they talked to that was shocking, but *how* they talked. They did not distort the gospel, but they used words for it that their hearers could relate to. Even the message was being reproduced non-identically. We know that these unnamed speakers were bicultural people, so perhaps it was easier for them to make this jump. Being at home in Greek culture, yet having the Jewish faith, they could better express and explain the gospel. They were among the first to pay attention to context. So they distinguished the event of Jesus, as the core of faith, from the Jewish cultural understanding of it as Messiah. To do this opens the door to diversity. It shapes and aids the reproduction, not the replication, of churches.

Bruce notes that this step forward at Antioch goes beyond the response of one Ethiopian, or Cornelius and his household: 'The scale of Gentile evangelisation in Antioch was something entirely new.'[27] Then another surprise emerges. It is noteworthy that this very significant step was not begun by named, authorised leaders. The evangelists were unknown, uninstructed lay people, convinced by the good news of Jesus and convinced that it was for all. Stephen Neill tells us that the three great churches of earliest Christianity—Antioch, Rome and Alexandria—were all founded anonymously.[28] What a message that might be, when today we might think that the best way forward is finding better, ordained, formally trained, modern missionaries.

In response, this time the Jerusalem church sent not Peter and John, but Barnabas, a native of Cyprus (Acts 4:36). His shared past with the founders of the Antioch church and his known good and encouraging character are suggestive, but not conclusive, that the church in Jerusalem was opening up to principled diversity within unity. There may be threads of such thinking in Luke's comment on how Barnabas operated. He saw 'evidence of the grace of God' and reacted with gladness; he also encouraged them to 'remain true to the Lord' (Acts 11:23). Bishop Steven Croft describes what he did: 'Note that Barnabas does not come to Antioch and apply a definition. He comes with open eyes and ears and sees the grace of God. What is happening in Antioch may not look a lot like what he knows church to be in Jerusalem.'[29]

Put all this together and we learn that such discernment comes from the heart and the character, as well as the mind. Earlier in the Acts story, the Jewish Sanhedrin member Gamaliel did something similar. This fits with Jesus' words, 'Those who are not against us are for us.' We too should make our assessment by fruits, not by past external forms. If there are people encountering Jesus, wanting to be centred in Jesus, living lives more like Jesus, becoming like Jesus, drawing others to Jesus—in other words, evidence of the grace of God (Acts 11:23)—then it's Church.

Here, for the first time, the word 'church' is used to describe neither a local group which is in Jerusalem nor the whole Church, however widely spread. Here too the disciples were first called Christians. A group with some degree of separate identity from the Jewish population was recognised. This is evidence of reproduction beyond synagogue replication. Did Barnabas sense the value of Paul's bicultural background and so bring him there from Tarsus? Yet they model ongoing relational connection and mutual responsibility, across the cultural diversity of churches, through the gift from Antioch to the poor of Judea. That gift is transmitted by Barnabas and Saul. Reproduction leading to diversity was not seen as the route to independence. It maintained connection across difference. That is part of what the word 'catholicity' means.

These are the surprises, sent by the Spirit, embodied in a variety of unpredictable encounters. Through these chapters and the disturbances they contain, the stage is set for Acts 13 and the Spirit's call. That calling is thus better understood as the climax of a longer process, rather than the beginning of a whole new stage. Yet we must note the evident sense of surprise and shock. The Church did not expect or plan any of these developments. The text shows that without their permission, the missionary Holy Spirit gave them a set of experiences beyond what they expected, with people they least expected. In addition, the Church was propelled beyond mission by addition and helping others become 'like us'. There was a change to mission mainly by multiplication and diversification, with the characteristics of non-identical reproduction.

Another way to talk about it is the change from centripetal to centrifugal mission. The first sucks everyone in and the second impels people out. The early believers did not know any of that language, but the story reveals these dynamics.

One application to today

I have argued elsewhere that we can loosely map broad groups today on to the stages given in Acts 1:8 (as in Diagram 1), without pretending that this was Luke's intention.[30] Thus, attenders at existing churches could be described as *Jerusalem* people. Those on the fringe of such churches are rather like those living in *Judea*. They already sometimes attend existing churches and any missionary journey among them is still centripetal. This is legitimate, as they themselves would normally see increased commitment in terms of deeper attachment to an existing church.

The de-churched could be likened to those in *Samaria*. They have in common an unfortunate story of distance, distrust and dislike. The non-churched, who are ignorant of the core of Christianity, or believe themselves rightly dismissive of it, might be likened to the Greeks and Romans. They thought the Jews were strange for their lack of idols, their insular cultural particularity and their moralistic stances. While Greeks and Romans do not represent the ultimate *ends of the earth*, they were at least a yet further stage out towards it. Thus, the progression in Acts 1:8 has already become one useful framework to assess the mission of contemporary fresh expressions of Church. Please notice, too, that many more people live in the non-churched and de-churched ellipses of the diagram than in the churched or fringe circles.

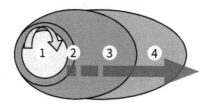

    1 Jerusalem… the churched
    2 Judea… the fringe?
    3 Samaria… the de-churched?
    4 The ends of the earth… the non-churched?

Notice what happens to the orginal centre, and the mission shape.

Diagram 1. The eccentric effect in Acts

Why centrifugal understanding is insufficient

However, the view that the change, in the Acts story, is from solely centripetal to dominantly centrifugal obscures a further dimension, which most authors miss.[31] All of them only grasp one dimension of the change—from centripetal to centrifugal. Thus, they leave Jerusalem at the centre of the picture. This distorts the story by reading back into it Christendom assumptions that put the Church at the centre of society. My diagram above shows something radically different. Two major corrections are needed.

The eccentric effect

The first major amendment is that the progression from 'Jerusalem' to 'Judea' to 'Samaria' to 'the ends of the earth' is not concentric. It is eccentric, once the Judean boundary has been passed. This brings a quite different perspective. The centre of the story shifts away from Jerusalem. In the Samaritan episode, Peter and John travelled to Samaria and the converts were not brought back to Jerusalem. The same was true of the Greek converts in the Antioch church. This eccentric pattern then grows even more distinct. Paul travels further west and more churches are born, not just in Asia but beyond it, and the non-Jewish Christians are not circumcised. This indicates both cultural and religious diversity. The eccentric shape suggests a disturbance of previous patterns. It certainly created controversy in the early Church. We need to realise that this is typical of reproductive development. It always raises the question of how continuity and change are both honoured, for reproduction contains both.

One family analogy dealing with continuity and change, or similarity and difference, is that it is physically obvious, biologically demonstrable and legally true that I am father to, but I am not either of, my sons. We are all members of the Lings tribe. These two young men are in some ways like me and in other ways importantly different from me. We are biologically connected, lovingly related and in possession of individual identities. We are similar and different.

Unity as uniformity, or growth as replication, cannot cope with those realities. This is what the early Church had to face. The eccentric effect fits with the reproductive strand at work; it embodies disturbance yet maintains connection. There is, then, a great difference between replication and non-identical reproduction of the Church. If the body of Christ is supposed to reproduce and, in effect, have ecclesial children, we should expect that they will have the DNA of Church but will not be identical to their parents. We know that this is how it is with human beings, and this is also what we are seeing with fresh expressions of Church. They are Church and they are fresh. They are related to us and they are different from us. It's actually normal.

The eccentric progression is enshrined in the geographic poles of the book of Acts. The journey goes from Jerusalem to Rome. Thus, simple centrifugal thinking is a serious distortion of the actual story and its intentions. All of this can be argued without naming the destruction of Jerusalem in AD70. The significance of that event is not lost on Neill:

'Until that date Jerusalem had been without question the mother Church of the whole Christian world... Since AD70 the Christian Church has never had one local centre.'[32] Resource churches and sending churches, please note!

'Concentration and dispersal' modifies the theory

The second major adjustment picks up another important dynamic within the overall story. Bob Hopkins had an idea that modifies simple centripetal-to-centrifugal thinking.[33] He detects three phases, not one step, in the mission within the book of Acts. He spotted it because, every so often, Luke uses a phrase about increasing and multiplying. The three phases involve Jerusalem, Antioch and Ephesus. In Hopkins' words:

> It seems that the writer of Acts structured the story to highlight three phases in the growth of the New Testament Church. Each phase showed parallel characteristics developed through the narrative and can be identified by three very similar repeated summary verses which bring each phase to a conclusion. These are found in Acts 6:7, 12:24 and 19:20.

This modifying theory sees that there is a repeated dynamic within each of the three phases. Each begins with *concentration* of resources in that place, both in terms of numbers and over time. This is followed later by *dispersal* of that resource. But it is also possible to detect an intriguing progression. The first dispersal was by persecution in Jerusalem, over which the Church had no choice. The second was by calling at Antioch, inviting cooperation. The third dispersal is not directly recorded. It is attractive, but unproven, to think that it might have been by design. Possibly, the Church understood that it was normal. There are bits of evidence to indicate that Ephesus acted as such a dispersal centre. This cannot be taken as conclusive. However, if broadly correct, then Hopkins' concentration and dispersal theory, published in 1988, is an independent ally to my later theory of the reproductive as a strand of Church identity and its normal practice over time.

Hopkins' theory is important to set alongside the eccentric pattern. The dynamic of concentration and dispersal suggests that the centripetal and the centrifugal are not opposed. They are better thought of as phases within a longer pattern. The movement still heads towards the ends of the earth and will be eccentric, from wherever the Church starts. This then reconciles well-known texts such as Jesus' words, 'Come to me' and also, 'Go therefore and make disciples of all nations.' This yields a rhythm to ecclesial reproduction. The missional going, to others unlike us, will at some stage involve a calling for them to come to Christ and into his body, the Church. That Church will, in turn, need to move through a period of concentration before it is likely to be called once more to dispersal. The dispersal impels reproduction; the concentration helps reproduction take place. What is also diagnostic is that the pattern repeats.

We can then see that reproduction should be connected to a sufficient maturity. In most creatures, the ability to reproduce is one mark of maturity, and the presence of maturity is the right background for responsible reproduction. How I wish that were true of the Church! What is unlikely and unhelpful is thinking that either going/dispersal or coming/concentration can be endless without the other phase. So Bob Hopkins' theory holds together centripetal and centrifugal phases as necessary to one another. It offers reconciliation, without domestication, between the missional and pastoral.

It may be significant that it is at Ephesus that Paul gets the insistent call to Jerusalem and Rome: 'I must also see Rome' (Acts 19:21, RSV). If conflict in Jerusalem and prison in Caesarea had not intervened, would this have been the clear start of the third phase of dispersal? Some scholars think that the book of Romans was written in Corinth, in the last three months before Paul set out for Jerusalem.[34] That makes his comments in Romans 15, about wanting to go on to Spain, yet more intriguing and suggests a fourth dispersal after Rome (see Romans 15:24, 28). In the perspective of Acts 1:8, Rome was not 'the ends of the earth', only the centre of a foreign empire.

After the expansion of the early Church, the danger that arose was in the way that Rome became the new centripetal-minded 'Jerusalem'. Yet Rome, or any other place, such as Canterbury or Geneva, can never be the final terminus. The eccentric effect, with its repeating pattern of concentration and dispersal, expresses the outward thrust brought by the Spirit towards the ends of the earth. These features are perennial. In today's mission in a global society, 'the ends of the earth' does not just mean geographical spread. It may better be thought of as a cultural progression outwards. In such a view, Judea would stand for a familiar journey to one's own spiritual heartlands; moving out to Samaria is a safari among the disagreeable and disenchanted, while the ends of the earth suggests an expedition to people-groups that was hitherto unimaginable.[35] In each successive case, the cross-cultural dimension will be more acute, the need to express gospel and Church within the culture more pressing, and the necessity of reproduction, not replication, more obvious.

The absence of a specific command to the Church to reproduce

Some might say, 'If it is that important, why is there no command in the New Testament for the Church to reproduce?' After all, Dulles' first test says, 'The clearer and more explicit, the better'. The answer is that this would have been foreign to the very process outlined in Acts. The whole point is that this reality was quite unlooked for, and gradual discovery was the process to which the story bears witness. What Acts shows is an emerging instinct for Church reproduction, growing out of surprising practice prompted by the Holy Spirit.

Bear in mind, too, that the New Testament documents are not systematic theology, so we should not assume that reproduction, as a specific doctrinal strand to the Church, should appear as a command. If you are still unconvinced, reflect that the word 'mission' does not occur in the New Testament, nor is there a command to do mission.[36] Yet a vast edifice has been built around the word 'mission' with its own theological discipline. The justification is more complex than the presence of a direct command, which does occur for some other marks of the Church, namely baptism and Eucharist.

In addition, there are several elements of being Church today, regarded by some traditions as essential, that have very thin New Testament support. A catalogue would include the necessity of bishops, the existence of priests, the requirement that Eucharist must be led by the episcopally ordained and the baptism of all presenting infants, let alone the even more unfounded practices of confirmation and centrally devised liturgies. I list these neither to dismiss nor to justify them, but to point out that some quite major features of being Church are argued primarily theologically, drawing on biblical themes and fragments. Some have far less substance than does the case here.

What Acts shows us

This chapter shows how, in fulfilment of Acts 1:8, the Spirit led the young Church beyond its inherited centripetal view of addition and replication, into a pattern of diverse reproduction. The long list of unsought surprises led to a centrifugal thrust characterised by an eccentric pattern. It moved the centre away from its initial geographical, historical and spiritual starting point. That pattern also had a broad rhythm, containing successive periods of concentration followed by dispersal. By these means, the Church grew by dynamics characteristic of reproduction rather than replication.

The story of Acts, in particular chapters 8—15, underlines the surprises within the calling to reproduce, and exposes how the capacity to fulfil the calling was limited by inherited assumptions. These were made more difficult to deliver by the opposition of traditionalists. We also see that any capacity the Church may have is no substitute for partnership with the missionary Holy Spirit. He inspires and impels, making use of persecution if necessary, directly calling some and sending to the Church the most unlikely seekers. Once more, we need real modesty about our capacity. This serves to underline the essential bipartite partnership of Spirit and Church.[37] That unfolds between Christian content and cultural context.

Most people do not realise that the Church in Acts is a story with two main threads. The best-known one is about how the good news of Jesus Christ travelled from Jerusalem to Rome. The gospel travelled from the edge of empire to its centre. The second thread is less well-known. It traces how the Church was changed. That movement was from the religious centre—in other words, Jerusalem—to its edge, the ends of the earth.

Both threads are the work of the Holy Spirit. We might say that the Spirit empowers the first missionary journey from the edge of culture to its centre. But we need to add that the Spirit disturbs, in order to make the second or ecclesial journey from the centre of Church to its edge. I think we live in a time when both these journeys are being explored again. Such dynamics makes more sense of the Acts story, which looks rather haphazard compared with the clear final command of the risen Christ that initiated the story of the Spirit-led mission of the young Church.

Will the Western churches have similar courage to make a journey from their centre to the edge, to come out of their churches and gladly let go those whom God calls to disperse? An international Roman Catholic consultant, and member of a religious order, is Gerald Arbuckle. He has written several books connected to his longing that the freedoms started by Vatican II will be realised. One of his comments from experience, about how today's diverging mission best happens, is that 'the new belongs elsewhere'.[38] That fits with the realisation that when the early believers spoke to Greeks, it did not happen in Jerusalem but in Antioch, just as Philip spoke to Samaritans elsewhere, and Peter spoke to Cornelius in Joppa. The new flourishes more easily elsewhere. The new then needs protection from the rest, by those in the centre who carefully listen, value and understand it, like the apostle James in Acts 15.

Notes

1 L. Newbigin, *The Household of God*, p. 148 (my italics).

2 J.V. Taylor, *The Go-Between God: the Holy Spirit and the Christian mission* (SCM, 1972).

3 L. Alexander, 'What patterns of Church and Mission are found in the Acts of the Apostles?' in S. Croft (ed.), *Mission-shaped Questions* (CUP, 2008), p. 133. Dunn agrees: 'Is there evidence for fresh expressions of Church in the New Testament?' in S. Croft (ed.), *Mission-shaped Questions*, p. 54.

4 Taylor, *The Go-Between God*, pp. 32–33.

5 This term has perhaps been coined, certainly popularised, by M. Frost and A. Hirsch, *The Shaping of Things to Come* (Hendrickson, 2003), especially pp. 18–21.

6 L. Newbigin, *The Gospel in a Pluralist Society* (SPCK, 1989), p. 121.

7 R. Allen, *Missionary Methods: St Paul's or ours?* (Lutterworth, 2006), p. 13 (my italics). It was originally published in London by World Dominion Press in 1912.

8 Alexander, 'What patterns of Church and Mission', pp. 134–36.

9 Taylor, *The Go-Between God*, pp. 120, 121.

10 Quoted in P. Weston, *Lesslie Newbigin, Missionary Theologian* (SPCK, 2006), p. 171.

11 Paul recognised this perception as being held by his Jewish accusers in his trial before Felix in Acts 24:14. Taylor, in *The Go-Between God*, calls this stage an 'adventist sect within Judaism', p. 84.

12 F.F. Bruce, *The Book of Acts* (Marshall Morgan & Scott, 1970), p. 183, follows G.W.H. Lampe, *The Seal of the Spirit* (Longmans, 1951), p. 72.

13 J.D.G. Dunn notes that both Samaritans and the eunuch *per se* were excluded: *The Acts of the Apostles* (Epworth, 1996), p. 113.

14 Bruce, *Acts*, p. 190, cites Irenaeus, *Against Heresies* 3.1.2.8, but notes that we have no independent source of the Ethiopian Church before the fourth century.

15 I am obliged to a 2003 email from an informal colleague, Stephen Rymer, for alerting me to this feature.

16 Bruce, *Acts*, p. 213, footnote 68; Dunn concurs: *The Acts*, p. 130.

17 M. Riddell, *Threshold of the Future* (SPCK, 1998), p. 22.

18 E. Haenchen calls this Scene 6 of Acts, seen as an overall play, 'The great surprise': *The Acts of the Apostles* (Blackwell, 1971), p. 359.

19 M. Riddell, *Threshold of the Future* (SPCK, 1997), p. 25.

20 Newbigin, *The Gospel in a Pluralist Society*, p. 124.

21 L. Newbigin, *The Open Secret: Introduction to the theology of mission* (SPCK, 1995), pp. 59–61, expands on the meaning of this action of the

Spirit. See also Riddell, *Threshold of the Future*, p. 25, and Peter's own interpretation, Acts 11:17.
22 Newbigin, *The Gospel in a Pluralist Society*, p. 124.
23 Antioch was the third largest city of the empire after Rome and Alexandria, a free city, the seat of Syrian provincial government and proverbial for immorality. See Bruce, *Acts*, p. 238.
24 Bruce, *Acts*, p. 237, is clear that Greeks means Gentiles, not Hellenists.
25 J. Dunn, 'Is there evidence for fresh expressions', p. 55.
26 Bruce, *Acts*, pp. 238–39.
27 Bruce, *Acts*, p. 239. S. Neill, *A History of Christian Missions* (Penguin, 1980), p. 24, agrees that they 'made Christian history at Antioch by preaching directly to Gentiles'.
28 Neill, *A History of Christian Missions*, pp. 24–25.
29 Croft, *Mission-shaped Questions*, p. 194.
30 G. Lings, 'Discernment in mission', *Encounters on the Edge* 30 (Church Army, 2006), pp. 16–20.
31 The church historian Stephen Neill writes: 'It became clear that the movement of the Church was to be not from the circumference inwards to Jerusalem, but outwards from Jerusalem to the circumference': *A History of Christian Missions*, p. 22. Alexander, 'What patterns of Church and Mission', p. 140, similarly claims: 'This centrifugal pattern… is exactly what we see in Acts.' Theologian and evangelist Michael Green writes, 'Luke is at great pains to stress the links between the apostolic Church in Jerusalem on the one hand and the spreading circles of Christian outreach on the other': I *Believe in the Holy Spirit*, p. 137. C. Van Engen also talks of 'ever-widening… circles': *God's Missionary People* (Baker, 1991), p. 42. M. Arias and A. Johnson, arguing from the Johannine commission, write that 'this gospel is inherently ex-centric—going out of the centre': *The Great Commission* (Abingdon Press, 1992), p. 97.
32 Neill, *A History of Christian Missions*, p. 23.
33 It first appeared in a partial version in B. Hopkins, *Church Planting: Models for mission* (Grove, 1988), pp. 11–12. It is developed in B. Hopkins and R. White, *Enabling Church Planting* (CPAS, 1995), p. 5.
34 C.K. Barrett, *The Epistle to the Romans* (A&C Black, 1971), pp. 3–4.
35 I develop and apply this thinking in 'Discernment in mission', *Encounters on the Edge* 30, pp. 21–26.
36 With the two cases of the English word 'mission' in the RSV, one (Acts 12:25) is about taking the gift to Jerusalem, for which the Greek word is 'service'. With Peter's 'mission' to the Jews (Galatians 2:8), the Greek is 'apostleship'.

37 Kevin Giles, *What on Earth is the Church? A biblical and theological inquiry* (SPCK, 1995), p. 79, quotes Raymond Brown: 'The distinguishing feature of Lucan ecclesiology is the overshadowing presence of the Spirit.'
38 G. Arbuckle, *Refounding the Church* (Geoffrey Chapman, 1993), pp. 119, 149.

8

Christendom's eclipse of a reproducing Church

In his second test, Dulles asked for:

> *A Basis in Christian tradition.* Not all Christians set the same value on tradition, but nearly all would agree that the testimony of Christian believers in the past in favour of a given doctrine, is evidence in its favour. The more universal and constant the tradition, the more convincing it is.[1]

A tough question needs to be faced. If the idea of the Church as reproducing is well supported in scripture and by connections with the Trinity and the life of Christ, why has it been so notably absent in most of Western Church history?[2]

The modest value of tradition

The term 'tradition' can be understood in several ways. Here, I mean it in its widest sense—the ongoing story of the Church since its start.

My view is not only that the test of tradition is less important than that of scripture, but also that where it deals with the Church, its views are derived from other doctrines, as we saw in Chapter 4. So the tradition about the Church itself does not determine what is true. In addition, Church doctrine has been reactive throughout its history. It has shifted, in relation to either its mission or the changes in the surrounding culture. This tendency is demonstrated by the very title of Eric Jay's two volumes: *The Church: Its changing image through twenty centuries.*

Thus, the Church's history is unlikely to be a secure starting place as a test. Yet the most demanding part of Dulles' wording about the test of tradition is: 'the more universal and constant, the more convincing it is'. Questions are raised by his use of the test, which falls well below this requirement. For example, he charts the rise of the institutional model of Church, as dominant from the late Middle Ages up to World War II. Yet he himself discards its widespread long life as an adequate justification. He also, rightly, critiques this model for having only meagre biblical backing.[3] It seems that the Church can hold certain convictions about itself for many hundreds of years and yet later find them inadequate. This is a flaw in the tradition test. I merely follow Dulles in treating this test as a supplement, finding our major support in 'scripture' and 'theological fruitfulness'.

In responding to the second test, I'll show how Church tradition contains both good insights and past distortions, and it is to the latter I turn first.

Why the reproductive strand was usually absent in Christendom

It was bound to be so

The absence of the reproductive element in Church identity for many centuries could seem a damaging omission, yet it turns out to be anything but. The point is that the meaning of this element is only now being made clear, explicit and positive. Until now it has been unclear, ignored and out of sight. Therefore, it is not a surprise that previous understandings of the Church did not disclose it, and would be unlikely to do so. This book claims to add a missing strand to ecclesiology. From that viewpoint, the very absence of the theory in Church history is part of the case for it.

Christendom saw the Church as an institution

In Europe, the first reason for the eclipse of the reproductive strand was the predominant institutional model of Church. Any growth was by replication, because the Roman Church believed, in the words of Vatican I, that 'the Church has all the marks of a true Society… It is so perfect in itself that it is distinct from all human societies.'[4] Any 'perfect' society could construe change only as loss or weakness, so any growth would be by copying, under ecclesial control, in new areas of territory. When Protestants disagreed with it, the belief was only replaced by an equal certainty about a Church with reformed marks—usually the word, sacraments and Church discipline. The Acts of Uniformity in 1559 and 1662, concerning public worship in the Church of England, sprang from the same mindset, coupled with a fear of political anarchy. In the 16th century, ecclesial certainty and coercive nationalism were powerful partners. In the words of Anglican Church historian Mark Chapman: 'Uniformity and obedience were at the heart of the settlement.'[5] The result was a Church which was both monolithic and monopolistic. It could not conceive of diverse mission within its own borders. Those outside the fold were likely to be persecuted, whether they were Muslim or Anabaptist.

This institutional mindset would ideologically exclude organic reproduction because it involves both continuity and change. The continuity would be agreeable, but the change would be highly suspect—schismatic, if not also heretical. Moreover, the institutional model cannot reproduce, because reproduction is itself an inter-personal model, not an institutional one.

Christendom was 'mission accomplished'

Secondly, the reproductive element was excluded because Christendom had apparently completed its mission task,[6] by political and often armed conquest of European peoples and an imposition of the faith on them. One result was the gradual, top-down administrative creation of dioceses and then the introduction of a parish system based on tithing.

Bishop Stephen Cottrell, at the 2007 National Anglican Church Planting conference, argued against the romantic illusion of the origins of
the parish as missional. He told us that Europe was evangelised by the
monastic orders and that the parish system was a consequence, not the
cause, of that mission. Either way, the mission had been accomplished.

Dan Beeby writes that 'the curse of Christendom' was that 'therefore
there was no need for a mission'.[7] Rodney Clapp gives another angle:
in Christendom the realities of Church and world became one. Thus,
there was 'no longer anything to call the world'. The social, political
and military functions of the world 'were all baptised'. So the Church
became chaplaincy, being 'part of the power structure itself'.[8] Bosch
argues that this paradigm remained until the mid-20th century in both
Protestant and Catholic thought.[9]

The reformers were 'indifferent to mission' for they saw their task as
Church reform and Protestant survival, until the Peace of Westphalia
in 1648. Bosch admits that 'very little happened' about mission, with
a notable exception in the Anabaptist movement.[10] However, some
say that the reformers' sermons give hints that they did believe fully in
evangelism. Sometimes they would be trying to gain Catholics to the
Reformed Church and creed, but at other times they refer to gaining
converts for Christ.[11]

Internal conflict also became a larger issue in a divided Church. The
missiologist Wilbert Shenk writes, 'Christendom has become so at
home in European culture that it has become the folk religion and
Western ecclesiology has developed in this insular context. It was
non-missionary and focused on conflicts between various Christian
groups.'[12]

The pastoral and administrative mindset

Thirdly, in practice, any growth of the parish system was by administrative division of existing territorial units, served by paid clergy, paid
for partly by plots of glebe land. Any new centre focused on provision

of a church building via patronage and/or local taxation. One example would be the admired St George's Deal building, where I was Vicar from 1985 to 1997. It was built in Queen Anne style between 1707 and 1717, by partnership between Canterbury Diocese, the Admiralty and a tax on coal coming into Deal.

The model was 'very clericalist and wholly pastoral'.[13] Mission only meant baptising the newborn, catechising the young, conducting compulsory worship and teaching the ignorant faithful. They were seen as insiders because Church and society were one. 'All were necessarily Christian and until Elizabeth's reign all infants were baptised very quickly after birth,'[14] is Bishop Colin Buchanan's assessment. The attitude is summarised in the response in 1575 of the Bishop of London to some Anabaptists who were fleeing persecution in the Netherlands: 'In England there is no one that is not a member of God's Church.'[15]

Protestant Church leadership ministry was concerned with word and sacrament, which defined its government, structures and pastoral work. The reproductive element was out of sight and considered unnecessary. This attitude was exposed in the resistance and incomprehension that met William Carey and others advocating world mission in the 1790s. It was unthinkable that growth could or should be by organic multiplication, centred on a community sent out in mission with a calling to non-identical reproduction.

The divorce of Church and mission

When individuals in the Protestant churches began to hear the call to mission worldwide, partly as a result of the Evangelical Revival, their response was organised by voluntary groups, not churches, much less denominations. The churches were indifferent, even hostile. These voluntary societies were very different from the churches. They were based on contribution of funds by individuals who had one common concern to spread the gospel. They embraced all classes and both sexes, and were not mainly made up of clergy. Often they were linked to the abolition of slavery and a desire to overturn its consequences.[16]

The ongoing tragedy of this divorce was that 'in the thinking of the vast majority of Christians, the words "Church" and "Mission" connote two different kinds of society'. Newbigin explains further. The first kind is 'devoted to worship, and the spiritual care and nurture of its members',[17] while the second focuses on spreading the gospel and 'passing on its converts to... "the Church"'. There is almost no overlap between them. The emerging organisations institutionalised a separation of Church and mission, until formal links were made in 1961 at the World Council of Churches. With this wide, and regrettable, gap between the Church and missionary societies, we can understand why the very idea that the 'Church in mission' should be reproductive would fall in the gaping chasm between the two. It could not find a foothold on either face of this historical divide.

An exclusion of the reproductive element

With all these dominant historical factors, of course, the reproductive element of the Church was excluded. The absence in the tradition is not telling evidence against the reproductive theory but is evidence about its exclusion on other grounds. The reproductive strand was unthinkable.

In dwelling upon these ill effects of Christendom, I am applying Dulles' own method in relation to the test of fruitfulness. Where there is reasonable doubt about a previous mistaken belief, he urges that it will be necessary to 'unveil the positive reason that made people accept error'.[18] I have therefore explained why the context and mindset of Christendom made the theory of the reproductive strand virtually absent from people's thinking in all but the earliest centuries, until recently. The features of Christendom meant that anything even remotely like ecclesial reproduction would only be found beyond its territorial edges. As a result, its presence is very uneven across history. If the Church had been seen as reproducing non-identically, this would have made its attitudes in mission more humane, spiritual and organic, and would have promoted its earlier healthier expansion into other parts of the world.

Towards recovery of the reproductive strand

The following two examples of the recovery of the reproductive strand of Church identity are important precedents. I highlight them also because they represent hinge-moments in the development of the tradition. They disprove any claim that the tradition has nothing to add.

Some Catholic changes in mission mode

In the period called the Counter-Reformation, there were a variety of Roman Catholic missions beyond Europe and Christendom. Some, sadly, practised a mission model a long way from contextual reproduction. At best it was replication and at worst it was sheer imposition. It assumed that there was nothing of value in the host culture, thus destroying all idols and leaders of opposition, with enforced baptisms rapidly following. This model was clearly seen in the Spanish conquest of South and Central America.[19]

Francis Xavier and other Jesuits brought a change from this disgraceful mode of mission. Xavier began his work not as an ordinary missionary but as a powerful apostolic representative. Yet he worked among the illiterate poorer castes of South India from 1542 to 1549. Then, during his short stay in Japan from 1549 to 1552, he 'reconsidered his missionary method'.[20] He learnt the language and studied its philosophical roots. He adopted social and dress customs and attended local forms of higher education. This all meant the creation of ways of being Church that included elements of difference. It meant giving some worth to local cultures and religions, thus breaking with the previous view.[21]

There are similar patterns to be seen with Matteo Ricci in China (1583–1610), and Robert Nobili in India (1605–56). Nobili drew on the apostle Paul and remarked, 'I too shall become an Indian to save the Indians.'[22] In this, Nobili is consciously reproducing a pattern, rather than copying it by pointlessly attempting to become like a Greek or a Jew.

I am not arguing that a conscious theory of non-identical Church reproduction was present in the work of these pioneers. However, I do claim that these stories demonstrate how they modified their view of the missional and ecclesial task. This changed the way they approached culture and ideas of what the Church could be. The modified view meant that these missionaries started churches that were different from the churches that had sent them, making Christianity as little foreign as possible, even considering what words for God should be used. It meant working with cultural values like the importance of the family and veneration of ancestors.

Notice the shift away from enforced replication and a positive change to fit the context—later called 'inculturation'. In Nobili's case, as happens today, his innovations caused disturbance back in Rome. The adaptations to dress and baptismal practice were only accepted, after being contested, in 1623.[23] Nobili also saw the need to diversify missions further. This included forming a further Church for Hindu penitents, because he found himself largely limited to high caste connections. All these features were moves away from monolithic views of Church with replication as the only possibility. They are shifts towards the non-identically reproductive. These shifts offer one group of precedents for our own more recent discoveries at home, both developments arising because of cross-cultural encounter and the movement towards non-identical reproduction.

Henry Venn and 'three self' thinking: a Protestant contribution

Henry Venn (General Secretary of CMS from 1841 to 1872) was one of the earliest Anglican mission theorists to campaign for the foundation of indigenous churches as a goal. We know that he studied Xavier and other sources. He was concerned at the lack of both vigour and self-reliance in the 'native people' and their churches' 'lack of rootedness' in the indigenous culture.[24] His theory emerged in policy statements issued, by stages, until 1866, but his mind was shaped by the CMS financial crisis of 1841, when he was first appointed. The crisis pointed up the heavy dependence of the mission churches on paid leadership provided by CMS, coupled with the high mortality rate of those sent. It raised the spectre of what would be the fate of those churches if suddenly cut adrift from this financial and ministerial support. By 1846, Venn was speaking to CMS conferences about 'introducing a *self-supporting principle* into the Native Churches'.[25] This idea developed and is now remembered as the 'three self' formula.

The source of Venn's convictions

However, Venn's deeper personal roots are of greater interest. As the son and grandchild of abolitionists, he had strong and positive convictions about the equality of all human beings. These were confirmed by the ability of the Africans whom he met from childhood onwards. He cited to others the comment made to him by an African merchant: 'Treat us like men, and we will behave like men… treat us as children and we shall behave like children.'[26]

Several significant points arise. Firstly, the amount of trust placed in others by leaders and pioneers will tend to be governed by their view of humanity, formed by a mixture of theology and experience. Bosch tells us how Protestant missionaries have found this difficult because of their 'emphasis on humankind's total depravity'.[27] A contrast would be the more positive Catholic view of humanity held by Roland Allen, who developed Venn's ideas through painful comparison between the foreignness of the mission-founded Church in China and the records of the apostle Paul. He advocated trusting not only in the word and the Holy Spirit,[28] but also in the indigenous people who were young in the faith. Venn shared this willingness to trust.[29]

Secondly, the African merchant's poignant comment addresses our expectations of human growth. Venn's letters show that he continued to work with this human analogy. He talked about how behaviour appropriate in childhood 'is fraught with mischief in manhood'. Where there was 'infantile feebleness', it was because the missionaries thought that the natives were 'not trusted to go alone'.[30] He likened the missionary to a parent learning to let go. He saw the need to move beyond his earlier proposed pattern, which began with missionary control, then moved to 'Native agency under European superintendence', and thirdly to 'Native ministry the crown of the Native agency'. The further necessity he then saw was of 'a Native Church, the soul of Mission'. He likened the missionary to external scaffolding around a building: 'when the building is completed it is taken to pieces'.[31] With the exception of this scaffolding picture, his controlling analogy about the starting and sustaining of churches is a human one.

Here is a view of how the Church grows which is close to non-identical reproductive thinking. Significantly, the main analogy is human, not plant-based—so much so that Peter Williams' title for his study of Venn is '"Not transplanting": Henry Venn's strategic vision'. The vegetable analogy is poor in making explicit a clear process of development to maturity in the first generation. It is not good as a model that embodies ongoing change. With human reproduction, both continuity and change are quickly obvious. There is family likeness *and* individuality, as well as the intention for growth to mature interdependence between parents and their adult children. I therefore suggest that the human-based term 'self-reproducing' is always preferable to the vegetable-based analogy of 'self-propagation' or the managerial flavour of 'self-extending'.

Letting the Church grow up
In the year of Venn's death, the CMS journal *The Intelligencer* published an article[32] recommending that the native Church be constituted on

> … an independent, organic basis of its own; a Church which while it should be in the closest and most intimate relation with the mother Church which first gave it being, should nevertheless stand on its own bottom as the native Church of India, and not be merely a poor and feeble imitation of a far distant Church across the sea.[33]

The terms 'independent', 'organic', 'mother' and 'gave it being' all fit the reproductive strand. The repudiation of 'imitation' is also striking. What is different from my claim is that, in Venn, this is a useful analogy drawn from humanity. In my view it is an image of an essential feature of Church identity. It is not only pragmatically useful to act like this. The Church should think that such processes are theologically normal, and normative in its work. Yet, in Venn we see a witness in the tradition, going a long way towards that sort of perspective. Moreover, it is another precedent showing that moves in this direction tend to be learnt beyond Christendom and born out of the observation of practice.

It is also clear that Venn's language is not about the birth process. Indeed, this is not where Venn found the most longstanding problems. The difficulties arose for him in the recognition by older churches of the existence and maturing of the new Church, a Church that was both similar and different because of its context. Yet, *The Intelligencer* itself picked up that inevitability of difference, reverting to biology and alluding to a kingdom parable: 'The gospel is a seed sown in a different soil and that soil will modify the product, and a Christianity will be raised up which, in all that does not compromise essential principles, will be so modified as to be in sympathy with the national peculiarities.'[34]

Years after Venn, people dispute whether his theory was idealistic, in view of some difficulties that arose after the appointment of the first African bishop. Venn has critics and staunch defenders. The defenders blame undue dependency on the white missionaries, some of whom were apparently omnicompetent and controlling. Some would now be dubbed 'racist'. In Yates' view, there were 'cultural and sociological factors which Venn could not have foreseen'.[35] These were the source of whatever weaknesses there were.

Despite the debate, there is this hard evidence, in the tradition, that continued further reproduction is something that a church should do, out of its being. Venn has been a source of encouragement to those in English Church planting and fresh expressions of Church.

What we learn from Venn and those who follow him

I find it significant that this precedent towards recovering the reproductive strand occurred in Africa, where the incoming missionaries met a culture not so much dominant as subservient. Thus, the dangers of replication and creating dependency were more alluring. Later, Roland Allen also argued that it was over-complication of what must be included within the essence of both the gospel message and the Church that was problematic.[36] This was fatally coupled with a lack of trust towards the indigenous people, who had been given the word and the Spirit. Venn, as a theorist reflecting on the weakness of others' practical work and his experience of meeting fully human and trustworthy Africans, was ahead of most of the practitioners. The 'three self' theory was a valuable attempt to help newly created churches find their identity. It included being self-propagating—or, in better language that fits Venn's own view of human beings—self-reproducing. It is this third dynamic that has few precedents in past tradition. When steps towards it have been taken, they have met resistance and criticism, although others argue that those criticisms are flawed.

Similar support could be found in the Edwardian mission thinker Roland Allen. One of his characteristic terms is 'the spontaneous expansion of the Church'.[37] This term fits perfectly with the reproductive strand of Church identity. Spontaneity springs from identity. A still later witness to this trust in people, and in the reproductive element, would be Vincent Donovan, pursuing similar instincts among the Masai a further 50 years later, having read Allen.[38]

Recent advocates of the reproductive strand

Church and life cycle theory

Christendom's influence on blindness to the reproductive strand is underlined by the observation that, as Christendom continues to dissolve, so the reproductive instinct has emerged. Advocacy of something like Church reproduction first surfaced in writings intended for westernised nations through an American Church Growth thinker, Bill Tinsley.[39] This debt was acknowledged by Bruce Patrick, then director of the Baptist Home Mission department in New Zealand. A few years later Patrick published a booklet for his denomination called *The Life Cycle of Reproducing Churches*.[40] I, among others, brought this text back to Britain in 1992.

Reevaluated over 20 years later, the ongoing value of the booklet is now limited in a wide variety of ways. It thinks only in Baptist independent congregationalist terms. It knows nothing of cell or house-based Church. It is dated by dependence on a full-time ordained minister, and is ignorant of indigenous lay leadership. It has managerial, target-driven concepts of planning within a tight sequential process. Church reproduction is now seen to be more complex, with overlapping, messier, organic patterns. It is mistaken in assuming that a church must revolve around Sunday services and that starting public worship necessarily marks the birth of a new church. Both those features are now disputed.[41] Moreover, being publicly accessible is not an essential feature of being a church. Early Church practice did not include it, and contemporary underground churches under persecution cannot be accessible in this way.

This list could suggest that Patrick's work is so flawed as to be without value. Yet, it helpfully suggests that planting churches is an organic process and that what is born is a new life. It opens up topics like the parallels between human and Church development, which are rich in understanding, and is excellent in describing the changing, and sometimes adversarial, stages of relationships between a sent and a sending church. It also sees clearly the need for growth to maturity, and it includes positive affirmation of the topic of reproduction, holding rightly that this process should continue in the next generation of churches.

Differences between life cycle thinking and my view

Tinsley and Patrick were pragmatic. They saw the need for more churches, in a time when the DAWN process[42] was being advocated in the West, to emulate Church growth in some Asian countries. Church planting was its major strategy and the life cycle was one management tool. My approach, however, is theological and argues that the calling and capacity for non-identical reproduction is part of the identity of Church. It is also rooted differently—not in a sense of need, but in the biblical record. It has a different theological impact via the discovery of the fruitfulness it brings to some theological issues. I suggest that because this approach is true, it should be used, not that it is tactically necessary and therefore should be invented. For me, mission has been the trigger, but it is not the major justification.

A further difference is that Tinsley and Patrick were interested in having more churches, whereas I am more concerned to follow the patterns of relational diversity from the Trinity, and of continuity and change from the incarnation. Both of these features map very well on to the human analogy of non-identical reproduction, which embodies them both. Non-identical reproduction is a more nuanced concept than the cruder 'more churches' view. I repudiate replication and cloning, because reproduction is always two-sourced, leading always to some measure of difference. One feature linking all the above criticisms is that they address the tendency towards church replication. They are in painful tension with Patrick's chosen analogy of human reproduction. He may use the word, but, with hindsight, it falls short of the fuller and better grounding that the theological foundations would give it.

For all those reasons, although I am personally grateful to Patrick's booklet for developing my sense of possibilities, I consider that our methodologies and conclusions are sufficiently different to justify claiming that I bring a further contribution to the Church, understood as community-in-mission, with a capacity and calling for non-identical reproduction.

Other contemporary voices in the tradition

There are a few other pointers to acknowledge in the ongoing recent tradition in the United Kingdom. Anabaptist Stuart Murray heard my initial public presentation on this topic at a conference in 1993 and has kindly commentated favourably in his 1998 book, *Church Planting: Laying foundations*.[43] There he accepts that I am making a point that goes beyond the views of those who think functionally or only in mission terms: 'Self-propagation, or reproduction, is not just an admirable quality of some churches, but integral to the definition of the Church.'[44]

My fellow Anglican Michael Moynagh, in his second book on mission today, *Emerging Church.intro*, makes similar comments, including a quotation from my 1992 sabbatical report.[45] This is now expanded and built into his online guide to fresh expressions,[46] arising from our conversations and joint presentations over the years. Accordingly, there are also references to the theory of Church reproduction in his more recent and weightiest book, *Church for Every Context*.[47]

What Dulles' second test teaches us

This chapter has shown that the value put on tradition by Dulles' second test is reduced by his own use of it and limited in that his Catholic investment in tradition would be unacceptable to many other denominations. The chapter has disclosed how the dynamics within Christendom eclipsed the reproductive strand, but also how it is being uncovered as that masking feature dissolves. The precedents from Catholic and Protestant sources that point towards it have in common an encounter with a non-Christian culture.

Facing the failure of previous missions, working cross-culturally and starting out from nothing have all helped to reveal these dynamics, which Christendom was inherently unable to do. More recent life cycle thinking has been contrasted with my understanding of non-identical reproduction to show differences in method, theological approach and practice.

The value of the test from tradition has been shown to be flawed and partial. However, closer inspection shows why the evidence for reproductive thinking was so patchy, why more recently it was more likely to be unearthed, and what it now contributes to the ongoing tradition.

Notes

1 A. Dulles, *Models of the Church* (Gill & Macmillan, 1988), p. 191.
2 I have not included the Eastern Churches because their perceptions of mission are different via their understandings of unity and worship, and Dulles' tests deal with a Western context.
3 Dulles, *Models of the Church*, p. 43.
4 Dulles, *Models of the Church*, p. 37.
5 M. Chapman, *Anglicanism: A very short guide* (OUP, 2006), p. 2.
6 S. Murray, *Post-Christendom: Church and mission in a strange new world* (Authentic, 2011), p. 129: 'If the Empire was Christian, evangelism was obsolete.'
7 H.D. Beeby, *Canon and Mission* (Bloomsbury, 1998), p. 3.
8 R. Clapp, 'Practicing the politics of Jesus' in M. Budde and R. Brimlow (eds), *The Church as Counterculture* (SUNY, 2000), p. 17.
9 D. Bosch, *Transforming Mission* (Orbis, 1991), p. 377.
10 Bosch, *Transforming Mission*, pp. 243, 248.
11 See M. Parsons, *Calvin's Preaching on the Prophet Micah: The 1550–51 sermons in Geneva* (Edwin Mellen, 2006), pp. 181–227, and M. Parsons, 'Luther on Isaiah 40: the gospel and mission' in M. Parsons (ed.), *Text and Task: Scripture and Mission* (Paternoster, 2005), pp. 64–78.
12 W. Shenk, *Transmission*, issue in tribute to Lesslie Newbigin (1998), p. 5.
13 C. Buchanan, *Is the Church of England Biblical?* (DLT, 1998), p. 281.
14 Buchanan, *Is the Church of England Biblical?*, p. 281.
15 Murray, *Post-Christendom*, p. 168, noting that he also condemned them to death.
16 A. Walls, *The Missionary Movement in Christian History* (T&T Clark, 1996), pp. 241–52.
17 L. Newbigin, *The Household of God* (SCM, 1953), p. 194.
18 Dulles, *Models of the Church*, p. 193.

19 J. Comby, *How to Understand the History of Christian Mission* (SCM, 1996), pp. 69, 87. Also S. Neill, *A History of Christian Missions* (Penguin, 1987), p. 156.

20 Comby, *How to Understand the History of Christian Mission*, p. 88.

21 Bosch, *Transforming Mission*, p. 479.

22 Comby, *How to Understand the History of Christian Mission*, p. 92, citing a letter, 20 November 1609, quite early in the lifetime of Nobili.

23 A summary of the longer story of increased tension over such variations, including the resultant suppression of the Jesuits, is found in Bosch, *Transforming Mission*, pp. 449–50.

24 W.R. Shenk, *Changing Frontiers of Mission* (Orbis, 1999), p. 53.

25 W.R. Shenk, 'The contribution of Henry Venn to mission thought', *Anvil* 2.1 (1985), p. 35.

26 P. Williams, '"Not transplanting": Henry Venn's strategic vision' in K. Ward and B. Stanley (eds), *The Church Mission Society and World Christianity* (Eerdmans, 2000), pp. 149–50.

27 Bosch, *Transforming Mission*, p. 450.

28 T.E. Yates, 'Anglicanism and mission' in S. Sykes, J. Booty and J. Knight (eds), *The Study of Anglicanism* (SPCK, 1998), pp. 434,438.

29 Shenk, *Changing Frontiers*, pp. 53-55.

30 Williams, 'Not transplanting', p. 156.

31 Williams, 'Not transplanting', p. 156, and T.E. Yates, *Venn and Victorian Bishops Abroad* (SPCK, 1978), p. 16.

32 Some thought it might be a final memorandum from Venn, but most think that this is unlikely: Williams, 'Not transplanting', p. 170.

33 Williams, 'Not transplanting', p. 171, citing CMS archives.

34 Williams, 'Not transplanting', p. 167, citing *The Intelligencer* (1869), p. 99.

35 Yates, *Venn and Victorian Bishops Abroad*, p. 136.

36 R. Allen, *Missionary Methods—St Paul's or Ours?* (Eerdmans, 1962), pp. 87–92.

37 D. Paton and C. Long, *The Compulsion of the Spirit: A Roland Allen reader* (Eerdmans, 1983), p. 33. It is the title of his 1927 book published by Lutterworth Press and reprinted in 2006

38 V. Donovan, *Christianity Rediscovered* (SCM, 1982), pp. 32–35.

39 In 1988 Tinsley wrote on the life cycle in conjunction with Fuller Theological Seminary, having published a book on Church planting, *Upon This Rock: Dimensions of church planting* (Home Mission Board of the Southern Baptist Convention, 1986). He went on to become Director of Missions and Executive Director for Minnesota-Wisconsin Baptist Convention in 1993.

40 B. Patrick, *The Life Cycle of Reproducing Churches* (Baptist Union, 1988).

41 We now recognise that different starting points are legitimate and necessary in a diverse set of mission contexts and cultures. Putting on an act of worship is but one option and is only suitable for a minority of cases: G. Lings, 'Discernment in mission', *Encounters on the Edge* 30 (Church Army, 2006), pp. 5–15.

42 DAWN is an acronym for Discipling A Whole Nation.

43 S. Murray, *Church Planting: Laying foundations* (Paternoster, 1998), p. 57.

44 Murray, *Church Planting: Laying foundations*, p. 60.

45 M. Moynagh, *EmergingChurch.intro* (Monarch, 2004), p. 48.

46 www.freshexpressions.org.uk/guide/about/principles. Reproduction is one of his list of ten features.

47 M. Moynagh, *Church for Every Context* (SCM, 2012), pp. 114, 166.

9

Reproduction and the classic 'four marks' of the Church

The Christian tradition has long used four words—one, holy, catholic and apostolic—to describe the Church. Its call to be 'one' could be rooted in John 17. The call to be 'holy' could be traced to 1 Peter 1. 'Apostolic' might be grounded in Ephesians 2; it is also prominent in the lists in 1 Corinthians 12. The term 'catholic' goes back to Ignatius and was first used before about AD108, but the prior presence of catholicity is derived from two concurrent factors: though groups around the Mediterranean were called churches, at the same time there was a sense of one overall Church, as in Ephesians 4.

If non-identical reproduction is to be accepted within the ongoing tradition, it must engage with these four words. Equally, using Dulles' sixth test, the reproductive strand needs to demonstrate features of the Church that the words do not adequately explain. Its fruitful contribution is in adding to the four marks. I am not saying that the reproductive strand should sit equally alongside the four marks and be added to the historic creeds. I am merely showing how it meshes with these features, which are widely accepted attributes of the Church.

The choice of the four marks

The four marks have a good claim to being a standard. They have been used for years; they appear in some creeds and are used in liturgies in some denominations. (I write as an Anglican, knowing that liturgy acts as 'a primary source of Anglican theology'.)[1] Bishop Steven Croft calls them 'a brilliant example of distilled ecclesiology'.[2]

However, the four marks have not settled all Church disputes. During the Reformation, other features were highlighted. Two Protestant 'notes' are found in the 1530 Council of Augsburg: 'The Church is the congregation of saints, in which the Gospel is rightly taught and the Sacraments are rightly administered.'[3]

Yet I don't want to use 'word and sacrament', partly because they are reforming features, not founding ones. Moreover, they describe only the Church's public worship, telling us little about what Church is. Equally damaging, they are centred on leadership, are weak on community and say nothing about mission. Christ's commands do urge word and sacrament on every expression of Church, but the way we do public worship doesn't answer issues of Church identity, so they are of little use here.

Part of the difficulty in a two-way conversation between the reproductive strand and the four marks is their varied interpretation over time. Dulles spends his eighth chapter showing that the four marks meant different things according to each of his first five models.[4] It is clear that they do not have a fixed meaning within the broad tradition of the Church. This may explain why Dulles does not make them into his tests.

Meeting this diversity of meaning and wondering if there was a unity, I summarised some contemporary Anglican sources on the four words to explore whether this would bring convergence or maintain divergence.[5] I found congruence. Moreover, all authors accepted that there are untidy edges between them, not neat separation. All the marks are thus held modestly. If the variety and modesty are legitimate, it is easier to think that the Church's calling and capacity to reproduce may affect the way we understand the four marks. Dulles himself would be open to this, citing Pope Paul VI at Vatican II: 'The Church is a mystery. It is a reality imbued with the hidden presence of God. It lies, therefore, within the very nature of the Church to be always open to new and ever greater exploration.'[6]

The reproductive strand in interaction with the four marks

I offer one consensus on the broad meaning of each mark, and this frames the conversation with the reproductive strand. To some extent the four words can be paired with each other, for it is clear that they derive their meaning partly through their interconnection and overlap.

Apostolicity

I take apostolicity to mean a dimension of the Church that exists and has relationships that *connect across time*,[7] *yet stays faithful*, looking back to its origins in God, Christ and scripture, which give both authenticity and authorisation. It also looks forward with 'momentum', to borrow a word from Avis. Apostolicity is concerned about how foundational values are faithfully transferred. By it the Church also looks forward through apostolic mission and sends members out and beyond itself.

The reproductive strand and apostolicity

Apostolic concern for faithfulness is essential in cross-cultural mission, to resist syncretism. Looking forward must remain connected to looking back. The Church faces backwards in faithfulness to the gospel in Jesus so that it may move onwards in missional creativity. Therefore, the apostolic mark involves a test of genuineness. Some people have interpreted this as the preservation of identical practices in public worship, but I think it goes deeper than maintaining outward conformity. Identical replication of practices is an inappropriate test. I have offered a deeper apostolic test for the reproductive idea through several chapters on the biblical basis, and theological chapters on the Trinity and Christology and the way it sits in the historical tradition.

The reproductive strand then adds to the future dimension of the apostolic mark. The calling is to create further missional churches, not just to initially found and then add people to existing ones. Chapter 4 put up a case that the Trinity are 'community-in-mission', which means that being apostolic is deeper than just being sent *by* God. It is about being sent to reproduce some patterns *of* God's community-in-mission identity and activity.

The missions of the Trinity discussed in Chapter 4 were focused in the person and patterns of Christ. I argued in Chapter 5 that the incarnation acts as a precedent for the reproductive process, showing how both continuity and change are diagnostic of non-identical reproduction. At its heart, Chapter 6 unpacked the 'dying to live' instinct in the seed parable of John 12. That instinct sits on a telling reproductive basis, going back to the words in John: 'As the Father has sent me, even so I am sending you' (John 20:21, RSV).

However, the reproductive strand should learn from those who warn that too much focus on Christ has led the Western Church to an over-emphasis on the historical.[8] The Spirit has an equally key role in apostolicity, which is shown in the book of Acts, teased out in my Chapter 7. There the Spirit disturbed monolithic inherited patterns, bringing diversity. This was described as an eccentric effect, disturbing the centrality of Jerusalem. A reproductive understanding of the apostolic would expect a continued eccentric non-identical progression, as successive generations of young churches come into being.

Interaction with the reproductive also means that the apostolic is focused on living communities, not just on truths or authorisations, with their debates over whether 'apostolic' means doctrinal inheritance or valid succession of leadership. The reproductive strand agrees with those who stress 'that the Church as a whole is charged with continuing the apostolic role of being sent',[9] and that this role is not just for designated teachers, apostles or missionaries. But it goes further. Being apostolic, for an existing church community, means more than learning to face outwards to draw others to it. It includes the possibility of some members leaving and starting a further community elsewhere. That was the case with the Trinity, the incarnation and, then, Christ's calling of his disciples. Planting fresh expressions of Church by reproduction is closer to this divine pattern than much of the 'come to us' mission practised by existing churches, let alone the barely missional existence of many local churches. The reproductive idea sharply critiques this practice as well as the regrettable cases of fresh expressions of Church being created for the internal tastes of discontented Christians.

Another significant difference compared with past understandings of the apostolic dimension is that the reproductive strand validates the call for the Church to multiply, not just to add. It does not repudiate these other dimensions of growth by the Spirit, but insists that reproduction by multiplication is a further valid, yet often ignored, dimension of the call to the people of God.

The reproductive strand agrees that mission cannot be separated from the Church's bread-and-butter tasks of 'the triple ministry of word, sacrament and pastoral care',[10] but nor can it be limited to them. Too often there is an overwhelming tendency to undertake those ministries within a framework of inviting others to come to us, rather than understanding how to go and create Church amid their culture. In all these ways, the reproductive works with the apostolic, yet it brings significant critiques to its past interpretations.

Reproduction, by definition, leads to the birth of authentic, related but non-identical churches. The apostolic mark alone cannot encompass this, not even with straight multiplication. Principled diversity, by which there can be churches that remain apostolic in faithfulness yet differ from inherited shapes, needs engagement with the more recent views of 'catholicity'.

Catholicity

Catholicity has a complementary relationship to the apostolic. My Anglican sources (the House of Bishops, Avis, Brown and Cray) held in common that catholicity is about the dimension by which the Church exists and has relationships that *connect across space*,[11] *and across difference*. It expresses the wholeness of the Church in each place, through insisting on an enduring connection between its twin callings to be both universal and particular to each place. However, universality should not degenerate into mere uniformity.[12]

Catholicity enshrines the idea that all Christians are in relational connection. This repudiates a view of ourselves primarily as individual Christians or even as independent individual churches. This connectivity is also with the communion of saints, for ultimately there is one Church and one new heaven and earth. Connection with others unlike us also informs the mission to all, that the faith may become more universal in geographical scope and yet remain particular in cultural diversity. In this sense, catholicity is a mandate for mission and for the view that the Church must truly enter cultures. As such, it is hospitable, but that value is held in tension with apostolic faithfulness to Church origins.

The reproductive strand and catholicity

Reproduction sits well with Ignatius' understanding of 'catholic' as being where Jesus Christ is, among his people. But wholeness is not the same as completeness, just as no one localised church is the universal Church. One suitable analogy for understanding the Church is human development. Just as a baby is seen as human, though not yet adult, so the reproductive strand engaging with catholicity will wish to embrace, rather than reject, Christian groups that may not yet have all the marks desired of Church. By encouragement, and trusting that they have the potential and intention to grow to Church maturity, we can welcome and nurture individuality and youthfulness.

The reproductive strand also fits with the tension within catholicity of the call to be both universal and specific. The planting of fresh expressions of Church for areas and cultures as yet unreached is an expression of the desire that there might be followers of Christ everywhere. Yet 'everywhere' needs the particularity of 'somewhere'. Non-identical reproduction, rather than replication, by its nature finds it easy to embrace diversity, and not just because of culture and context. Diversity is expected as normal, not seen as deviant. This kind of reproduction is an evocative image by which to hold the tension between universal and particular. For the Church to expand in a specific way, it will connect across space but will also welcome the greater diversity that this connection will engender.

The reproductive strand concurs with catholicity seen as an invitation to cultural hospitality. However, Chapter 5 showed that if the fuller pattern of Christ is reproduced in his followers, then, while hospitality begins in incarnation, it moves towards counter-cultural engagement. For Jesus, this occurred though his focus on the kingdom and his selection of a group of disciples, chosen out of the world but not withdrawn from it. Here, the marks of catholicity and holiness inform one another.

Reproduction also reminds all fresh expressions of Church that they came from an outside yet relational source. They were generated, humanly speaking, either by a founder or by a group from another sending church. They are inherently part of something greater than themselves. You could say that newly born churches should know relational catholicity with their apostolic forebears. Here, the time and space dimensions of being Church meet in an obvious way. Young churches should be very conscious of a wider belonging, or catholicity, that gave them birth. Such a birth, in vulnerability, reminds them of grace and gift from beyond, rather than power and ability from within. Catholicity may serve to deliver them from being egocentric, a developmental preoccupation of the young.

Current literature on emerging Church and fresh expressions of Church is often weak in this area. Both the influential Anglican English source St Thomas Sheffield and the widely read writings of Free Church Australians Frost and Hirsch reduce the dynamics of Church from four marks to three—'Up' for holiness, 'In' for Unity and 'Out' for being apostolic. They include nothing on catholicity.[13] Both use the controlling diagram of a triangle (Diagram 2). Each point represents one mark, rightly held in relationship to the other two. But a good representation of a dynamic three cannot excuse the omission of the fourth, catholicity, factor. To introduce another preposition to their formula, I would call catholicity 'Of', alluding to the universal Church as the body *of* Christ.

An alternative has been a cruciform shape (Diagram 3), but it has two disadvantages. The more each mark is pursued, the further it moves from all the others, so the marks are torn apart. Also, this representation is two-dimensional. It offers no sense of time. A more suggestive shape would be three-dimensional, suggesting depth in space and time, which is required by understandings of apostolicity and catholicity. It is helpful to use a regular tetrahedron, or three-sided pyramid (Diagram 4). Here, all four sides connect to all of the others, and all four faces are equal in size. Moreover, the shape is stable and will rest on any base. Thus, all four marks are honoured, yet none of the four is privileged above the others, with no one word in the four controlling. Moreover, from every angle there is always a hidden face of the tetrahedron to symbolise the mystery of the Church that is greater than all our words about her.[14]

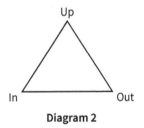

Diagram 2

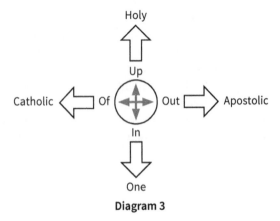

Diagram 3

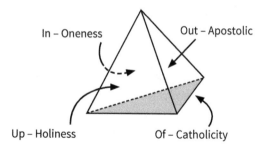

Diagram 4

I suggest also that the reproductive strand teaches all expressions of Church that they need one another and that they belong relationally, before and above belonging by law. It affirms from catholicity that all belong, across their diversity, yet all are only expressions of Church. None can fully express Christ, or even the universal Church, because each is particular. Thus, the reproductive in conjunction with catholicity should bring modesty, interdependence and mutual need into all inter-church relationships. The challenge is two-way. Both inherited expressions of Church and fresh ones belong to the one Church and to each other. We are connected through Christ as overarching, and generationally through the reproductive process of seeing further churches brought to birth. The reproductive values catholicity and critiques current understandings of Church planting that lack it.

Holiness

Recent authors on the word 'holy' have in common the language of calling, being set apart, being positively different from those outside, but without a world-denying withdrawal. I suggest that this mark expresses the dimension of how the Church exists with a diagnostic relationship of *belonging to God*. This belonging to God, and for his purposes, connects holiness to the apostolic mission and to the interdependence of catholicity, by learning from God's own unity in diversity. To exist for God becomes also the call to become more like God, morally and spiritually. As Dulles says, 'Finally, the Church must be characterised by holiness; otherwise it could not be a sign of Christ.'[15] A focus on spiritual disciplines makes us take on God's moral characteristics: 'Be holy, because I am holy' (Leviticus 11:44).[16]

The reproductive strand and holiness

The reproductive strand resonates with an emphasis on calling. Without a calling, the reproduction of churches could degenerate into ecclesial imperialism or self-centredness. The reproductive also needs the call to holiness, for it sets a goal for every church that is born. Belonging to God brings a deeper identity that should resist the temptation of being too Church-centred. Newbigin is consistent in his view that calling, with all its gifts and privileges, cannot be separated from apostolic identity: 'They are chosen not for themselves, not to be exclusive beneficiaries of God's saving work, but to be bearers of the secret of his saving work for the sake of all. They are chosen to go and bear fruit.'[17]

The reproductive strand, which instinctively thinks of fruit, takes such a specific calling seriously, and it adds a particular kind of theological fruitfulness to this link between holiness and apostolicity.

The emphasis on holiness reminds those who are starting churches that novelty is no substitute for integrity, character and spirituality. Doing what has become popular or fashionable is also no substitute for seeking and following the calling of God. Worship at any expression of Church should never descend to self-indulgence in either classical or contemporary tastes. Rather, it is to be a response to God, so that we may be transformed to become more like God, in grace, character and purpose.

Holiness is also linked to 'dying to live' dynamics. Chapter 6 teased out the 'dying to live' theme, showing how it is a shorthand for reproducing the broad patterns of Christ, in his death and resurrection, in the ongoing mission of the Church. Christ's own holiness is connected to his apostolic identity and demonstrated in his self-giving. He described it through the intentionally dying seed in John 12. This link holds for the Church also, so holiness is rightly said to include the willingness to sacrifice. Michael Ramsey speaks of the Church as 'expressing the Lord's death and resurrection, wherein its "holiness" consists'.[18] He adds that to believe in this Church 'is to die to self'. That includes the incoming Christians' comfort and preferences, as well as inherited ways of being Church and of presenting the gospel, so that these realities may live, reborn afresh elsewhere.

The reproductive strand also welcomes the more recent emphasis on the kingdom-based 'now and not yet' provisionality of the Church. This brings a greater transparency about our flawed capacity to live out the call to holiness. It will often include a flawed capacity to reproduce—as the biblical stories of the matriarchs demonstrated—not just flawed spiritual and moral lives. The reproductive analogy inherently values the small and vulnerable. This sits well with being painfully aware of the Church's inabilities. Yet, where this realism is coupled with healthy honesty about weakness or spiritual and moral failure, it can lead to greater reliance on grace and on hope placed in a lifelong transformation by the Spirit. Then the reproductive birth of further churches is once more characterised by a sense of gift by the Spirit, rather than human power.

When holiness is being reproduced, the other side of that coin appears. Flawed lives that are being slowly transformed are attractive by their integrity and their realism about life in community. The pursuit of holiness in a diverse yet well-integrated community has long been appealing, at least since the writing of 1 Peter. Here are links between holiness and oneness, as diverse oneness is inclusive and attractive. Such attraction then itself becomes part of the content of the apostolic message and is one way in which the characteristic Spirit-based language of the Church as foretaste deserves its label. The reproductive strand welcomes the call to holiness, not least the reemphasised provisional framework. At the same time it makes explicit the call to holiness in the community-in-mission. This strengthens the sacrificial link from holiness to apostolicity, which we see in Christ.

Oneness

I suggest that the fourth mark of 'oneness' complements the third mark of 'holiness'. It describes how the Church exists with relationships that live out *belonging like God*. It handles the way the Church community understands its internal relationships, because of its identity derived from beyond itself. Common to the contemporary writers is that oneness finds its deepest source and understanding from the relationships of the Trinity, and from Christ's prayer in John 17 that those who follow him will be one. Today's trinitarian base for unity immediately puts diversity on the table alongside it. Any unity that disallows diversity has become suspect.

The reproductive strand and oneness

The reproductive strand is committed both to relational connection and to difference based on persons. It welcomes the relatively recent shift in the understanding of oneness to an Eastern trinitarian view of unity in diversity. That emphasis increases the overlap between understandings of catholicity and oneness. *Mission-shaped Church* suggested that oneness today deals more with the dynamics of diversity within a local group of Christians and with how they belong together in ways that follow trinitarian unity and diversity. It dealt with catholicity more as wider connections across space and with bonds between groups of Christians in different places or cultures.[19] This is artificial for two reasons. Firstly, the earliest use of the term 'catholic' is about the local church and about its wholeness there. Secondly, at least in theory, the oneness of the Church is universal both in time and space, meaning that catholicity and oneness intertwine.

The reproductive strand contributes to a significant departure from an older view of oneness. I wondered why the order of the four marks is as it is. At one level, the answer is that this is how the words appear in the creeds. However, the deeper questions are about why that order was penned and whether it implies a controlling order which gives power and priority to being one. If true, this power is increasingly odd today, not least as the visible Church is clearly very far from being 'one'.

It seems that this instinct goes back to a focus in the theology emanating from Cyprian. Today, the alternative trinitarian view by Eastern Orthodox theologians has challenged it, and awareness of context has led to disbelief of it.

Cyprian's influence, training and background

Kevin Giles claims that too much doctrine of the Church has been static, institutional, legalistic and authoritarian.[20] He roots this danger in the views of Cyprian, who wrote *On the Unity of the Catholic Church* in AD251. The book's influence lasted so long because of the vacuum in ecclesiological writing that followed it: 'There was no other book written on the doctrine of Church for more than a thousand years—until Wycliffe wrote *The Church* in 1378.'[21]

The historical background was that the persecution in 249 led to large-scale public denials of the faith. When it ended, the issue was how to deal with those who had lapsed. Cyprian found himself in some ways supporting the protest of the hardline presbyter Novatian. However, after failing to become bishop, Novatian formed a dissident 'puritan' group that lasted for centuries. Cyprian utterly rejected these schismatic responses. In this context he wrote *On the Unity of the Catholic Church*. Then, his public martyrdom in 258 added prestige to his views.

Cyprian was dealing with the problem of schism and rival baptisms. It led him to look for arguments to express oneness and catholicity that were visible and consistent. These viewpoints then became arguments for excluding those with whom he was disagreeing. Cyprian was also a lawyer by training and Roman by culture. Jay describes his approach as 'practical, legalistic, and logical'.[22] So his arguments all favour external measurable marks of the one Church. As Giles puts it, 'The Church for Cyprian is an empirical, geographically extended institution. It is the spiritual counterpart of the Roman State, a well ordered society unified under one ruler, the bishop.'[23]

The Roman influence

Cyprian's instincts sit in a cultural context. They endorse churchy equivalents of the security brought by a united, well-ordered society, operating under one ruler and remaining one empire.[24] Without this united identity and security, there was the lurking perpetual fear amid Roman society that the empire might fall into chaos. Then the barbarians at its gates would take over. We know that Cyprian lived in this cultural fear of chaos and that he regarded the world as in the process of collapse. The place of safety and salvation was the Church.

Cyprian reveals instincts for the need for defence and the assumption that there is only one way of doing things, when he likens the Church to a military camp.[25] Each Roman legion carried on their backs the tools necessary to build a camp or fort. It was characteristic of the Roman army that there was one plan. A fort built near Scotland would be identical to one in Turkey. This is a physical, cultural example of Roman uniformity: there is one way of doing things. In this culture, there was a strong tendency for oneness to mean uniformity. Cyprian's cultural background taught him that schism meant fragmentation; it raised the fear of chaos, challenged the ordered view of authority. Whatever its face, schism must be unholy. 'Cyprian held there is only one Church, and those who break away, however pure they appear, are agents of the devil in their breach of fundamental charity.'[26] To break away 'was the worst of sins'.[27] It was even worse than lapsing, because it entailed deceiving others.

Oneness and singularity

Moreover, Cyprian thought in the Greek cultural terms of his day. An ordered society was based on a monolithic and unchallengeable hierarchy. This guaranteed the stability of society. An example of this mindset is that Greek philosophers were surprised and alarmed when the circumference of a circle, in relation to its diameter, was proved not to be an integer, such as 3, but the strange value now entitled 'pi': 3.14159 and so on.

Oneness must mean singularity: one empire, one ruler, one bishop, one Church, one baptism. In *On the Unity of the Catholic Church*, Cyprian draws more on factors such as Christ's choice of one man, Peter,[28] or the robe of Christ remaining undivided, than he does on allusions to the unity of Father, Son and Spirit.[29] Two comments in his letters show his thinking: 'The Church is one and indivisible' and 'If there is one Church, there can be no baptism outside it.'[30] Hence, he insisted that the necessary baptism of heretics was not rebaptism.

This interpretation of oneness as singularity interlocks oneness with catholicity. In understanding the Church, visible oneness and catholicity (universality) become the same. This is a wider concept than Cyprian's. Dulles tells us that the mark of apostolicity, as true belief, was used against heretics, arguing that they were departing from apostolic faith. By contrast, a lack of catholicity was the charge against schismatic groups like the Donatists, who could demonstrate that their practice was only local, not universal.[31] For Cyprian, to be schismatic or out of communion with the bishop or ruler, who gives unity to the Church,[32] could only mean, legally and logically, being outside the Church. Hence his famous phrase, 'There is no salvation outside the Church.'[33] Consistent with this, there is only one salvation, as in Cyprian's other well-known tag: 'He cannot have God for his father who has not the Church for his mother.'[34] Then, any sort of plurality of the Church in different places can only be derived from and utterly dependent on the centre. So Cyprian uses the analogies of the rays of the one sun, branches of one tree, and streams in one river. Without their source, each dies or ceases to exist.[35]

Such was the climate in which this fourth mark was used and defended. It shows how oneness became the driving factor controlling all the others. Its cultural and doctrinal preeminence is clear. It is crucial to note this strong historical and cultural bias towards oneness as the ruling concept, and to note that oneness was interpreted as singularity and uniformity.

Challenging the power of Cyprian's view of oneness

I have shown that the priority given to oneness is unconvincing. It was derived from historically particular and now superseded cultural, political and even mathematical assumptions. They are no longer convincing as proving uniformity. By contrast, the 21st-century Church faces, firstly, a felt disgrace of institutionalised and organic disunity, as well as intractable difficulty in solving it. Secondly, in a postmodern context, denominational identity is becoming seen more as an acceptable, though provisional, mutually affirming plurality. Thirdly, both emerging and inherited churches display evident diversity of practice. Fourthly, for decades many have seen contextual mission, and diversity through engaging with cultures, as necessary. All these factors mean it is no longer credible to understand oneness as singular uniformity. Being 'one', in these senses, is not the most characteristic or determinative feature of Church identity. Salvation may no longer be exclusively linked to formal membership within any one visible expression of Church.

Moreover, fifthly, our deepest theological base for reevaluating oneness is the Trinity. Its implications for all the marks have been explored in this chapter. The reproductive strand makes common cause with this, although it must be a lesser feature. The reproductive understanding repudiates the linkage between singularity and oneness. It builds on the sending of both the Son and the Spirit, and on the three differentiated persons of the Trinity. It adds that such dynamics are, in limited senses, to be reproduced in the Church. It further justifies modifying singular oneness by showing that the incarnation of God the Son held together both continuity and change. This dynamic applies both in this fresh expression of God the Son and in his calling of 'dying to live'. Both are passed on to the Church. Continuity sits easily with singularity and uniformity, but change does not, and yet both are required. So the non-identical reproduction strand gladly receives the trinitarian base and demonstrates how it should be applied to the Church. Reproduction embraces an untidy yet profoundly relationally connected diversity. The reproductive strand profoundly challenges this inherited meaning of oneness.

Summary and an analogy drawn from human reproduction

I have argued why the four marks deserve attention as long-honoured features of the Church tradition. Some freedom to modify their meaning was justified through Dulles' demonstration of their previous wide historical interpretations. Despite this historical variety, I have identified some coherence across four contemporary interpretations of the marks and engaged with them to suggest that the four words can be paired, as well as overlapped.

This chapter has shown how the reproductive strand learns from all of the marks but also brings fruitful development to them and beyond them. There is nothing in the reproductive strand that excludes any of the four marks. Indeed, it will operate better when informed and educated by all of them. This attentiveness will give a healthy balance to what is reproduced in all fresh expressions of Church.

While the reproductive concept has an utterly junior role to the four marks in terms of history, it brings features of its own. This strand of Church identity goes beyond an apostolic focus on past or present growth by addition, adding non-identical reproductive multiplication. It nuances catholicity to deliberately include those young churches that may well be incomplete but are intending to mature. It explains further why ecclesial diversity is to be thought normal within catholicity. Conversely, all fresh expressions of Church and all those theologising from them need to name and value catholicity, and some sources in the past have ignored this need. The reproductive strand helpfully links holiness to apostolicity. Its instinct about 'dying to live' also connects in a fresh way to the emphasis on sacrifice within holiness. Perhaps the most substantial modifications brought by the reproductive element are concerned with what it means for the Church to be one. It turns down all claims to ideological uniformity as well as patterns of replication. The weight of this, and the unearthing of an undue reliance on Cyprian's power play about being 'one', profoundly question whether oneness must be the controlling term among the four.

As befits the topic, what the reproductive offers can be likened to the changes brought by having a new family member. It is different from any other changes that can occur—for example, existing family members becoming larger and more mature, or more frail, succumbing to temptation, illness or dementia. A new arrival affects all the other members of the family; while not discrediting the family identity, it brings someone unique and not seen before. Examples might include the addition of a third child, which changes the dynamics in a previously 'four square' family and begins a new pattern of relationships. This is a disturbance, but it is development, not destruction. Another example would be the birth of a girl in a family that previously had only boys, with attendant fresh dynamics in the interactions and expectations. Such changes by addition to a mature family will be enriching, although they will require adjustments.

In the family scenarios above, although birthdays declare who is the oldest, it is destructive to ask, 'Who is the most important family member?' Their interdependent interaction, not their priority, is more promising and provides a better view of persons. So, although I am intrigued by questions about whether any one of the four marks should be put first, I think them unhelpful. My earlier illustration of the four marks as a tetrahedron refuses to assert the primacy of any of the four.

The arrival of the reproductive strand will bring to the broad tradition a renewed emphasis on the Church as an interconnecting set of four living dimensions and relationships, not least between generations of the Church as fresh ones are born. These connections have deep roots in the Trinity and the patterns of Christ. In turn, they emphasise the communal, missional, interrelational and developmental aspects of the life of the Church, and these are legitimate causes of joy rather than doubt or dismissal.

This chapter has explored how the reproductive strand makes friends with these four key ecclesial words from the living tradition. It rightly receives from them but, importantly, also gives to them and explains what they alone cannot account for, in the creation of the more recent diverse generation of fresh expressions of Church. The reproductive strand of the Church does distinctive work in engaging with the ongoing tradition and meeting Dulles' sixth test of theological fruitfulness. It then becomes more plausible but hopefully modest to say, 'I believe in a reproductive Church.'

Notes

1 E. Jay, *The Church: Its changing image through twenty centuries*, Vol. 1, *The First Seventeen Centuries* (SPCK, 1977), p. 188.

2 S. Croft (ed.), *Mission-shaped Questions* (CHP, 2008), p. 189.

3 Council of Augsburg Section 7.1. The Anglican emphasis on ministry and worship, centring on word and sacrament, is located in its 39 Articles of Religion and in the Ordinal. The wording of Article 19, which defines the visible Church as being where these two features occur, draws on the Augsburg text.

4 A. Dulles, *Models of the Church* (Gill & Macmillan, 1988), p. 137.

5 The four sources are the House of Bishops, *Eucharistic Presidency* (CHP, 1997), pp. 20–21; M. Brown, 'What do we mean by Church?', a private paper for the Pastoral Measure 1983 Review Group, 2002; P. Avis, *The Anglican Understanding of the Church* (SPCK, 2000); G. Cray (ed.), *Mission-shaped Church* (CHP, 2004), pp. 96–98.

6 Dulles, *Models of the Church*, p. 18.

7 M. Volf concurs: *After Our Likeness: The Church as the image of the Trinity* (Eerdmans, 1998), p. 117.

8 *Eucharistic Presidency*, p. 19, para 2.20.

9 M. Brown, *What Do We Mean by 'The Church'?*, p. 7; H. Küng, *The Church* (Search Press, 1968), p. 355, concurs.

10 P. Avis, *Mission and Ministry* (lecture to the Porvoo Theological Conference, September 2004), p. 4.

11 Volf, *After Our Likeness*, p. 118, concurs: 'The catholicity of the Church in space…'.

12 P. Avis, *The Anglican Understanding of the Church*, p. 65, acknowledges the latter distortion: 'Catholicity… in the past has often been a byword for authoritarianism, uniformity and crushing of local traditions.'

13 St Thomas Sheffield, under its previous leader Mike Breen, popularised a triangle to emphasise three directions: 'up', 'in' and 'out' to correspond with holiness, oneness and apostolicity. M. Frost and A. Hirsch, *The Shaping of Things to Come* (Hendrickson, 2003), p. 77, also use a triangle, dubbing the points 'communion', 'community' and 'commission'.

14 This sits well with Minear's conviction that no image of the Church is complete in itself; see *Images of the Church in the New Testament*, 2nd edition (Westminster Press, 2004), pp. 11–27, 221–27. Croft has a similar conclusion: 'Like any summary of the essence of the Church, the different New Testament images need to be used together rather than in isolation': *Mission-shaped Questions*, p. 192.

15 Dulles, *Models of the Church*, p. 133.

16 The wording is echoed in 1 Peter 1:16.

17 L. Newbigin, *The Gospel in a Pluralist Society* (SPCK, 1989), p. 86.

18 A. Ramsay, *The Gospel and the Catholic Church* (Hendrickson, 2009), p. 45.

19 Cray, *Mission-shaped Church*, p. 99, although p. 96 does use 'oneness' for relations between Churches.

20 K. Giles, *What on Earth is the Church?* (SPCK, 1995), pp. 213–16.

21 Giles, *What on Earth is the Church?*, p. 213. Jay concurs: *The Church*, Vol. 1, p. 65.

22 Jay, *The Church*, Vol. 1, p. 65.

23 Giles, *What on Earth is the Church?*, p. 213.

24 R. Allen echoes this of Paul's period: 'one empire… one law, the one peace': *Missionary Methods: St Paul's or ours?* (Eerdmans, 1962), p. 14.

25 Cyprian, *Letters 46 and 54*, cited in Giles, *What on Earth is the Church?*, p. 213.

26 Hall, 'Cyprian', p. 144.

27 W.H.C. Frend, *The Early Church* (Hodder & Stoughton, 1965), p. 112.

28 H. Bettenson, *The Early Christian Fathers* (OUP, 1969), pp. 262–63.

29 Bettenson, *The Early Christian Fathers*, p. 265, Cyprian common text, section 7.

30 Bettenson, *The Early Christian Fathers*, p. 271, citing Cyprian's letters nos. 74 section 4 and 71 section 1.

31 Dulles, *Models of the Church*, p. 124.

32 Jay, *The Church*, Vol. 1, p. 67.

33 Jay, *The Church*, Vol. 1, p. 68, gives Cyprian's *Letters* 72:21.

34 Bettenson, *The Early Christian Fathers*, p. 265, citing Cyprian, *De Catholicae Ecclesiae Unitate*, Common text, section 6.

35 Bettenson, *The Early Christian Fathers*, p. 264, and Cyprian, Common text section 5.

10

The useful outworking of the reproductive strand

Three questions

I have tried to deal with three related questions about the reproductive identity of the Church. The chapters on the Bible, the Trinity and Christ all tackled the fundamental question, 'Is it true?' The chapters on the long tradition and the classic four marks of the Church respond to a second question: 'How far is the idea universal?' A third question about the idea is 'Is it useful?' They all matter, but probably in that order.

This third question takes us back to Dulles. Four of his seven tests assess the usefulness of an idea. A very intriguing notion could be true but of absolutely no practical value, which would be a reason to ignore it. An idea could also be useful to those who think it, but dead wrong. Genocide would be a horrible example. Yet, if an idea can be shown to be helpful, enriching and constructive, then it should be made known, encouraged and applied.

Dulles' third test

Dulles' third test is the 'capacity to give Church members a sense of their corporate identity and mission'. Any valuable theory about the Church should provide a framework that aids this kind of self-understanding. This theoretical test complements his seventh, its practical partner. I'll examine test seven immediately after this one.

An obvious resonance

Test three is so sympathetic to the theory of a reproducing Church that readers might think I invented it. Naturally this theory builds the 'capacity to give Church members a sense of corporate identity and mission'. Research into fresh expressions of Church stories has shown the high priority that young churches place on fostering a corporate identity, which they find has a vital connection to effective mission.[1]

Another way the third test is fulfilled is that a young church which grasps this strand of Church identity knows that this is not the end of the process. Its longer aim is to grow to maturity. Within that, by discerning the Spirit's calling and enabling, it can begin further expressions of Church among yet further groups of people. Reproduction's dynamic is therefore better thought of as a spiral than a circle; it is an ongoing story, not a complete episode. Reproduction embodies, not just assists, ongoing corporate identity and mission.

Intrinsic linkage of Church and mission

The need and the way to connect two different bits of theology—revived trinitarian understanding and the *missio Dei*—were explained in Chapter 3. Let me take it further.

Past competition and separation

In the past, missiology and ecclesiology became divorced.[2] This divide between the two disciplines led to unhealthy patterns whereby ecclesiology was seen as a home-based task, focusing on internal issues such as authority, ministerial orders and sacraments, while missiology was done abroad. Material on these subjects was usually delivered in different training institutions. Barriers between the two disciplines have grown. Moreover, in the past, when missions abroad were successful, success was measured by Church values set from home, and the values were often imposed on the local culture abroad. Equally negatively, when a local work stopped being a mission and became a 'church', often it ceased being missionary.

Competition for priority between the disciplines has brought distortions. For example, Avis' shorter book on Anglican Church doctrine relegates missiology to one of a number of 'departments or sub divisions' of ecclesiology.[3] By contrast, others favour the priority of missiology, like Bosch, who argues, 'Ecclesiology therefore does not precede missiology.'[4]

I am disappointed that today it is possible to read books on one discipline that barely mention the other. Plenty of mission-minded leaders speak and blog, issuing rallying calls to mission, and appear to think that, in their focus on mission, it is both possible and desirable to ignore the Church completely. This is like working for a mission harvest while thinking of the Church as a burning barn. Another distortion is to present encounter with Jesus as something totally separate from belonging to his Church. Others can talk up discipleship as crucial, but without any Church reference. So I was pleased to see the subtitle of Alison Morgan's recent book: 'The plural of disciple is Church'.[5]

Developing a base to hold them together

Trinity seen as 'community-in-mission' insists on an intrinsic relationship between Church and mission, not just a functional connection.

This view of the Trinity helps to resolve tensions between the clashing priorities of missiology and ecclesiology. From this perspective, all are mistaken who think that either missiology or ecclesiology is a subsection of the other. I challenge the claims of some missiologists. It is not just that mission is in the nature of the Church. The reproductive strand makes explicit that Church is in the nature of mission.

Ecclesiology and missiology can be reunited. Both disciplines will be entirely and equally necessary for the birth of further churches and the understanding of existing ones. I was delighted that a contemporary authority in the Church planting field, Stuart Murray, wrote in connection with my 1993 lecture on the topic, 'Adding "reproductive" to the lists of epithets normally associated with ecclesiology such as "one", "holy', "catholic" and "apostolic", might be a significant component in the integration of missiology and ecclesiology that is important for the health of both disciplines.'[6]

Missiology and ecclesiology are more than a complementary pair of foods such as fish and chips. It is better to view them through the fabled question 'Which came first, the chicken or the egg?' The two are intimately related and ultimately inseparable. The saying's point is that it is mad to try to say which came first. All that is certain is that the complete removal of one factor will eventually end the life of the other. I'd claim that no way of thinking about Church and mission, other than the reproductive, holds the two disciplines so powerfully together. It's a kind of glue, or theological Araldite. Another analogy is to see Church and mission as an excellent marriage. Here are two intimately joined persons, separated only with difficulty, danger and divorce. They belong together, need each other and will grow by mutual loving commitment, valuing their difference within their foundational unity. And their union might lead to children!

Response to a pair of objections

One fear is that my views create a back door into what is called ecclesio-centric thinking—that is, too much emphasis on the Church. I think not, for the following reasons. The trinitarian community-in-mission argument refuses to assert Church over mission, or vice versa. I have also affirmed the priority of the kingdom over the Church, though holding to a significant connection between them through the 'foretaste' argument. Eschatology also helps to reduce undue focus upon the Church, by stressing its flawed nature in this age while drawing the Church into God's greater future. Yet, when the kingdom fully comes, it is the Church that will continue as a community of faith, hope and love. What will cease is mission, as well as many gifts that are useful to it (1 Corinthians 13:8–13), ordained ministry, baptism and even Eucharist.[7] Thus, a high view of the Church does not need to be an unhealthy self-focused one.

Many of the same arguments answer a second charge, that this theory might make reproduction an end in itself, which is not a new objection.[8] Croft rightly raised it over past distortions around the arrival of cell church. He used a relevant analogy, which is that the purpose of marriage cannot be reduced to having children.[9] Let me state that the reproduction of churches is not the ultimate goal. The Church exists firstly for God the Trinity and then for their wider restorative purposes, of which reproducing is but one calling and means. To have a high view of the Church is not to have a narrow view of its mission.

I think that Dulles' third test is comprehensively passed. In addition to clearly contributing to corporate Church identity and to mission, the special contribution of the reproductive strand is in forging deeper bonds between the two halves of this test. It counters much of the unhappy divorce between ecclesiology and missiology.

Dulles' seventh test

This test, complementing number three, is as follows: 'Fruitfulness in enabling Church members to relate successfully to those outside their own group.'[10] This assesses practice.

Some limitations in the data available

We do now have much more hard data about attendance among the diverse and prolific fresh expressions of Church, in the Church of England. For any depth on this, readers should consult the 2014 and 2016 reports of Church Army's Research Unit. The first report analysed all known examples of fresh expressions of Church in one quarter of the English dioceses. The second repeated the analysis for a second quarter and was able to make further comparisons.[11] As a result of that research, I am sure that any working knowledge of the theory of the reproductive strand of Church is still largely limited to theoreticians of the movement, some clergy and trained pioneers. It is not yet widely known by lay leaders or the members of many fresh expressions of Church. We can't say that they acted because they knew this theory.

Relating successfully to those outside their own group

However, we do now know much more about their motives for relating successfully to outsiders. Leaders were interviewed by phone and asked to fit their story into a choice of eight possible motives that we had observed occurring over time. The two most common choices selected were a pair: identifying groups of people culturally distanced from the existing Church, and an attendant desire to diversify styles of Church on offer. The first is more missional and the second more ecclesial. The second is linked to the reproductive strand and its non-identical character. The Christians intuitively sensed a need to start further churches that were different in some appropriate way, including any of the following: a different starting point, a stronger sense of community, a different size of congregation, different dynamics to raise participation, or meeting on different days, in different venues or at different times.

The third most common motive was that they believed that the Church should grow, not by addition but by beginning a further church. In that sense, although the theory of the reproductive Church might be largely absent, the instinct for it was present and has been fruitful in relating to outsiders.

Why is it necessary to relate to outsiders? Imagine your church as a kind of pillar box. There are some great things about it. It has that nice red colour and you can't miss it on the pavement. It is equipped with a sensible rectangular hole at the top for your letters. It even has regular collections (which makes it even more like a church!). However, if you want to post a family-sized bottle of Coke, a giant Toblerone bar or a DVD box set—oh dear, you find they are all the wrong shape.

Today there are people who are interested in spirituality but suspicious of religion. Many have never really met the Church community but are pretty sure it wouldn't suit them; they might not even know where their local one is. In the trade we call them the non-churched. Many others carry the disappointments and bear the scars they got by belonging in the past, while others have just drifted off as life has changed. We called them the de-churched. There are people from both groups who are discovering that Jesus is brilliant, but they suspect that the Church sucks. None of these people fit the postbox shape of the way into Church.

Another problem is that there are even people who have belonged to Jesus for years but Church is driving them away. They find that its worship doesn't fit with real life, the quality of its community is low, it seems focused on itself, and Christians fall out quicker than Smarties from an open tube.

So, 40 years ago, a slowly growing stream began to flow. Christians began to ask, 'How can we reimagine Church so that it is true to Jesus but is the right shape for those people who don't do Church?' They set off down that path. Then, it was called Church planting. Today, it's seeing the birth of fresh expressions of Church. Our research examined who attended these young churches. We asked the leaders to distinguish between three groups present: firstly, team members who had begun the new church and Christians who had joined since; secondly, the de-churched; and thirdly, the non-churched.[12]

We found that proportions of the three groups varied. There were some differences by type of fresh expression of Church. Some attracted more de-churched and others more non-churched. There were also links to the length of time a church had existed; quite often they seemed to reach a plateau, or perhaps a natural unit size. However, it made little difference whether these young churches were led by ordained or lay people, or by men or women.

Yet two headlines stand out. The first is that among the second set of ten dioceses, in rough terms, 40% of the attenders at fresh expressions of Church were existing Christians, 27% were de-churched and 33% were non-churched. Secondly, on average across the same dioceses, for every one person sent out, there were now 2.6 more people attending—in other words, 260% growth over time. These figures varied across individual stories and even whole dioceses.

Church Army's Research Unit was not only interested in numbers, but also asked questions about ways in which these young churches were growing in maturity. We do not crudely equate 'success' with mere numbers. Yet, it is undeniable that both headlines reveal a story of Christians relating successfully to those outside their group, and in proportions that are either rare or totally unknown in the wider Church. Bob Jackson, in *Hope for the Church*, drew trenchant conclusions from earlier similar data that I gathered in the 1980s and 1990s.[13] He argued that planting is the most fruitful strategy the Church of England has.

This all happened not because these young churches knew the theory of church reproduction but because they practised it. We now have firm evidence that reproducing churches has this effect. It will be interesting to see in the next ten years, if the theory becomes widely known, what further difference that might make.

Though I have made it clear that more people are motivated by the practice than the reproductive theory, I suggest that Dulles' seventh test is passed. The practice of starting fresh expressions of Church—at least an outworking and perhaps born of some dim awareness of the theory—demonstrates significant fruitfulness in enabling members to relate to those outside their own group.

The next test is moral.

Dulles' fourth test

Test four reads: 'Tendency to foster the virtues and values generally admired by Christians.' Dulles cites the following: 'faith, hope, disinterested love of God, sacrificial love of fellow men, honesty, humility, sorrow for sin and the like'. He continues that if 'a doctrine or theological system sustains these values, they will be favourably inclined toward it',[14] adding that the reverse is also true.

Ellen Charry, in her fine but demanding book *By the Renewing of Your Minds*, takes this test yet further. Her deepest conviction is that 'God is not just good to us but for us'.[15] She argues that 'the classic theologians based their understanding of human excellence on knowing and loving God, the imitation of or assimilation to whom brings proper human dignity and flourishing.'[16] She has invented a word for this process, the adjective *aretegenic*, from the Greek words for 'virtue' and 'to beget'. It means 'conducive to virtue'.

Charry argues that unless a doctrine results in virtues, at best the way the doctrine has been communicated is flawed. At worst, it is probably untrue because it lacks aretegenic character. More simply, 'If something is harmful to us, it must be false and certainly cannot be the truth of God.'[17] She continues, 'Classical thought believed that truth, beauty and goodness are affective; that is, they change the seeker by bringing her into their orbit and under their influence.'[18] This raises the stakes surrounding any fresh claims to truth. Does that view produce virtue? According to Charry, these concerns cannot be divided. She concludes, 'The pastoral functions of doctrine, then, are to clarify and, when necessary, revise the teachings of the Church in order to invite believers to be transformed by knowing God.'[19] The first step is to 'reconnect truth and goodness'.[20]

In relation to the classic marks of the Church, hymns praise the beauty of holiness and the beauty of the (apostolic) feet of those who bring good news. The psalmist calls unity 'good and pleasant' (Psalm 133:1). Years ago, David Watson argued that love is the one central mark of the Church.[21] Virtues exercised unselfconsciously are beautiful. But how do such churches fare in relation to Dulles' specific list?

Virtues and a reproducing Church

I'm not saying that these virtues are more present in fresh expressions of Church than elsewhere. Dulles only asks for a tendency to foster their presence, not an ability to outshine other churches. Nor do I need to prove that every fresh expression does this. We are talking about overall practice, which is under examination for its tendency to produce such virtues. But if it was true that fresh expressions of Church had a tendency to produce the opposite vices, that would be evidence against the theory. In looking at Dulles' list of virtues and values, I immediately notice that such qualities would be ideal in any team beginning a young church. But is there any evidence that fresh expressions of Church have the tendency to foster these virtues?

It does take *faith* to set out into the unknown, a characteristic in creating fresh expressions of Church. In consultations with leaders, I often hear them talk about 'making it up as I go along'. Non-identical reproduction, rather than replication, makes deeper demands of faith, because we don't know the result at the start. This fosters dependent prayer, which is related to faith. The mission task involves explaining the faith to others, which takes faith. I have watched how, as their journey continues, faith grows in the young community as the discernment unfolds, as new challenges emerge and gifts in ministry are discovered. Often leaders and members sense that the task is beyond them and only by grace and faith can it be fulfilled.

I have noticed that *hope* is engendered in at least three ways. Partly, it is in association with the possibilities of a new life. Just as, when a married couple prepare for the birth of a child, energy is released, so it is with a team preparing for church reproduction. There is also increased hope that a fresh chance, beyond the confines of past expressions of Church, may be a more fruitful way forward. I also detect hope in the creative partnership with the Holy Spirit, to discover and fashion what is needed in pursuing a fresh mission and the resultant creation of a young church. Such hopes are not always realised, but they are usually there.

Regarding the *disinterested love of God*—altruism is difficult to detect, unless you have known someone well over a period of time. One pointer towards it might be the observed desire for others to know God. More costly is the willingness to amend existing ways of being Church, including worship, away from those forms which suit the planting team, in order to suit the context. This instinct puts sacrificial spirituality firmly on to the agenda of every young church.

The *sacrificial love of others* connects to the previous virtue. What closely embodies this virtue is the 'dying to live' instinct[22] drawn from the ministry of Christ. The attitude of those sowing the seeds of gospel and Church must be to put those in the receiving culture first. It is paralleled by the self-sacrificing attitude of parents to their children, not least of mothers. This feature should characterise sending churches in relation to those they plant. The attitudes advocated by the reproductive theory, for all fresh expressions of Church and their sending bodies, are not always followed; nevertheless, the theory itself fosters this attitude of sacrifice.

Honesty is related to truth and realism. Pressures brought by internal ambition and external demands, especially for quick progress to financial self-sufficiency, militate against the fostering of this value. Against this, I notice that younger churches are aware of the failure of past models. They also evaluate themselves more often, because they are more experimental and have less of a track record to rely on. Indeed, some leadership teams get tired by ceaseless external and internal evaluation. Evaluation indicates a desire for honesty, though at times it can look like teenage self-absorption and doubt. Some younger churches have external steering groups. From my participation in a number of these groups, I am aware that the wider Church is seeking a level of honesty and realism about its life and progress.

Humility is a virtue that is well placed to offer correctives to any new churches tempted to arrogance. Yet the reproductive theory helps uphold this virtue by its insistence on the Church's flawed capacity to reproduce, for which grace is needed. It also teaches that all churches had a sending or parent body, which should foster a sense of interconnectedness that resists pride and self-sufficiency. Moreover, reproduction as part of the nature of the Church forestalls future complacency. To plant is only to begin; it is never to arrive. The future aspect of the coming kingdom makes this clear. Like the leaven, the

Church is never to stop growing and permeating the dough. The language of 'expressions of Church' should teach humility. All are partial and all need the others.

Sorrow for sin shows itself periodically. Young communities experience tensions. In addition they know that quality of community matters internally and in their common witness. Because they are smaller, carry fewer passengers and live closer to the edge, when failure of community life occurs, the results are more obvious and the costs higher.[23] This is not quite the same as sorrow for such failures, but it is related to it.

In relation to all these virtues and the capacity of the reproductive strand to foster them, we must not be idealistic. Sara Savage writes about the positives and dark side of parish life, in which 'the heavy costs of maintaining the positives are mainly borne by the clergy'.[24] Rightly, in my view, she states, 'It is not possible to shed the problems discussed in this chapter simply by starting new forms of Church.'[25] Although she suggests that fresh expressions of Church will have a honeymoon period, they should not be deceived by it.

With this healthy caveat against misplaced idealism, I arrive at the view that the reproductive strand of Church identity does, in the above ways, help foster this set of desirable virtues. That does not imply, however, that they are always embodied in every fresh expression of Church.

Dulles' fifth test

Dulles calls his fifth test 'Correspondence with the religious experience of men today'. He explains that this test has two applications. One is that religious experience has a part to play, held alongside scripture and tradition, in establishing what is true. The second is a missional connection. Writing about a significant change of context, he says, 'Granted the tremendous cultural shifts… it is to be expected that men today will approach the Christian message from a new point of view.'[26] Then he argues that some past, honoured models of Church will be too culturally bound to past images and concerns.

This test could be taken as cultural captivity, allowing secular beliefs and patterns to dominate, and thus be dubious. It would be open to charges of relativism and syncretism, or establishing truth by majority voting. However, seen at best, it is an argument for churches that relate well to the culture they are for. That is one intention of the reproductive theory and all the best fresh expressions of Church. The reproductive strand of Church identity is well placed to be part of the response to the widely perceived collapse of the credibility of the Christendom-type Church. The reproductive Church provides a set of positive images that contemporary people could applaud, for it embodies values that people welcome today.

An emphasis on the reproductive strand places a high value on the Church as organic, rather than institutional.[27] It also fosters a sense of vulnerability and weakness rather than strength, which, in an age suspicious of power, has attractions. This connects to the vulnerability of the incarnation and to Jesus' words about tiny seeds or lambs sent among wolves. The sense of weakness and yet potential is starkly put in the observation that if the Church does not reproduce, it will die.

The reproductive strand also accents the relational nature of being Church. This applies to the loving engagement between those sent and those to whom they are sent, and also between the sending and sent church. It overlaps with seeing Church as creative,[28] which stands in stark contrast to its perception as negative, world-denying, unchangeable and sterile. Favourable secular local press coverage given to fresh expressions of Church stories bears witness to this resonance and the positive connections being seen.

The reproductive also favours understanding the Church as contextual. The soil and seeds analogy demonstrates this view. In addition, the 'dying to live' process underlines the reproductive strand's deep commitment to the expectation that what emerges will be related to the past but different from it, because of context. This non-identical identity from their sending and sponsoring bodies is what gives fresh expressions of Church greater freedom to work with people not previously reached. This approach is thus differentiated from much evangelism which is wedded to a 'come to us as we are and learn to like it' attitude. Starting further churches is also attractive to some because it fits with the value placed upon choice and newness. These last two may be tactical advantages and contemporary images, but in themselves they cannot become the rationale, as critiques by Hull, Milbank, and Davison and Milbank[29] rightly make clear.

The reproductive strand also highlights that Church can be viewed as developmental and not static. Our world is interested in personal, psychological, economic and social development. It thinks that change is inevitable and necessary. This is positive as long as it is linked to the next factor.

The reproductive also opens the possibility of seeing Church as ecological. I mean this in the sense that true ecclesial reproduction always takes place in sympathetic relationship to an environment. Ecology has a profound interest in what is indigenous. It values balance with surroundings, and sustainability. All of these concerns inform the birth and growth of sustainable community. They help a new group to live well in its context, and promote the greater health of that context. This should be true of churches as well as wider communities. This contrasts helpfully with past views of the Church as destructive, detached or parasitic, or as institutional, hidebound and impervious to context.

I have taken Dulles' seventh test in a positive way, because he would not endorse capitulation to contemporary thinking. The reproductive strand to Church identity can engage widely with values that many people hold today. It can help them to see the Church as a group of people who are capable of principled and sympathetic change. It brings to the fore the creative, personal and contextual side of Church as an organism, which will also need to be an organisation but in ways that serve the organism, not the other way round.

For each of these tests of utility, evidence shows that the Church as reproductive engages with them positively. In some places, the Church needs to heed their wisdom; in others, such as tests three and seven, it most strongly fulfils them and highlights values that the whole Church does well to attend to.

The reproductive element makes some surprises normal

The Church Army research on around 1100 Anglican fresh expressions of Church[30] has revealed some unexpected features. Contrary to the impression created by publicised large transplants, most fresh expressions of Church are small. The average size so far is around 50 attenders. What we are seeing is the multiplication of many, varied, young and small churches. Moreover, start-ups have increased four- to fivefold since 2004. This is a very different scenario from what Anglicans knew for decades—a steady number of long-existing churches, the majority of which were in slow decline and a minority of which grew in numbers. In a reproductive Church, the multiplication of small groups looks more normal.

Though the fresh expressions of Church have grown significantly from their start, we now also know that a steady 48% of them reach some kind of numerical plateau.[31] In the past we would have been likely either to accept a plateau or to denigrate it. In a reproductive church we should ask two questions: have you reached your natural unit size, and when might it be right under God to begin another church? Once again, this is not normal denominational thinking but is natural in a reproductive church.

More churches bring the need for more leaders, and the next discovery has been that half of those started are lay-led. The surprise is that 36%

are laity without training or accreditation—those we have called the 'lay-lay'. They are more often women, serving in their spare time and voluntarily. When we dig deeper, we find that the young churches they lead are no less effective in mission and are taking much the same steps forward in ecclesial maturity.[32] It all suggests to me that, in the reproductive Church, we need to accept that formally trained ministry exists to serve the Church as it emerges, rather than to organise churches around the ordained ministry that we already have. Such a view also fits with a wider change in the role of the full-time ordained.

There are more strands to this than I can trace here, but the heart of them is that priests of the future need to see their ministry as *episcope*—an oversight of the leaders of a number of churches. In that role they provide vision, act as a focus of unity, model catholicity and interdependence between the churches, care for the local leaders, and enable, as well as authorise, vocations.[33] These roles are ideal to support a reproductive diverse set of non-identical churches.

There are various ways in which the fresh expressions of Church show their non-identical character, including how they exhibit both continuity with past churches and changes from them. Let me take you through three groups of changes, showing also the continuities that exist, because there have been precedents.

Changes of practice that involve flexibility

The day, time and venue of meeting are now all more flexible. The instinct behind this change is to take context seriously. As we have seen, the incarnation is the theological basis for it. About half of fresh expressions of Church meet during the week, and the same is true about the choice of a venue other than a church.

A deeper change is the thought that our past instinct for parish and territory is not an ultimate value. It is one way in which context works. There is nothing wrong with parish; what is wrong is to think that it works for everyone. So we have seen the birth of churches from shared relationships, quite often related to a shared stage of life. We call them network churches and special interest group churches. This reworks the application of being apostolic, or missional.

Another deep change is the movement away from thinking that congregation is the norm, and the realisation that Church is multi-level. We observe cells for up to twelve, clusters for groups up to 50, congregations of up to 200, then even larger celebrations and diocese, and so on. That gives flexibility in choosing the right size of group to respond to a context. It also establishes that neither oneness nor catholicity means being much the same size.

Yet we've seen such changes before. Mid-week Communions and the 1970s house churches demonstrated variety of day and venue. Chaplaincy and cross-cultural mission have always operated in context and beyond parochial thinking. Moreover, Anglicans have always resisted congregational*ism* and, in theory, held that Church has many levels. These examples of reimagined change are only sharpening a past trend.

Changes linked to belonging

We are seeing the end of a format in which people passively sit in church pews or chairs. Instead, lay people participate in a variety of ways and they are trusted. That change is not unique to fresh expressions of Church but it is characteristic of them. It comes about partly because their leaders are not control freaks, unlike many clergy, though the latter dress it up as necessary 'quality control'. Many kinds of fresh expression of Church exhibit and foster a greater freedom to explore in worship. Messy Church is the widest and best-known example. The leaders trust their people and the word and Spirit given to them.

This is related to the next change—the centrality of being a community around Jesus. Most of us were brought up to think that worship was central, so this represents a radical and significant change. All religions worship; it is not especially Christian. Encountering Jesus, though, is characteristically Christian. That is what leads to worship and gives it bite and authenticity. This change appears in various kinds of fresh expression of Church.

The next factor sits alongside the first two. With less passive people, and community being central, it is intriguing that only about half of the fresh expressions of Church have an ordained leader. Historically, this is at least unusual. Yet all the signs are that these are young churches.

Have we ever been here before? Passivity was challenged by the arrival of family services 40 years ago. Trust in the people was urged by the writings of Roland Allen in the Edwardian period, and in the 1960s by Donovan, the Jesuit missionary. Similarly in the world Church, the Base Ecclesial Communities, of which there are hundreds of thousands, place stress on the quality of community, as do most forms of monasticism. In 1982 the Anglican John Tiller urged changes in our understanding of ordained ministry. He argued that clergy existed to enable local lay ministries to flourish. There are precedents to learn from. The changes are evolution, not revolution.

Changes within Church identity

One focus is that we are looking for discipleship, not attendance at church services, as characteristic of being Church. We are followers of Jesus, not visitors to ancient buildings. This is a vast subject, but it is encouraging that around 80% of all the fresh expressions of Church we surveyed have taken some steps down that road. This trend connects with holiness as one mark of the Church.

The fresh expressions of Church amply demonstrate the theory of the non-identical reproduction of churches. They show that it is normal for churches to give birth to further churches. We observe that these churches are like and unlike the churches that send them, just as our children are ours, but are not us. The same should be true of each generation of Church. This is how change and continuity stay connected. Yet the new shows something that the old could not express, which is one element of how good catholicity works.

With the dissolving of Christendom, the Church is no longer at the centre of events. Yet the edge is a natural Church location. The pre-Christendom story runs through Galilee, not Jerusalem, in the catacombs, not the forum. The early Church included lepers, slaves, women and the mentally ill, all seen as people on the edge of society. A number of fresh expressions of Church engage with the poor and cultural groups that are not much regarded by society.

What of precedents? The method in Methodism was about discipleship in accountable groups. The birth of non-identical reproduction of churches and the journey to their own maturity was in the 'three self' thinking of missionary leader Henry Venn. A number of groups in Church history, not least the monastic and Anabaptists, have had a prophetic effect by living at the edge.

Perhaps what is new is that such a wide range of changes are occurring at much the same time.

New but old

Yet I want to say that the heart of being Christ's Church has not changed at all. I borrow Archbishop Rowan's words in 2004: 'We are seeing what corporate forms of life actually happen—when people meet Jesus.'

All these recent discoveries are the outcrop of what happens when you get a reproductive Church. This is the practical evidence that churches are reproducing, not just that the numbers are increasing. This book shows that there is a sound theory behind this evidence. It makes sense of what we are already seeing. If we accept the theory, then all this is the new 'normal'.

In one way, it is but an echo of what was written back in 1927 by Roland Allen in *The Spontaneous Expansion of the Church*.[34] If expansion is spontaneous, then it arises from the Church's calling and nature. Allen argued that it should be natural, and only various fears (which are still around today) prevented it. I've tried to go further and show a wider biblical and theological basis. Now it is the time for the Church to wake out of its sleep and realise a glorious truth about itself.

This suggests that the Church is rather important and significant in the purposes of God. To the question of whether a high doctrine of the Church is believable today, I now turn.

Notes

1 Many examples occur in the 55 stories in Church Army's *Encounters on the Edge* series, or shorter versions of stories on the Fresh Expressions website.

2 Divorce is used by Roland Allen for the relationship between mission societies and the Church in *The Spontaneous Expansion of the Church* (Lutterworth, 2006), p. 117.

3 P. Avis, *The Anglican Understanding of the Church* (SPCK, 2000), p. 3. Avis can take the opposite view. See the Porvoo Theological Conference 2004: 'Mission precedes Church... The Church exists because God's mission is under way.'

4 D. Bosch, *Transforming Mission* (Orbis, 1991), p. 372.

5 A. Morgan, *Following Jesus: The plural of disciple is Church* (Resource, 2015).

6 S. Murray, *Church Planting: Laying foundations* (Paternoster, 1998), p. 60.

7 The last in the list is argued on the basis in 1 Corinthians 11:26: 'until he comes'.

8 Murray, *Church Planting: Laying foundations*, pp. 20–23.

9 S. Croft, *Transforming Communities* (DLT, 2002), p. 59.

10 A. Dulles, *Models of the Church* (Gill & Macmillan, 1988), p. 192.

11 www.churcharmy.org.uk/fxcresearch: the site also provides separate shorter reports on each diocese covered.

12 In later years, Church Army's Research Unit tested the extent to which the leaders' views were accurate by a smaller survey of attenders. This report, 'Who's there?' can be found on the Research section of the Church Army website.

13 B. Jackson, *Hope for the Church* (CHP, 2002), p. 35.

14 Dulles, *Models of The Church*, p. 192.

15 E. Charry, *By the Renewing of Your Minds* (OUP, 1997), p. 3.

16 Charry, *By the Renewing of Your Minds*, p. 18.

17 Charry, *By the Renewing of Your Minds*, p. 233.

18 Charry, *By the Renewing of Your Minds*, p. 235.

19 Charry, *By the Renewing of Your Minds*, p. 232.

20 Charry, *By the Renewing of Your Minds*, p. 238.

21 D. Watson, *I Believe in the Church* (Hodder & Stoughton, 1978), pp. 356–68.

22 This phrase reoccurs in G. Cray (ed.), *Mission-shaped Church* (CHP, 2009), pp. 30–31, 88–89, 115.

23 A number of these dynamics are highlighted in C. Dalpra, 'Chasing the dream' and 'The cost of community', *Encounters on the Edge* 37 and 38 (Church Army, 2008).

24 S. Savage, 'On the analyst's couch' in S. Croft (ed.), *The Future of the Parish System* (CUP, 2006), p. 21.

25 Savage, 'On the analyst's couch', p. 30.

26 Dulles, *Models of the Church*, p. 192. I take the non-inclusive language simply to mark this as a text of its time.

27 Jackson concurs in *Hope for the Church*, p. 141.

28 Dave Male wrote up the story of the Net, a fresh expression of Church in Huddersfield, and reflected on the current range of terms. He decided to use 'creating Church'. D. Male, *Church Unplugged* (Authentic, 2008), p. 4.

29 J. Hull, *Mission-shaped Church: A response*; J. Milbank, 'Stale Expressions: the management-shaped Church', *Studies in Christian Ethics*, 21.1 (online 2008); A. Davison and A. Milbank, *For the Parish* (SCM, 2010).

30 G. Lings, *The Day of Small Things* (Church Army, 2016).

31 This percentage adds up those cases that plateau very rapidly, those that do so over a few more years and those whose numbers fluctuate.

32 See the Church Army website for an eight-page report on this feature: www.churcharmy.org.uk/fxcresearch.

33 A fuller description of the history leading up to this and of these changes was given in a 2004 lecture by George Lings. It can be downloaded from the website of Church Army's Research Unit.

34 This book is still a stirring read and a trenchant exposure of the fears—doctrinal, moral and organisational—that quench spontaneous expansion, or non-identical reproduction, of the Church.

11

Rehabilitating the Church

If the Church has a clear calling to reproduce, yet a flawed capacity for it which needs dependence on the life-giving Spirit, this raises expectations of the Church's place in the purposes of God. It implies a high doctrine of the Church. This must not be idealistic, and must live with the shame of the Church and its current tarnished image.

I know that, for some people, the very term 'Church' is so inherently problematic that they want to avoid using it beside the words 'fresh expression'. They think that the downward gravitational pull from the inherited, traditional, institutional Church is too powerful—so ingrained as to make it an impossible image to escape from. I know too that in certain mission contexts it will be wise and right not to use this 'C' word. However, that is very different from thinking ourselves free to abandon the theological reality of the Church beneath what is growing locally.

This negativity to the Church occurs widely among mission-minded people, and among those whose past experience of the Church has been significantly negative. Dan Kimball has written a book titled *They Like Jesus but Not the Church*.[1] There might be plenty of reasons why that might be true. I have gathered some quotations over the years from a wide range of sources, including my own findings. I want to be realistic about the very Church of which I have a high doctrine.

The Church's tarnished image

- **The shame and down-drag of the Church:** To many outside the Church, 'Church is what some others do. It is noticed sadly, in their terms, not only as an alien and expensive building that I wouldn't know what to do in; worse, it is occupied by people I wouldn't be seen dead with. To them, Church stands for internal bickering over issues no one else cares about, inconsistent lives that make claims in words ridiculous, led by people who don't know what they believe and are probably to be distrusted with other people's children.'[2]

- **A longstanding problem:** 'The Church's history was already a problem in Western culture—the Crusades, witchcraft trials, support for slavery, and more were perceived by the culture as arguments against the truth of Christianity… Since that first edition [of my book in 1997] the situation has gotten worse.'[3]

- **Well-meaning irrelevance:** 'I was brought up with the middle-class Anglican stance which effectively means plenty of form and very little function and just a semblance of belief going through the ritual of going to church on Sunday morning but not allowing your professed belief to interfere in any way with how you lead your life.'[4]

- **Cultural captivity:** 'The 19th-century Church allowed itself to be captured by the prevailing class structure… The lower classes were tolerated, smiled upon and seen as worthy targets for the charitable. A truly working class style of worship, Church life, leadership and evangelism were never really allowed to develop.'[5]

- **Church abuse:** Philip Yancey writes partly for victims of Church abuse, where congregational life has been controlling, manipulative and dehumanising, or living out a guilt trip under the law, and in some cases involving physical or sexual abuse. He considers himself a fellow sufferer. Richter and Francis, in *Gone but Not Forgotten*[6] showed that half of the de-churched are closed to return because of the experiences they have been through.

- **Ethical failure:** The charge of being hypocritical is longstanding. Spectacular falls from pedestals by Christian leaders delight the press. Splits and poor relationships within the overall Church are commonplace.

- **Failure to build community:** 'The task of forming a new genuinely Christian way of life that acts as a sign of the kingdom to come can only be done in community. It is impossible for an isolated Christian to follow this path in order to undertake the search for a new style of life. Every Christian ought to feel and know that they are supported by others. It will be necessary to engage in a work that aims... at discovering Christian community so that people may learn afresh what the fruit of the Spirit is.'[7]

- **Clericalism:** 'The Church remains a strictly sacral society run by in-house personnel... The clergyman-priest enshrined in a privileged and central position remained the linchpin of the Church... making it impossible for the young Church either to execute its particular ministry or to survive without help from outside.'[8]

- **Fixation on public worship:** 'Jeremiah's criticism was "You keep saying the temple of the Lord, the temple of the Lord" (Jeremiah 7:4). We too have a heavy emotional dependence on, and heavy financial burden of, religious buildings and public worship, exaggerating the sense of the importance of place in guaranteeing the Church's future stake in an emerging society.'[9]

- **Loss of mission identity:** 'We must insist that a Church which has ceased to be a mission has lost the essential character of a Church, so we must also say that a mission which is not at the same time truly a Church is not a true expression of the divine apostolate.'[10]

- **Loss of faith:** 'In many parts of the Church there are clergy and laity who today apparently no longer believe in a God who acts. For many church-going Christians, God has become primarily an idea rather than an event and so our theology... and our spirituality... lack any real sense of expectation.'[11]

- **Devious intransigence:** 'It is totally unrealistic to suppose the C of E will accept and implement a massive programme of radical reform during the next 30 years. It will not accept such a programme, it is incapable of implementing a programme. Those who can produce only radical and dramatic solutions to current problems will therefore remain largely without influence.'[12]

I take no pleasure in this list and I am aware that many readers could add their own or others' horror stories. By including this catalogue of woes, I do not intend to engender despair or guilt. I simply need to make the reader aware that I am not starry-eyed about the Church. We know her shame. It is our shame. At points we have probably all been complicit in aspects of it, and perhaps we long to disassociate ourselves. Yet, at the same time, I believe more strongly than ever before in a high view of her identity, purposes and calling. This raises two rather different questions:

- Is the Church so tarnished, corrupt and broken that mission-minded people are better to continue with a Churchless mission, abandoning the Church and talk of it?
- Or can the essence of the Church be redeemed by an insistence on its true character and purpose in being missional?

Unless there are good answers to these questions, why bother with the argument that Church is intended to reproduce? Should we talk in generic terms about fresh expressions *of Church*, even though it may be a love–hate relationship that adventurous types have with the Church? Come to that, why not cut the Gordian knot and focus everything on mission? Something similar could be argued to prioritise the kingdom.

My reasons are drawn from scripture, elements in the tradition including theological thought, and current experience.

Indications from scripture

Old Testament clues from the way Yahweh operates

My reading of the Old Testament tells me that God's preferred way of mission is through his people. From the very first, God chose to work with and through those created to be in his image. Adam and Eve were to look after the creation and be the most characteristic sign of God's presence in the world. That is part of what 'image' is about. Next in the story of mission, we see that the nations will be blessed through Abraham and his seed. Much later on, within the exilic literature, this universal mission call is refocused, as God's servant is called 'a light to the nations' (Isaiah 42:6; 49:6, NRSV). Of course, God is free to work beyond his people, as he did with the Persian Cyrus, who was also called a servant, but that freedom does not remove God's people as a major strand of his mission, as he promised to Abraham.

The language of '*my* people' is a characteristic description of the Jewish people. Their role was to be the community and location where God is normally to be found. They often failed to deliver this promise. However, their failure did not take away either their identity or their high calling, although it did bring periods of judgement, most notably in the exile. This pattern of exalted purpose and debased performance is like the Church's current state. Election combined with failure is not a new problem.

Abraham has lasting significance. What is true for Abraham has important significance for his descendants. Expressing that same continuity, Newbigin writes, 'The whole core of biblical history is the story of the calling of a visible community to be God's own people, His royal priesthood on earth, the bearer of His light to the nations… and the same is true in the New Testament'.[13]

Lessons from the New Testament treatment of Christ and his Church

In Chapter 3 I explained why I am not impressed by those who claim that Christ never intended to create a faith community centred in him. The wedge driven between Jesus' command to his followers to make disciples and what came to be called the 'Church' is an artificial one. Rowan Williams explored the question 'When does the Church begin?' at the 2011 Fresh Expressions conference in Oxford. It was very clear that, in contrast to the customary response, he places the beginning of the Church before Pentecost. He traced it back through the Easter events, the call of the disciples, and the history of 'the people of God', back towards Adam and Eve in the creation accounts.

Ephesians expresses deep, strong and even surprising links between Christ and the Church. If there is one image of the Church for which Ephesians is noted, it is that the Church is to be seen as 'the body of

Christ' (Ephesians 1:23; 2:16; 3:6; 4:4, 12). It is odd to venerate Christ as head (1:22; 5:23) and despise or dismiss his body, although, when confronted with a paraplegic Church, we can emotionally understand the error.

The expectations in Ephesians 3 are high. Verse 10 says, 'His intent was that now, *through the church*, the manifold wisdom of God should be made known.' This includes the disclosure of a mystery (3:9; 5:32), that Jews and Gentiles (that is, insiders and outsiders) are reconciled to God in Christ and to one another in the one *body* (2:16). This thought is related to 3:20–21: 'Now to him who by the power at work within us is able to accomplish abundantly far more than all we can ask or imagine,' (no surprises so far), 'to him be glory *in the church* and in Christ Jesus to all generations' (NRSV, my italics). What a connection, and what a surprising order of words; what a high doctrine of the Church!

Going on in the same epistle, I spot another reason why I am never free to despise or dispose of the Church. Ephesians 5:25 says, 'Christ loved the church and gave himself up for her.' Within sentences the author goes on to tease that love out, explaining that Christ nourishes and cherishes the Church as a human being does their own body (v. 29). It may be that these two verses are the nearest to proof texts and are the Christ-centred core justifying a high view of the Church.

Does our talk about the Church often reflect this dignity of identity and purpose? Or has it all been eroded through failed expectations? Has the Church itself succumbed to an ecclesial form of Alzheimer's and forgotten its identity? In the 1970s, Michael Griffiths wrote about the Church under the title *Cinderella with Amnesia*.[14] Has the Church become dysfunctional, descended into inconsequential self-absorbed trivialities and become an object of palliative care? By contrast, across all the epistles, Paul (who had plenty of immature, troubled and troublesome churches to deal with) never gives up on the turbulent young churches and is breathtakingly audacious about the linkage between Christ, the Church and God's mission.

Similar work about the Holy Spirit and the Church could be done. This would include how the Spirit inhabits the Church, transforms and inspires the Church, as well as surprising and alarming her. That perspective links to the Spirit's disclosures in the book of Revelation. The book begins with pertinent and sharp advice to various churches, but it ends with the perfected Church—the new Jerusalem, the bride of Christ, the city of God. It ends with a Christ-centred community, which in turn embodies the disclosed rule of the kingdom of God; mission has been completed.

Scripture strongly suggests that the mission of God and the people of God are deeply mutually linked. So Newbigin writes, 'We must insist that a Church which has ceased to be a mission has lost the essential character of a Church, so we must also say that a mission which is not at the same time truly a Church is not a true expression of the divine apostolate.'[15]

Elements in the tradition

Trinity and missionary ecclesiology

Chapter 4 outlined my understanding of the connections between the Trinity and the Church. I suggested that the phrase 'community-in-mission' is an acceptable term for the Trinity and for what is being reproduced in the Church of God. Moreover, this twofold identity is diagnostic for Church reproduction. Chapters 5 and 6 showed what is reproduced from the example of Christ the missioner of God, who proclaimed the kingdom and yet was more important than it.

I want to apply all that thinking to the hope of rehabilitating the Church, showing that it must be seen in relation to mission and to the kingdom. These other two factors have tended to trump it. It seems to me that over the last 100 years there has been an understandable loss of confidence in the Church. This has led to a search for more attractive and life-giving big ideas, such as mission and the kingdom.

The Trinity show us that mission alone is not enough. Mission itself overflows from the loving community life of God. This bears on one of this chapter's original questions—whether the essence of Church can be redeemed by an insistence on its missional character. Put another way, is it enough to take on board *missio Dei*? I believe the answer is no; partly, it fails to do justice to the Eastern understanding of the Trinity and the community nature of the Church.

A motoring analogy may illustrate the point. Liken the Church to an old Morris Minor car (I enjoyed three of them) and an image of attractive quaintness bumbles across the screen of the mind, but realists know that the vehicle is limited for contemporary transport and long-distance trips. Offer to add missional power to this beast by dropping in a BMW two-litre engine and there would be dramatic changes. I would, however, have questions about the gearbox, suspension, brakes, steering and seating. Adding the woof of mission to a clapped-out Church is about the same sort of change. The need today is much deeper and more radical. I use 'radical' to mean the search for roots. Our Christian roots are to be in who and how God is, here understood as community-in-mission, in reproducing the dynamics of Christ's ministry and cooperating with the surprising Spirit.

Researched experience

Sometimes I am asked what best sums up all I have learnt in 20 years of research life in Church Army. My reply has been, 'the centrality of community'. I have seen it manifested as the fresh starting point in mission, often arrived at intuitively by pioneers wanting to connect with the people furthest away from us. I have then noticed that growing community works in mission to all sectors of society, not just those furthest away. Few people hate being loved. Truly loving, accepting, authentic community is always attractive as well as demanding.

Evangelism works when local church life makes watching people ask questions. As a whole, fresh expressions of Church are making some missional impact. They embody both missional effectiveness and ecclesial reimagination. This result is no accident. The latter is the community that gives authenticity to the former. I have also learnt that community was the most effective and enduring dynamic in the missionary life of the early Church. The study that made me change my mind was Alan Kreider's *Worship and Evangelism in Pre-Christendom*.[16] As such, we are only rediscovering old ways—part of what 'fresh' means.

Kreider demonstrated that the early effective way was a community who lived a Jesus-shaped distinctiveness. This was fed by the practices of their spiritual lives, including public worship. They did little direct evangelism and banned outsiders from coming to worship. That is utterly different from our investment in worship as the so-called shop window of the Church. More recently, I have come to see that this emphasis on community is not merely tactical wisdom and ancient practice. The centrality of community connects with the deepest strands of our theology. Who God is and what the Trinity show us they are like are foundational for being Christian and being Church. Such a foundation offers a profound reason to have a high theology of the Church and also sets a high bar for the journey that, too often, she still has to travel.

Theological connections between Church, mission and kingdom

I now want to suggest a way of holding mission, Church and kingdom together by setting the Church as part of a triangle of three interrelated forces.

Some ecclesiology seems to float free of either mission or kingdom, which is odd. It seems to deal with what, to me, are secondary and tertiary ecclesial issues, such as questions of ministerial orders, the ordering of worship and sacramental discipline. The primary ecclesial questions deal with deeper questions: what is the Church, why does it exist and what for? What relationships and qualities are essential to its life? In writing and practice, too often the tail of ministry wags the ecclesial dog.

In other literature about engagement with society, Church is the poor relation to both mission and the kingdom. Sometimes it seems there is competition for primacy between advocates of mission and those of kingdom. An example might be John Hull's critique of *Mission-shaped Church* both for its lack of a kingdom emphasis and, in his view, its proselytising view of mission.[17] At other times, mission and the kingdom are presented as allies. But there can be a tendency to marginalise the Church. The links to Christology and Trinity explain why such a view will not do, but I now need to give some contours of the two-way relationships that I suggest exist between mission, kingdom and Church.

Diagram 5

The triangle (Diagram 5) models that the three factors connect relationally, while demonstrating that none is identical to the others. The shape gives room to explore the dynamics along its three sides and to enquire what might be in the middle of the three. The problematic relationship between mission and Church is where we started. A healthy balanced relationship will be suggested. I then will outline the connections round the other sides of the triangle for a more balanced picture.

Relating mission and Church

I have put the label 'Mission' at the top corner, partly in deference to *missio Dei* thinking. Mission, being in and from God, can be represented as coming from above. To some extent it is true that the other two proceed from it. As a matter of history, the mission of God precedes the creating of the people of God, the Church. The creation is the first chapter of the mission and the beginning of the kingdom on earth. In the salvation story, the coming of God the Son as Jesus of Nazareth precedes the community founded by him. I agree with *Mission-shaped Church*: 'the Church is the fruit of God's Mission'.[18]

Thus, one can draw the process as a straight line from the mission of the Trinity, focusing in the sending of the Son, which led to the creation of the Church. But it is not so simple as thinking that the Church is just a product of mission. No sooner is Church the *consequence* of mission than it becomes also the *conductor* of mission. Taking the fruit analogy, the Church becomes also the bearer of the gospel; it becomes the sower as well as the fruit—so the line then runs upwards from Church to mission. The initial progression has become more complicated. Beyond the triangle image, it is like suggesting that the twin strands of mission and Church intertwine in a helix. In this process, first one, then the other, is perceived as dominant. If, first, mission led to Church, then Church goes on outward in mission, which leads to yet further expressions of Church.

Another pair of words develops the theme of reciprocal connection. It is not only true that the Church is the bearer of the gospel message. The term 'bearer' suggests that the gospel is a package which the Church carries in its hand but which is essentially separate from the body that bears it. Yet the New Testament also tells us that the Church is more than the *bearer* of the message; it also *embodies* the message. This is related to the doctrine of the Holy Spirit. Through the gift of grace and the transformation the Spirit brings, we the Church experience the first stages of being in Christ, not just Christ being in us. We enter into something of the loving life of the Trinity and we get our first glimpses of heaven. The Spirit is a real deposit, not just a promise of some inheritance later. We see Christ in one another, and the way we treat each other will be taken as the way we treat him.

This is truly astonishing stuff, but it is encouraged by the language of the New Testament about what the Holy Spirit does. His fruit actually grows in us. We are the new creation in Christ that 2 Corinthians 5 talks about. In these ways, mission and Church are bound together and there is a two-way relationship going on.

Relating mission and kingdom

The mission of God initiates a process by which the kingdom of God comes into being on earth. That suggests that we are putting mission before kingdom. The acts of God lead to the disclosure of the rule of God. So the signs in the Gospels are missional, in that they embody the good news, as well as being indicators of the coming-and-already kingdom. I am taking 'mission' here in its most basic and apostolic sense—that God is a sender who has sent the Son and the Spirit. This is how mission or 'processions' in the Trinity were understood in the Eastern Church.

However, there is traffic in the other direction. My understanding is that the outworking of mission is historical. God reveals himself, acts and sends, in space and time. Thus, the word 'apostolic' is often used to refer not just to mission but to key acts and truths in the past, carrying authority into the present. But along this right-hand side of the triangle, the historical meets the eschatological. There is energy coming from the kingdom to mission. Although we timebound beings struggle to understand this, the 'not yet' kingdom is advancing into the present from the future. Hence, both the kingdom and the Spirit are foretastes of a future that is real now and yet also 'not yet' fully disclosed. Or, to borrow bits from varying biblical analogies, the banquet is prepared and the canapés are already being enjoyed. The city of God is laid out with many mansions, and signs and waystations to it may be seen.

Once more, there is both an initiative from mission and a reciprocal response from kingdom. Not only that, but the two are bound together. No kingdom of God will become present without mission, though we could say it already exists in the future. So we are commanded to pray and work for its coming. Equally, no mission can be authentic unless it leads to an advance of the kingdom and is conducted by its values. Nor can mission be complete until the kingdom is revealed in all its glory.

How do Church and kingdom relate?

Chapter 3 laid out my present understanding that there is an intentional overlap between the kingdom and the Church. It repudiated the claim that either reality swallows the other, yet explored the idea that the two are not identical, with the kingdom being wider and wilder. By taking four different terms—'instrument', 'agent', 'sign' and 'foretaste'—it argued that 'foretaste' best expresses the idea. Foretaste is necessary if the other terms are to be honourable, not hollow, and capable of being fulfilled.

Each of the four successive terms has a higher and more human-like role for the Church to play, by the Spirit, in the scheme of God's mission. It simply is part of the picture, and we are not free to dispense with it. The Church is a way in which the gospel is embodied, hence showing itself to be a foretaste of the coming kingdom, partly because it is directed by the values of its king. Once again we meet a reciprocal relationship. Hence we have the daring image in the New Testament that the Church is the body of Christ, who is the Lord or King of the kingdom.

Linking back mission, kingdom and Church to the Trinity

Let's push this further. The triangular pattern of mission, Church and kingdom is not unlike the pattern of the Trinity. This isn't modalism: I am not saying that each member of Trinity is only concerned with one point of the triangle. I am aware that all three persons in the Godhead are involved in all three outcomes. However, I do notice that there is a set of perichoretic relationships between the three features, which I am suggesting must be held in relation to each other: mission, Church and kingdom. What happens in any one affects the other two. Let me now link this to what I have learnt from Tom Smail and his book, *Like Father, Like Son*.

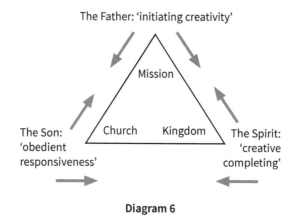

Diagram 6

Smail characterises the nature of God the Father—as the image of father itself suggests—as 'initiating creativity'. Thus, the Son and the Spirit in some sense proceed from the Father. The same dynamics are true of mission; hence I place both at the top of the triangle (Diagram 6). Smail uses the term 'obedient responsiveness' as characteristic of the incarnate Son. John's Gospel most notably traces this feature. The Son is also the visible focus of the mission of the Trinity.

Similarly, the Church, at its best, is the visible focus of both mission and the kingdom. Mission happens as the Son is obedient to the Father, and, in *missio Dei* thinking, that is true of the Church too. Furthermore, it is the Church, not the mission or the kingdom, which is called the body of Christ. Hence, I link the Son and the Church at the left-hand base of the triangle. This Jesus also promises the Spirit, from the Father.

The term Smail uses for the Spirit is 'creative completing'. The Spirit does not initiate, but completes. The Spirit completes the mission of the Father, promotes and extends the glory of the Son and fosters the bringing in of the kingdom. All the 'foretaste' language of the New

Testament is connected with the presence of the Spirit and the coming of the kingdom. The two are joined at the hip. In addition, both the Spirit and the kingdom are seen as inherently dynamic and powerful. Yet, neither is seen directly in itself, but only through signs that go well beyond mere talk. The effects of wind and the inbreaking kingdom are detectable and at the same time mysterious. There are intriguing parallels; thus, I place the Spirit and the kingdom in the remaining right-hand corner of the triangle.

Is anything at the centre of mission, Church and kingdom?

Here the precise parallel between the three and the Trinity breaks down, for I think that the centre of the triangle is Jesus. This is fashionable in the shadow neither of trinitarian thought nor of multi-faith awareness. But consider the Gospels. I suggest that the kingdom is not central to the Gospels. It is but the key message of the central figure. In that sense, Jesus is greater than the kingdom. Without the king, there is little worthwhile kingdom left.

Jesus is also the epicentre of God's mission. In him God is supremely revealed; in him salvation is accomplished once for all. In him we are not only being transformed, which is encouraging, but we are 'participants in the divine nature' as 2 Peter 1:4 (NRSV) tells us, which is astonishing. *Theosis*, as Athanasius says, means, 'God became man so that men might become gods.'[19] I complete the trip around the triangle, adding that Jesus is both founder and head of the Church. In all these ways he is central, and Rowan Williams is keen and right to keep telling us that the Church is event. It is the event of what forms through transformative encounter with Jesus. Spiritually and theologically, the Church is formed Christologically.

Drawing threads together

Rehabilitation, not oscillation and distortion

I have sketched one way to put the case that the doctrine of the Church deserves rehabilitating, but in dynamic triangular relationship with mission and kingdom. It needs that because the 20th century has witnessed a history of unhelpful oscillation between the priority of Church and mission, or of Church and the kingdom. So some theologians still express the priority of mission: 'There is a Church because there is a mission.'[20] Meanwhile, others say, 'Without the Church there is no authentic mission.'[21] And a third group can claim, 'Ecclesiology has become the central organising principle of 20th-century theology.'

It may be that this rehabilitation is occurring under our feet. It is much easier for me to write this chapter in the wake of our Church Army researched findings across half of the Church of England's dioceses. Over four years, by phone calls with leaders, we have taken snapshots of more than 1100 fresh expressions of Church. We found that they have had a significant missional impact, drawing a good proportion of people who had either given up on church attendance or had almost never been to church. They are the single largest contemporary example of community-in-mission in action, as well as putting flesh on the concept of the Church as intended to reproduce. They show that the reimagination of Church, seeking to be both faithful and creative, occurs. They exhibit both continuity with the past and change to meet the present. Sometimes, evangelism leads people to attend these young churches; sometimes, it is exposure to their common life which is the evangelism. By all these means, the kingdom is advancing. They are a living laboratory showing that the three—Church, mission and kingdom—can, as they should, be held together.

This chapter has argued that a high doctrine of the Church is overdue and that the term 'fresh expressions of Church' is useful, apt, necessary and valid. Other authors, as well as my own observations leading to new thinking, have persuaded me to hold to a high view of the Church, living better with the disappointments that thus come. I cite some of my mentors: 'There is no way of belonging to Christ that does not include the Church.'[22] 'Throughout this study we have assumed that, in one way or another, the Church is at the heart of God's mission.'[23] I wish I could find the source of the next view:

> The Church is to be the primary agent of mission and if it does not exhibit evident community and transformed lives then any amount of evangelistic events and Church projects will have limited credibility… That community is described in Scripture as nothing less than the body of Christ… This means that how the Church conducts its life is foundational to the whole work of proclaiming the good news of Christ.[24]

Ultimately the evidence for the credibility of the Gospel in the eyes of the world must be a quality of life manifested in the Church which the world cannot find elsewhere. (This comment comes from over 70 years ago.)[25]

Some may enjoy the way I myself put it some years ago in a lecture:

> A Church without evangelism has lost its heart.
> Evangelism without the Church has lost its body.
> Medical wisdom recommends the retention of the relationship.[26]

What then should we do?

I limit myself to one plea. Let us give resources and importance to fostering the quality of community life that bears the aroma of Jesus, that commends itself as embodying his values, that is inexplicable other than as the overflow of his life within us. Let's go deep with community, absorbing the writings of Jean Vanier and Scott Peck. Let us learn from Alan Kreider and the early Church. Let's drink from the well of the best of new monasticism today and the shorter writings of Claire Dalpra.[27] Why not reread the New Testament as a treatise on

Christian community and the love modelled there by the Trinity?

If we grow Jesus-centred community, it will have a missional effect. Be Jesus-like together and the kingdom will advance. Always hold mission, kingdom and Church in perichoretic relationships. Recover a high view of the Church, as long as your view of Christ is higher still.

Implications for theory and practice

If the triangular relationship between mission, kingdom and Church is broadly right, then certain other things follow, as with understandings of the Trinity.

- It is neither helpful nor ultimately possible to collapse the three into one. All belong to, are needed by, are related to and are different from the others.
- While it is possible to privilege the Father and mission in terms of procession, it should not be done so as to subordinate the other two (Jesus and the Church, the Spirit and mission), such that they are less than essential to the overall purposes of God.
- You cannot remove any one of the three without damaging the other two.
- To examine one without relation to the other two will be to invite distortion. Part of the identity of each one is known through its relationships to the other two.

In conclusion

I conclude that an element of a proper high doctrine of the Church is a calling and capacity to reproduce. This must always be related to the Church's roles in embodying mission and the kingdom. It means reclaiming part of the identity of the Church, not merely a function. It is an explicit addition to ecclesiology to be acknowledged and shared by all. It is far more than tactical opportunism or a desperate search for relevance. It springs from what the Church is, in the purposes of God.

This addition to doctrine establishes an ecclesiological foundation for seeing the birth of fresh expressions of Church. It rests on several sources teased out by Dulles' tests. Among its other virtues, the reproductive strand offers something to all the other ecclesial models. They would not have had the ability to include it, as it has been hidden by the absence of mission peculiar to Christendom. The last 40 years have helped to make explicit one element of being Church that should no longer be eclipsed. 'Reproductive' can now take its place as a sort of lesser fifth mark of the Church, serving the classic four of the ongoing Christian tradition.

This view sits well with the claim that the best analogies for the Church, and more churches, are interpersonal human ones, not horticultural images, much less non-organic ones. This emphasis is supported from the intentions for God's people in creation, as being in the image of God. It is expressly underlined in the Genesis covenant texts. It springs from the links between the interpersonal relations within the Trinity and ecclesiology. It is fostered through the connections between Christ and the Church. Although horticultural language is present in the biblical record, it should always be subservient to this interpersonal consideration. It then makes sense to argue that 'Church reproduction' is more accurate language than 'Church planting'. Images assist the creation of the mentality they assume.

Starting young churches is not just something the Church does out of a missional imperative or tactical choice, much less dire necessity. If it is true to itself, and the time is right, then Church reproduction will occur because it is in the nature of Church. There are also values that characterise this process and normally should accompany it.

1   The calling to reproduction is likely to be clear, despite the fact that the attendant capacity is often flawed. The infertility of the three Genesis matriarchs instances this, as does the stumbling into cross-cultural mission by the early Church. Calling reflects election, but capacity requires the intervention of grace.

2 It is bipartite. This trait is demonstrated from humans being created from dust and breath, through the incarnation of Christ as God and man, and by the Church rightly growing from theological inheritance and context, as well as partnership with the missionary Spirit.

3 Continuity and change are both present. This is exhibited in the incarnation and in Jesus' death leading to resurrection. It is embodied in Jesus' image of a dying seed leading to the life of a plant. Thus a fresh expression of Church, revealing both family likeness and individual difference across generations of churches, is to be regarded as normal.

4 The second and third values above mean that this reproduction is always non-identical, just as is the case with human reproduction. The analogy of a church DNA would support this, as does the principle that the eternal Word always seeks translation in context. Any attempts to copy or clone Church is therefore an error, for it denies these second, third and fourth values.

5 Costly 'dying to live' in starting further churches comes from Christ and is binding as an attitude, not merely missionally or tactically advisable. Those sent out in Church reproduction will expect to put aside their own cherished forms of being Church, in honour of the incarnation, and to discover what should emerge by Spirit-led engagement with the context.

To believe in a reproducing Church should change our priorities about all churches. Most of our resources, financial and human, have gone into maintaining the long-lived ones and providing a continuity of centrally trained and authorised paid leadership for them. Proper care of these inherited churches should no longer eclipse two things.

Existing churches need to learn how to explore giving birth to further churches, which are related to them yet different from them, and central resources should, as a normal instinct, make serious investment in those churches being born and those which are still young. They represent some of our best hopes for the future in several ways. They are the communities with the highest proportions of those on their way to faith and those under the age of 16. They are the ones with the courage to find what is true to the past but connects with the present.

This view of the Church should change our expectations. We do not yet think it is normal and normative that churches have the calling and capacity to reproduce. In every other organic field, however, it is one mark of maturity.

So the avid 'bad birdwatcher' Simon Barnes writes, 'The aim of every living thing is to become an ancestor; that is what evolution means. If you have bred things that will survive and breed in their turn you have made your mark...That is why there is joy unconfined for every human being who becomes a grandparent.'[28]

Such intentional, ongoing, ecclesial non-identical reproduction should be expected in what is another creation of God: the people of God, the body of Christ and the temple of the Spirit.

Notes

1 D. Kimball, *They Like Jesus but Not the Church: Insights from emerging generations* (Zondervan, 2007).

2 G. Lings, 'Living proof', *Encounters on the Edge* 1 (Church Army, 1999), pp. 13–14.

3 J. Wilson, *Living Faithfully in a Fragmented World* (Lutterworth, 2010), p. 2.

4 G. Monbiot, *Third Way* (August 2001).

5 R. Gamble, *The Irrelevant Church* (Monarch, 1991), p. 63.

6 P. Richter and L. Francis, *Gone but Not Forgotten* (DLT, 1998); followed by *Gone for Good?* (Epworth, 2007).

7 J. Ellul, *The Presence of the Kingdom* (Helmers & Howard, 1989), p. 123.

8 David Bosch, *Transforming Mission* (Orbis, 1991), p. 470.

9 G. Lings, 'Encountering exile', *Encounters on the Edge* 13 (Church Army, 2002), p. 5.

10 L. Newbigin, *The Household of God* (SCM, 1953), pp. 200–201.

11 M. Marshall, *The Gospel Conspiracy* (Monarch, 1992), p. 28.

12 T. Beeson, *The Church of England in Crisis* (Davis-Poynter, 1973), p. 187.

13 Newbigin, *The Household of God*, p. 24.

14 M. Griffiths, *Cinderella with Amnesia* (IVP, 1975).

15 Newbigin, *The Household of God*, pp. 200–201.

16 A. Kreider, *Worship and Evangelism in Pre-Christendom* (Grove , 1995).

17 J. Hull, *Mission-shaped Church: A theological response* (SCM, 2006).

18 G. Cray (ed.), *Mission-shaped Church* (CHP, 2009), p. 85.

19 Athanasius, *Contra Gentes*, 269:54.

20 Bosch, *Transforming Mission*, p. 390.

21 G. Wainwright, *Signs Amid the Rubble. Unpublished works of Lesslie Newbigin* (Eerdmans, 2003), p. 104.

22 G. Cray, *Youth Congregations and the Emerging Church* (Grove , 2002), p. 5.

23 A. Kirk, *What Is Mission?* (DLT, 1999), p. 205.

24 The quote sounds like Newbigin, but neither I nor Paul Weston have been able to source it.

25 Bishop of Rochester (ed.), *Towards the Conversion of England* (Church Assembly, 1945), p. 33.

26 G. Lings, lectures to students at Church Army's Wilson Carlile College of Evangelism.

27 C. Dalpra, 'Chasing the dream' and 'The cost of community', *Encounters on the Edge* 37 and 38 (Church Army, 2008).

28 S. Barnes, *How to Be a Bad Birdwatcher: To the greater glory of life* (Short Books, 2004), p. 165.

Acknowledgements

Readers of this book will have realised that its gestation period has been more protracted than for an elephant. Without companions on the journey, known and anonymous, it would have been impossible.

My first thanks goes to those innumerable local leaders who set out in faith to follow their calling and do what was at least rare, and maybe even unprecedented in their context. They helped bring to birth what we came to call 'church plants' and later 'fresh expressions of Church'. The healthy disturbance you caused is what stimulated my curiosity, fed my imagination and prompted me to ponder and scribble about what it all meant.

I want to thank Church Army and its two leaders over 20 years—Philip Johanson and Mark Russell—for employing me to have time and freedom to watch what others do and then comment on its significance. To be a watcher, during this period of the reimagination of the Church, has been one of the greatest privileges of my life.

Within the Church Army Research Unit, there are many to thank. Claire Dalpra stands out as my most longstanding colleague and most helpful critic, often helping me see the big picture, sift woolly drafts and so communicate better. At the level of detail, Andrew Wooding has borne the heat of the day, chasing errant semi-colons, hunting down ignorant homophones and disciplining bogus apostrophes.

If there is some truth in the invented maxim that 'behind every PhD lies an astonished author', then my supervisor Dr Martyn Atkins merits particular thanks, for that work was the most rigorous testing of the ideas that I entertained as possibly true. When I was persuaded against my better judgement to start down this arduous academic road, his wise advice, and especially his constant encouragement, were all that stood between me and the belief that the upward road was too steep to continue to climb.

Latterly, my thanks to Bishop Paul Bayes for many years of friendship and a characteristically generous and pithy foreword, and to all my friends in the fresh expressions of Church world who have written commendations that make me blush.

To Hannah, Martyn and Julian, I say thank you for being the living embodiment of my homely dictum about non-identical reproduction—that, in regard to families and also churches, we must remember 'our children are ours, but not us'. Having seen the Lings family DNA work out in three ways that are both related but disparate has been surprising, delightful, and also educational.

To Helen, my wife, I give my thanks for staying around during the writing years when I became an academic hermit and social recluse. You covered the birthdays and anniversaries I might have forgotten, rightly nagged me to tackle jobs round the house, and provided everything from meals to emotional support and keeping the links going with all our friends. As a true companion you also kept walking with me through it all.

Beneath it all is gratitude to God for a life lived vocationally. I sense that, by the grace of Christ, I was called to offer my life to him in 1965, before I urgently sought him. Unbidden, in 1969, came the beckoning finger towards ordination; why not swap the Bank of England for the Church of England? In 1984, the start of a fascination with beginning further churches came out of the blue. In 1996, at the wrong time as I thought, Church Army advertised for a director of research and my wife told me to apply. It has all been a surprise. I am grateful for the calls and glad I had just enough wit to go with them.

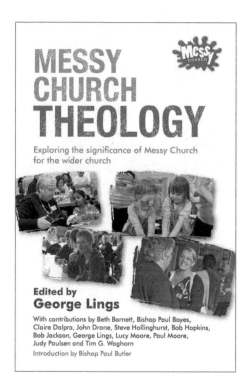

Messy Church Theology is the first title to encapsulate the theology of Messy Church. Through chapters by contributors from a variety of church and academic backgrounds and case studies by Messy Church practitioners, it gathers together some of the discussions around Messy Church and assesses the impact of this ministry, placing it in the context of wider developments within the church community.

Messy Church Theology
Exploring the significance of Messy Church for the wider church
Edited by George Lings
978 0 85746 171 1 £9.99

brf.org.uk

This book offers a map for pioneering a new future for the church. Decisions on what and how and when we change will inevitably affect growth or decline in a church, and also have a major impact on people. This is a book for leaders wanting to guide their Christian communities into a new future, and for church members wanting to be equipped for whatever lies ahead. Also included are over 100 questions for personal and group reflection.

Pioneering a New Future
A guide to shaping change and changing the shape of church
Phil Potter
978 0 85746 414 9 £7.99

brf.org.uk

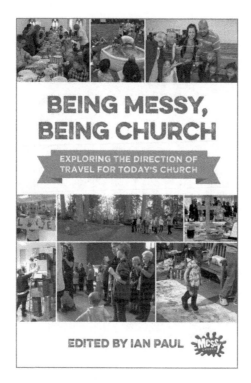

Being Messy, Being Church offers a series of thought-provoking essays exploring what Messy Church brings to the wider church, how these different forms of church community can coexist, and what this might mean for the future of the church. Essential reading for church leaders at national and local level.

Being Messy, Being Church
Exploring the direction of travel for today's church
Edited by Ian Paul
978 0 85746 488 0 £9.99

brf.org.uk

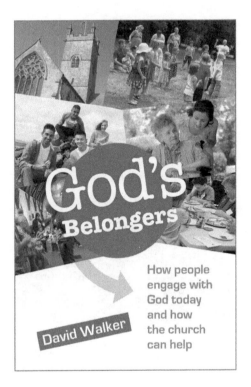

God's Belongers should transform our thinking about what it means to belong to church. Uniquely, David Walker replaces the old and worn division between 'members' and 'non-members' with a fourfold model of belonging: through relationship, through place, through events, and through activities. From his extensive practical research, the author shows how 'belonging' can encompass a far wider group of people than those who attend weekly services. This opens up creative opportunities for mission in today's world.

God's Belongers
How people engage with God today and how the church can help
David Walker
978 0 85746 467 5 £7.99

brf.org.uk